Delivering World-Class Technical Support

Navtej (Kay) Khandpur and Lori Laub

WILEY COMPUTER PUBLISHING

John Wiley & Sons, Inc.
New York • Chichester • Brisbane
Toronto • Singapore • Weinheim

Publisher: Katherine Schowalter
Editor: Theresa Hudson
Managing Editor: Angela Murphy
Text Design & Composition: Publishers' Design and Production Services, Inc.

Library of Congress Cataloging-in-Publication Data:

ISBN 0-471-15534-9

Printed in the United Srates of America

10 9 8 7 6 5 4 3 2 1

To Mary Ellena Ward, who gave me my first job in technical support and launched a satisfying and rewarding career

(Khandpur)

To my parents, Neyla and Wilmer Laub, for instilling in me a sense of purpose, the desire to make a difference, and an appreciation of accomplishment

(Laub)

Contents

About the Authors

Navtej (Kay) Khandpur is a management consultant in Technical Support Operations, Management and Strategic Planning. In his 19 years in the technical support field Kay has served in a variety of functions, from managing support operations to business planning for support delivery. Most recently he was with Tandem Computers, where he managed the company's customer satisfaction program for critical accounts. Kay has also taught graduate courses in the business school at the George Washington University in Washington, DC, and often speaks at technical support industry conferences. His credentials include a BSEE, an MSEE, an MS in Information Systems Technology, and an MBA; he is a member of Beta Gamma Sigma, the honor society for collegiate schools of business.

Kay is currently with Promentis Solutions (www.promentis.com), located in Santa Clara, California. Many of his clients are technology companies, from start-up ventures to Fortune 500 companies, whose goal is to deliver *mission-critical* support to their customers as cost-effectively as possible. Kay's work as a consultant has included support process implementation and improvement, strategy development, design and implementation of measurement systems, planning for support delivery operations, and contract program management for support technology selection and deployment.

Kay feels strongly that the quality and range of technical support delivered by a company can materially affect its profitability. He initiated this book in pursuit of his ambition to help develop professional, hands-on managers for this vital business function.

In his spare time Kay practices *kaizen* on his golf game, albeit with somewhat mixed results.

Lori Laub has created a new and dynamic vision in the service and support field by developing and implementing innovative programs designed to enrich technical support and customer service, increase employee contributions, and maximize company profits. She has built and managed several service, support and help desk organizations, is a frequently requested speaker at many prominent industry events, and has authored various articles for trade publications. Ms. Laub is a member of the Board of Directors for the Association of Support Professionals (ASP) and a Help Desk Institute (HDI) Advisory Board Member.

Currently, Ms. Laub is Vice President of Corporate Information Systems at Remedy Corporation, a leading developer of client/server software applications for systems support and business process automation. She also operates her own consulting firm, Excellence By Design, through which she has designed and implemented technical support and service strategy programs for industry-leading firms such as Knowledge Adventure, Inc., ImagiNation Network (a division of AT&T), and Compaq Computer Corporation.

Ms. Laub has held Vice President level positions at Great Plains Software, a prominent financial software company that was ranked first in customer service and support for six consecutive years, Intuit, a highly successful PC software company, Vantive Corporation, makers of a leading client/server based customer information management system, and Ziff Communications, a leading technology publishing firm. Her endeavors helped each of these companies make customer satisfaction a key corporate strategic asset, resulting in unparalleled reputations for outstanding customer support and more substantial bottom lines.

Preface

A NOTE TO THE READER

In recent years the delivery of technical support has begun to assume an increasingly important role in the operations of most technology companies. The renewed focus on customer satisfaction has meant that managers of more and more companies are trying to instill in their people a culture of excellent service, of caring for customers and getting things done for them. Technical Support Organizations are right in the middle of this, because they manage customer relationships.

In our many years in the technical support industry—as technical support representatives, managers, executives, and now as consultants—we have observed that successful technology companies have always had a world-class Technical Support Organization. The people are motivated, processes are well defined, the organization has good relationships both internally and externally, and most importantly, the managers keep a very close eye on operations. Managers are usually home-grown, and are familiar with the technical support environment. With the explosion in the number of companies, however, it has become difficult to develop technical support management talent in-house, and there are few programs available to recruit and train new technical support managers.

This book was written to help current and aspiring managers of Technical Support Organizations set up and run an organization that delivers world-class technical support to its customers. The authors draw on their experiences as practitioners, and as consultants called upon to assist Technical Support Organizations.

While both authors have experience in all the areas covered in the book, primary writing duties were divided to make the book possible. Navtej Khandpur was responsible for the Introduction and the chapters on Strategy and Direction, Process and Infrastructure, Performance and Measurement, and Planning and Budgeting. Lori Laub was responsible for the chapters on People and Culture, Products and Tools, Positioning and Marketing, and Partners and Affiliates.

Acknowledgments

This book would not have been possible without the help of a great number of people who gave of their time, experience, and wisdom. The authors would both like to thank Lou Muggeo for his keen insights and feedback on early drafts of the book, and his continuous support throughout. We should all aspire to be as good and effective as he is.

Others we would like to thank are:

- Helen Cheung, a statistician who knows how to make sense of numbers and apply them to business in a fair and honest way
- Bill Fallin, a friend and colleague who uncomplainingly critiqued all the chapters even when he was on vacation, and has put up with all sorts of questions and philosophical discussions over the last 13 years
- Emil Flock and Doug Carter, for their insights into the outsourcing process
- Willis Flood, a financial controller who knows more about technical support than many support managers, and who believes that the job of the finance groups is to make the operations people successful

- Lori Iventosch-James, a gifted measurement expert who understands the importance of operating and customer satisfaction measures, and knows how to develop the right ones
- Bob Johnson, the guru of technical support market trends, for his help and advice
- The service, support, and training team members we worked with at Great Plains Software, Intuit, and Tandem Computers, who adopted a can-do spirit to prove that service and support can be a key strategic differentiator
- All our clients, past and present, for giving us the opportunity to try out our ideas

There are no doubt others whom we should thank, and we apologize if we have not mentioned their names here.

Navtej Khandpur and Lori Laub

Introduction

1

TECHNICAL SUPPORT

Evolution

Supporting customers has always been an important part of the computer industry. Early technology was not as robust as it is today, so hardware failures were common. When a computer broke down the customer would contact the computer's vendor, and vendor personnel, called *service engineers* (or field engineers or customer engineers), would diagnose the failure and if necessary fix the computer using replacement parts. Computer hardware also required frequent preventive maintenance, when service personnel would run tests on the hardware, tune the system, and replace parts that were in danger of failing from a stock of spare parts kept on-site. In large installations vendor service personnel were often based on-site, and contacting the vendor was easy. Customers paid substantial amounts each year, often 20 percent or more of the value of the installed hardware, for hardware maintenance services.

The introduction of minicomputers gave rise to smaller computer installations and less expensive hardware. At the same time hardware became more reliable, so it became economically not viable to locate vendor service personnel at every installation. A customer would contact the vendor when service was needed, and a service engineer would be dispatched from a local office to perform the service. With the development and proliferation of personal computers, service functions became even more centralized and service engineers were rarely dispatched by vendors. Many vendors now perform remote diagnosis and if a new part is needed, it is shipped by the vendor for installation by the customer. Some customers purchase additional services, so a service engineer comes on-site and installs the part. All of these service models (and many variations) still exist and are collectively called the *computer service industry*: those activities involved with the maintenance and repair of computer hardware.

Software Support

Software support started on a similar path. Operating systems used proprietary technology and applications were often developed in-house, usually with the technical help of the vendor. When customers, who generally were quite knowledgeable about the technology, had problems with their systems they usually contacted the vendor of the computer system. The vendor's staff then worked with the customer at the customer's site to resolve the problem; like service engineers, support analysts were often resident at a large customer's site. These support personnel were variously called *systems analysts* or *field analysts* or *support analysts*, and were generally conversant with most aspects of the operating system and associated utilities. They were able to handle most customer issues on-site in a reasonably short time frame. For very complex issues they would call upon specialists located at regional and corporate offices, and analysts and specialists together would resolve customer issues. While some companies charged software license fees, few charged for software support, because hardware was very expensive and the hardware margins and hardware maintenance fees more than covered software support costs.

This started changing, slowly at first, when minicomputers became available, and rapidly after that, with the growth of the personal (desktop) computer market. Cheaper and more reliable hardware meant that hardware systems and service revenues started decreasing. The number of computer users started increasing, and as computer vendors started selling into more markets the variability in the technical expertise of the customer base started increasing. Software-only companies started to enter the marketplace, developing application software that ran on top of different platforms. Other software companies developed *middleware*, or software that ran on different platforms, that was itself a platform for more applications. The number of layers of software increased, and competitive pressure drove down software prices. Networks, once a rarity, started becoming commonplace with the development of Local Area Network (LAN) technology. The Internet, originally developed by the United States Department of Defense, found increasing commercial and personal use, and most recently the World Wide Web (WWW) has dramatically increased network usage.

Much has been written about all these industry changes, and interested readers may read any of the many computer history books available to get a historical perspective. For the others, Table 1.1 summarizes those changes that have had a major effect on the support industry.

TABLE 1.1   Factors Affecting the Support Industry

Factor	Past	Current
Number of computer systems	Few	Many
Cost of systems	High	Low
Number of users	Few	Many
Technical expertise of users	High	High/Medium/Low
Layers of software	Few	Many
Sources of software	Few	Many
Per-unit cost of software	High	Medium/Low
Product margins	High	Low
Degree of networking	Low	High

Technical Support

Computer systems environments are far more complex today than they were only a few years or even a few months ago, even though hardware technologies appear to be consolidating around a few common platforms. The complexity is brought about mostly by new software technologies, and the interfacing effects of networking technologies. The reliability of hardware in general means that more and more support is focused on software and networking. We call this evolving support paradigm *Technical Support*.

By our definition, Technical Support encompasses all product support that can be provided to a customer from a remote location, *support by wire*, as it were. Technical Support is therefore more than software support, and includes the remote service functions of hardware service. The purpose of technical support is to help customers successfully use products.

TECHNICAL SUPPORT ORGANIZATION

The *Technical Support Organization* is the organization in a company charged with addressing product-related issues raised by customers or users of the products. Technical Support Organization (TSO) is the generic name used in this book; the actual organization may be called something else in most companies (e.g., Customer Support Group, Customer Support and Services, Support Services, Software Support, or Product Support Center).

What a Technical Support Organization Does

The TSO typically addresses only product-related issues: defects with products (The product causes my computer to stop when I type in a certain sequence of commands.); questions on the usage of products (How do I use your products to access my network?); and questions on the customer's application of the products (How can I balance my books using your product?). Defect issues that cannot fully be handled by the TSO are generally passed on to the Research and Development organization; unanswered product-related questions may be passed on to the technical documentation group; and large-scale business application issues may be passed on to a separate consulting group. Sometimes customers call in specifically with suggestions on how the product may be changed; these *Feature Requests* are generally passed on to the Product Management or Marketing groups.

The TSO differs from other groups in a company that may talk to customers, in that the TSO does not typically handle business-related transaction issues (e.g., entering or tracking orders), order-fulfillment issues (e.g., shipping), classroom training, or face-to-face business consulting. A TSO's relationship to other organizations is shown in Figure 1.1. In some companies it is possible that all these functions are under one umbrella organization—for the purposes of this book, however, the definition of the TSO will be limited to the preceding.

Difference between a Technical Support Organization and a Help Desk

There is some confusion in the industry on the differences and similarities between a Technical Support Organization and a *Help Desk*. In some companies no distinction is made between the two, while in others the two are very different organizations with different roles. While both TSOs and Help Desks deliver support to their customers, and in fact generally use the same tools and technologies, we prefer to make a distinction between a Technical Support Organization and a Help Desk, identifying four areas where a Technical Support Organization differs from a Help Desk:

- Customers served
- Products supported
- Services offered
- Reporting structure

Technical Support Organizations tend to have an external focus. They generally support customers outside the bounds of the company, and are the conduit for post-sales customer contact with the company. Help Desks, on the other hand, have an internal focus. Help Desk customers are typically employees of the same company, and they use the Help Desk for day-to-day support of their company's computing environments.

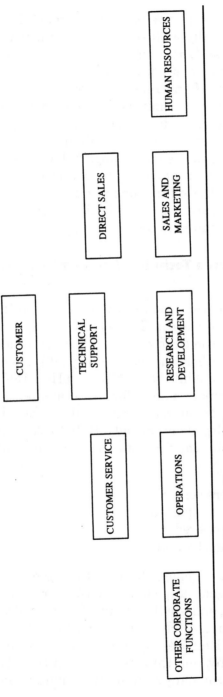

FIGURE 1.1 The Technical Support Organization.

6

The products and environments supported by a Technical Support Organization are generally created and sold by the company. The products may interface with the products of other companies, and in some cases a TSO will support some of the other products. That, however, is the exception and not the rule (except for Multivendor Support organizations, discussed in a later chapter). Help Desks, on the other hand, generally support their customers' computing environments, and this may include products from many different vendors, including the company. The products supported by a Help Desk are generally established by corporate policies and standards, and may include internal applications, such as payroll or order processing, used in the company for routine operations.

Technical Support Organizations deliver product support services, which may include business consulting services to end users on the supported products. Help Desks normally provide a similar scope of services, except for business consulting. On the other hand, many Help Desks are also responsible for asset tracking and maintenance. The Technical Support Organization usually contains the penultimate level of technical escalation—the last level of escalation before the Research and Development Organization. For applications that have not been developed in-house, issues that a Help Desk cannot address will be escalated to the Support Organization of the vendor of the offending product.

Last, a Technical Support Organization often reports to a Sales, Marketing, Operations, or Research and Development organization; though increasingly the organization reports directly to the chief executive of the company. Help Desks generally report to the Corporate Information Systems organization in a company.

With the increase in Multivendor Services, the distinctions between Technical Support and Help Desks are blurring in some companies. This is discussed later in Chapter 9.

FUNCTIONS IN A TECHNICAL SUPPORT ORGANIZATION

As in any organization, there are many tasks that are performed by the people in a Technical Support Organization. In the TSO of a small company the same people may perform multiple tasks; in larger organizations people are assigned to departments, each of which has its own charter in support of the mission of the organization. For example, if your group is small you may take on the responsibility for people management, marketing, and planning; whereas Technical Support Representatives (TSRs) may be responsible for providing support, and maintaining all support systems. In a medium-size support group each of these functions may be performed by a different department in the support group. In a large support group, one function may be performed by multiple departments. These departments all may be co-located at one site, or distributed across many building, cities, states, or even countries. The functions may be grouped into *key* functions and *support* functions.

Key Functions in a Technical Support Organization

There are three key functions in a Technical Support Organization:

- Support Delivery
- Planning
- Sales and Marketing

The Support Delivery function is the core business of a Technical Support Organization. It is the function that accepts and responds to support requests made by customers. The Planning function of the Technical Support Organization prepares the organization for changes in the environment; this may include planning and budgeting functions, as well as preparedness to deliver support for future products. The Sales and Marketing function is responsible for creating, packaging, and selling support offerings.

Support Functions in a Technical Support Organization

The key functions found in a TSO are supported by other functions like:

- People Management
- Technology Infrastructure
- External Interfaces

The People Management function in a Technical Support Organization supports the key functions by providing the mechanism for hiring, training, motivating, and compensating technical support employees. The Technology Infrastructure function provides the tools and technologies that enable technical support employees to do their jobs. The External Interfaces function is responsible for managing the relationships between the Technical Support Organization and other organizations, both within the company (such as Research and Development), and outside the company (such as support partners and affiliates).

Figure 1.2 demonstrates how the functions fit together.

Support Center

In the remainder of this book the part of the Technical Support Organization that is directly responsible for support delivery will be referred to as the *Support Center*. A support center is therefore made up of the collection of individuals and departments that interact with customers of the Technical Support Organization, handle the issues raised by those customers, and deliver support. Support Centers are sometimes also called *Call Centers*, *Response Centers*, or *Technical Assistance Centers* (TACs). Note that the Support Center is not necessarily at one location; it may in fact be spread over multiple locations.

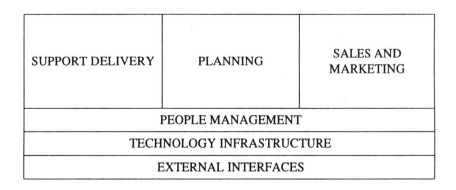

SUPPORT DELIVERY	PLANNING	SALES AND MARKETING
PEOPLE MANAGEMENT		
TECHNOLOGY INFRASTRUCTURE		
EXTERNAL INTERFACES		

FIGURE 1.2 Functions in a Technical Support Organization.

CUSTOMERS OF TECHNICAL SUPPORT

A Technical Support Organization exists to resolve product-related issues reported by its customers. But who are these customers? Customers of a Technical Support Organization are determined by its service policies and offerings. The service policies and offerings also define the products supported by the TSO, and usually the level of service that support customers may expect on those products. A small Technical Support Organization that supports a limited number of products may have only one support offering, and provide the same level of service to all customers. A large organization may offer multiple levels of support on different products, or combinations of products, and customers may make arrangements for the level of support that best fits their needs.

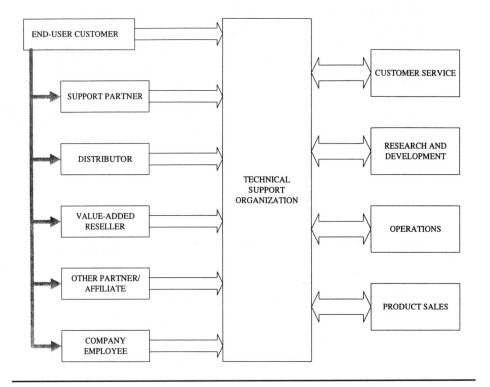

FIGURE 1.3 Customers of Technical Support.

The actual customers of a TSO may be end-user customers who actually purchased the product, proxies for those end users, partners of the company, or even company employees or others who need assistance from the TSO. The customer community of a Technical Support Organization is therefore larger than the traditional definition of a customer in most companies: individuals or entities that actually purchase the product (see Figure 1.3). We prefer to use the word *customer* instead of *user* when talking about someone who uses a TSO, even when that person may not be a customer in the strict sense of the word, because we believe that the terminology helps support personnel think of all users as customers. This mindset leads to a better quality of service to all users, and not only for those people who have actually purchased the product.

Consider an example: This book was written using a commonly available word-processing software package. If we had encountered issues with the product, we would have called the Support Center of the vendor of the software. If we were in a corporate setting we may have called a Help Desk in our company; and if the issue we had was complex and beyond the capability of the Help Desk to handle, a Help Desk technician may in turn have called the vendor's Support Center for assistance. The vendor in turn may have made arrangements with a Third-Party Support Organization to provide support on the word-processing package. If this outsourcing company had issues with the product, they in turn would have called the vendor's Support Center. Last, the Support Center could also receive support requests from within the company; for example, for technical assistance in a large presales situation.

An essential component in the management of any Technical Support Organization is a keen understanding of the demographics of the support user community. A good knowledge of the customers of the Support Center and their expected skill level can help determine the kinds and level of support to offer, and help set the operating standards in the Support Center. A Support Center that supports products sold into the consumer market will have to offer service in the evenings and on weekends, and at a level that is appropriate for the home user. This in turn may allow you to hire TSRs who are not very technically skilled but are excellent at dealing with home users of the products. On the other hand, a Support Center used by business customers that bet their business on products supported by the Center will have to be available during the customer's business hours, and hire technically superior people who can quickly restore a customer's operations.

TECHNICAL SUPPORT MANAGEMENT

The job of a Technical Support Manager is changing as rapidly as the Technical Support environment itself. What used to be a fairly straightforward job that involved knowing your company's products and having some communications skills has turned into a general management job that still requires some technical skills, but also requires skills in planning, marketing, sales, technology selection, partner management, people management, and finance. This is happening in almost all technology companies as growth in technology penetration, increases in support workloads, and pressures to cuts costs are placing new demands on all levels of support management. This situation is particularly prevalent in small and midsize companies, and even some large companies, that cannot afford to provide corporate support personnel to help out a support manager. Yet most companies are putting their support organizations under increased scrutiny, because that is one area of the company where costs are going up and the value is not always clear to company management.

As support organizations get larger, as they start charging for support, and as their revenue streams increase they will play a more important role in technology companies. Technical Support Organizations will be considered essential business units of technology companies; this has already happened in some companies, and many others are planning to move in that direction. In addition to managing a technical function, support managers will have to manage a business with revenues, costs, products, and services.

This represents a significant shift in focus, and a great career opportunity for support managers. As business managers they will have enhanced stature in their companies, and a successful stint in support business management could lead to bigger and better general management opportunities. We also see general management candidates in large companies being cycled through the technical support business to gain experience, just as those people are cycled through other company functional areas, such as operations, manufacturing, finance, and marketing.

As a practical matter, support managers will need to broaden their skills and experiences to cope with this changing environment. The most skilled support representative will not automatically be the best candidate for a support management job. All candidates will be expected to demonstrate their ability to view support as a business function, to understand its relationship to the other operating functions in a company, and to develop and implement a vision for the technical support business. We see a day when colleges and universities will offer courses in technical support management, and in the not-too-distant future, programs on general management with tracks for support managers.

AUDIENCE FOR THIS BOOK

There are two main audiences for this book: incumbent or aspiring managers of Technical Support Organizations, and managers or executives currently responsible for the success of the support business operation. As mentioned earlier, most incumbent or aspiring managers of TSOs frequently do not have the training or experience to step into a management role. They are not aware of all the things they need to do, or how to go about doing them. This situation is particularly prevalent in new and rapidly growing companies, where there is no established precedent from which a support manager can learn. Even in companies that have had Technical Support Organizations for some time there is often no formal training material on technical support management, and managers have to learn on the job.

This book meets the needs of these audiences by offering a comprehensive and practical discussion of the issues facing them, and discussing the advantages and disadvantages of different approaches they may take to address those issues. Consolidated into one text are all the factors that come up in the operation of a Technical Support Organization, and managers are given the tools they can use to make decisions and run the business.

A common organizational strategy in small but growing companies is to place the Technical Support Organization under the Chief Executive Officer, or under an executive of a well-defined area (e.g., the Vice President of Operations, the Vice President of Marketing, or the Chief Financial Officer). These senior managers are often unfamiliar with the strategic (or operational) details of Technical Support. This book will help these executives better appreciate the importance of the TSO and use it to further corporate strategy and goals.

Marketing and Product Managers in technology companies will also find this book useful. They will understand the value technical support brings to the business, and how the Technical Support Organization can gather competitive information that can be used to develop and market new products and programs. For example, a Product Manager could work with the Technical Support Organization to establish a conduit for requests made by customers for new features in existing products. A Marketing Manager may be interested in understanding how products are being used, in order to repackage the product and sell it into new markets.

Managers of Research and Development, and Engineering, will understand what actually happens to their products once they are shipped, and how usage and problem information reported by customers can be valuable in improving quality of products. Even cursory analysis of problem reports can point to major issues with products, and can result in early detection and correction of potentially damaging problems. Development managers will also get an understanding of how products can be changed to reduce the need for support requests; and if customers do call, how to reduce the duration of the support transaction by making products more supportable.

Managers of internal Help Desks and Customer Service groups will find similarities between their operations and the Technical Support Organization. They can use some of the concepts and techniques described in this book to help them run their operations.

Partners, integrators, and customers of technology companies may read this book to understand what happens behind the scenes when they report a problem or question, and how they can use the system to their best advantage. Our belief is that there will soon be college courses in Technical Support Management; this book could be used as a textbook in such courses.

A WORD ON STYLE

The approach taken in writing this book was to provide a comprehensive and rigorous discussion of issues of interest to our target audience. This is not an introductory text. We expect that our audience is familiar with the terminology, markets, and concepts of the technology industry, so little time is spent on underlying technologies. Focus is instead placed on Technical Support. We identify and discuss the issues the reader is likely to encounter, by first developing a framework for discussion, then identifying key issues, discussing the factors surrounding the issue, and finally discussing various approaches to address the issue. Whenever possible practical advice and tips that the reader can use are given.

Our goal is to not to direct the reader, but to discuss and guide. We want to give our readers a context in which to view and analyze technical support, and by discussing many factors around each issue we expect that the reader will apply the discussions to the context of the reader's own situation. We feel there are enough differences between companies and market segments, and so many and rapid changes in the industry, that to espouse one approach over all others would be wrong, if not irresponsible. For example, supporting customers of consumer software is not the same as supporting customers that use products for mission-critical applications. While there are clearly some techniques that apply equally well to both types of support, there are other factors peculiar to each segment that do not translate well to the other. There is no *standard* way to deliver technical support, and no *best* way that applies across all companies.

To deliver world-class technical support you must develop an organization and implement programs at a world-class level. We therefore want to help you understand the issues, develop a framework, then decide and implement what is best for your business.

STRUCTURE AND OVERVIEW

This book is organized into nine chapters, including this introductory chapter.

Chapter 2—Strategy and Direction

In Chapter 2, "Strategy and Direction," we discuss in some detail the value the Technical Support Organization brings to a company. We offer the reader some guidance on how to assess this value, and how to position the TSO in the company. An essential part of the job of a Technical Support Manager, indeed of any Technical Support employee, is to be able to articulate and communicate the benefits of the organization. The constant marketing of the organization within the company lays the groundwork for negotiations during the company's planning and budgeting process. This chapter will help the reader understand the linkage between customer satisfaction and customer loyalty, and be able to make a better case for the TSO during the planning process. We also spend some time going over current trends in the computer industry, and the implications these trends have for technical support. Change in the industry is constant and rapid, and while this presents challenges to technical support managers it also presents new and exciting opportunities. We examine some of the new developments in the industry, and make some predictions about the directions in which we think the industry is headed.

Chapter 3—Process and Infrastructure

The success of daily operations depends to a large degree on how the Technical Support Organization is structured, and how support requests from customers are handled. Chapter 3, "Process and Infrastructure," discusses how work gets done in a TSO, from the time it is received to the time it is completed. We will talk about both the process of how work flows in and through the organization, and how to structure your organization to optimize those flows. We will also discuss escalation of support requests, account management, and the hours of operation of your support center.

Chapter 4—People and Culture

One of the biggest challenges faced by Technical Support Managers is *people management*. Technical support is a demanding profession, and constantly dealing with customers' problems can be demoralizing. Chapter 4, "People and Culture," discusses how to create a culture for your TSO; and how to recruit, hire, train, motivate, and grow the people in the TSO.

Chapter 5—Performance and Measurement

Of course, if you manage an operation and manage people, how do you know how they are doing? Chapter 5, "Performance and Measurement," addresses this issue and helps you think about and define performance measures that reflect reality, are meaningful, and, most importantly, help you decide what actions you must take to run and improve your Technical Support Organization. We will discuss the different types of measurements, and give examples of each type of measure in different areas of measurement. We also talk about the characteristics of a good metrics system, and offer some suggestions on how to implement such a system.

Chapter 6—Planning and Budgeting

At many of the conferences we attend, many managers say that the most distasteful part of the job is justifying and getting resources to do the job. Chapter 6, "Planning and Budgeting," helps you make a business case for your organization, and gives ideas on how to go about getting resources using the language of the people who control resources. We will talk about some common techniques for forecasting and estimating staffing levels, and examine the relationship between staffing levels and service levels.

Chapter 7—Products and Tools

Now you have the resources, how do you decide where to spend money, what to buy, how to affect your work load? Chapter 7, "Products and Tools," covers how to influence the products you support, and how to select tools that increase the productivity of your support organization. We review support automation technologies in use today, and discuss how you can use those technologies to improve your support organization. We also discuss the impact of the Internet, and the World Wide Web, on technical support delivery.

Chapter 8—Positioning and Marketing

Many companies have found that segments of their customers have different expectations of technical support, and that some are prepared to pay for the right kind of support. How do you decide what kinds of support offerings you must have? Chapter 8, "Positioning and Marketing," discusses the need for marketing your organization's services and successes internally and externally. It provides information on selecting a strategy, developing and pricing your support offerings, getting the word out, penetrating the marketplace, and establishing lasting relationships with your customers.

Chapter 9—Partners and Affiliates

Finally, Chapter 9, "Partners and Affiliates," looks at relationships with third-party support providers, and examines how to expand your operations to support your customers on products not made or sold by your company. It also considers the option of outsourcing, reviews the special needs of partners, such as systems integrators, distributors, and value-added resellers, and offers sources for industry conferences, publications, and professional membership opportunities for technical support professionals.

Strategy and Direction

To have a successful Technical Support Organization, both company executives and technical support managers must have the same answers to two questions: What is the strategic value of the technical support organization to the company, and what does that mean in operational terms? The answer to the first question provides some insight into the mission and purpose of the Technical Support Organization. The answer to the second determines how much the company is willing to invest to realize that value and the support programs that are implemented in the organization.

It is incumbent upon all support managers to constantly align their sense of technical support's value to that of company executives. Sometimes this means that support managers must change their own perceptions to match those of company management, but more often than not it means that support managers must educate their executives on the value that the support organization brings to the company and its customers.

This chapter will discuss the value that technical support can bring to a company, and how to demonstrate that value. We then examine the roles the Technical Support Organization plays in a company, and show how a support manager can make an economic justification for technical support.

Last, we look at some trends in the industry, and discuss the impact we believe these trends will have on Technical Support Organizations in the future.

STRATEGIC VALUE OF TECHNICAL SUPPORT

It may be obvious to managers of technical support why a technical support function is essential in a technology company. However, many executives in technology companies do not fully realize the purpose of technical support, and sometimes wonder what the technical support organization does and what value it brings to the company.

The primary mission of any Technical Support Organization is to provide information and services to customers to help them be successful in their use of the company's products. By providing the right information and services, the technical support organization will increase or maintain the value of the products, as perceived by the customer, and improve customer loyalty and satisfaction.

Why Loyalty Is Important

Why is this important? There is a business imperative for technology companies to retain customers in the face of competitive pressures. Research has shown that the extent of customer loyalty can significantly impact the profitability of a company; an article in the *Harvard Business Review* ("Zero Defections: Quality Comes to Services," by Frederick F. Reichfeld and W. Earl Sasser, Jr., *HBR,* Volume 68, Number 5, September-October 1990) reported that a 5 percent reduction in customer defections in a software company boosted profits by 35 percent. The basic thesis is that reducing the defection rate (improving loyalty) results in a longer average customer life span. This in turn increases the likelihood of additional sales to existing customers, thus generating profit. Profitability is further enhanced when selling to existing customers, because the cost of selling to those customers is generally lower than the cost of selling to new customers, since existing customers generally require less of a sales effort.

Dynamics of Satisfaction and Loyalty

One of the contributors to high customer loyalty is customer satisfaction. Figure 2.1 shows four broad categories of customers: discontent and disloyal; discontent but loyal; content but disloyal; and content and loyal.

Discontent and disloyal customers are those that are not happy with a company's products, and will switch to another company at the earliest opportunity. Disloyalty can be high because competitive products are readily available and the cost of switching to competitive products is low. They may be dissatisfied for any one of a number of reasons, but there are two major rea-

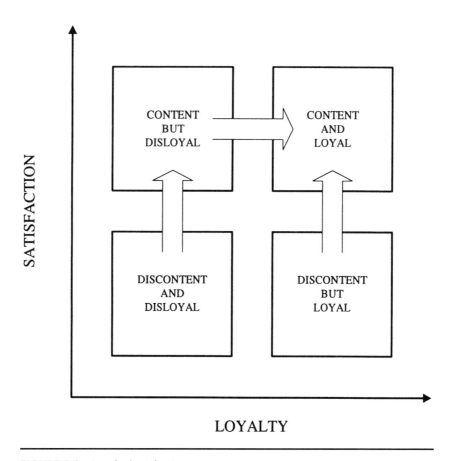

FIGURE 2.1 Loyalty/satisfaction categories.

sons: They may have had a very bad experience with the company or the product, or they are not the right customers for the product. The latter is a marketing issue, because the product has been sold to a customer who will not realize value from the product. There is not much a Technical Support Organization can do about that. Customers who are discontent and disloyal because of a bad experience with a company or its products can be salvaged by the Technical Support Organization by first making them content and then making them loyal. A company must decide how much value it places on such customers to determine what it is willing to do to salvage these customers.

Content but disloyal customers are found most often in commodity technology market segments; for example, where there is no clear market leader, competition is high, and many products are available with little or no differentiation between them. As before, it is easy for a customer to switch to a competitive substitute product. In these situations a Technical Support Organization must move customers to the content and loyal category by providing services and value that differentiate that product and company from the competition. Because the customers are happy with the product, they are more receptive to value-added services; however, the pricing for these value-added services must also be competitive with substitutes.

Discontent but loyal customers are found in market segments where there is little or no competition and few substitute products are available. This generally occurs when a company's products use new and/or proprietary technology, and the customer has purchased the product on the basis of one or more specific features not available elsewhere. This situation may also arise if the product has a significant cost advantage over that of its competitors. Customers in these segments face high costs of switching, so they tend to remain loyal to the company even if they are not satisfied. In theory, as long as a company can maintain the competitive advantage of its products, the satisfaction of its customers will not materially affect its profitability. Free markets being what they are, however, substitute products will appear in the marketplace, and dissatisfied customers will defect to competitors. It therefore makes strategic sense for the company to keep these customers satisfied even in the absence of competition. In these situations, the Technical Support Organization serves to maintain customer loyalty by providing support and moving customers in this category to the content and loyal category. Customers in this category can also provide a steady stream of support revenues, because the product is usually essential to them; if the product were not essential they would have either not purchased the product or settled for a lesser substitute.

Content and loyal customers are the most profitable for a company. They may be found in any market segment, and they value the benefits they derive from the company's products. Customers in this category tend to buy additional products from the company at low incremental selling costs, and further contribute to profitability by providing referral services. These customers are also willing to pay for value-added support services to further enhance the use of the products, and so provide another revenue stream for the company. Customers in this category expect a consistent level of service, so a Technical Support Organization must ensure that all support delivery functions are executed well and in a consistent manner. The company cannot afford to lose customers in this category, either to competitors or to other loyalty/satisfaction categories. To the extent that customers are happy with the product and ways of doing business with the company, a major reason for a change in loyalty or satisfaction is poor support. A Technical Support Organization must therefore provide mechanisms to quickly identify, escalate, and address product issues that may lead to slippage in loyalty and/or satisfaction.

In all the four preceding categories the Technical Support Organization plays a significant role in keeping customers content and loyal. The extent to which a company wishes to keep customers satisfied and loyal determines the strategic value it places on the Technical Support Organization.

ROLES OF TECHNICAL SUPPORT

There are many activities that go on in a Technical Support Organization to improve customer satisfaction and loyalty. In performing these activities, the organization as a whole plays five distinct roles:

- Consulting and training
- Service
- Account management
- Nonproduct revenue generation
- Competitive differentiator

Consulting and Training Role

The rapid pace of technological change means that new technologies are often sold to customers who have little experience with the technology. It therefore takes them some time to adapt to the new technology, and no matter how sophisticated and complete the product and its supporting documentation, some customers will need assistance with the usage and operation of the product. It is in the interest of the company to ensure the customer's success with the usage of the product, because product sales will be short-lived if customers cannot use the product. Support of this kind usually has to be delivered by the product vendor, because typically only the vendor has the technology and product knowledge required to deliver the support. This is a *consulting and training* role of a Technical Support Organization. Without further product and technology changes, the need for a company to provide this function may diminish over time as the marketplace gets used to the technology, and also as other sources of usage and operations knowledge become available. For example, the introduction of personal computers (PCs) was a major technology shift in the marketplace, so PC vendors set up large support organizations to help customers get used to the technology. Nowadays the PC is ubiquitous, and while many of the vendors still have large support organizations their customers are generally more knowledgeable and have other sources for help. On the other hand, consulting and training can be a lucrative business for a Technical Support Organization, especially if it goes beyond products and into the customer's business needs.

Service Role

Not only is the pace of change rapid, but products are also getting more complex. The features available in some products today were unimaginable a few years ago. A consequence of this complexity is that the product documentation hardly ever keeps up with changes in products. The documentation that goes out with new products is often out of date before the product actually ships, because last-minute changes were made to the product after the documentation was sent to the printers. This is evidenced by numerous updates and addenda to documentation. Another consequence of product complexity, compounded by the rapid pace of change, is that product quality is not as high as it could be. New products and new releases of existing products often contain defects that were not identified prior to product release; some companies even release products with known defects if in their judgment the defects will not significantly affect customers. However, even if a product is released with no known defects there may be defects that are still inherent; most quality assurance techniques are designed to show the presence of defects, not their absence. Technological changes in the marketplace could mean that the product is put to use in an environment that did not exist when the product was created, or in an environment that was not tested with that product. For example, products may be designed for and tested on particular hardware platforms, but new revisions of those platforms may be released after the product has started shipping. In this and many other similar situations a company must have a means of collecting and disseminating additional information about products as it becomes available. Customers expect a company to stand behind its products and fix problems with them. This is typically done by the Technical Support Organization in its traditional *service* role.

Account Management Role

Customers of a technology company like to give feedback to the company, on their views of the product and suggestions for new features and products. Customer communications of this type differ from traditional customer service communications, such as billing and order or shipment tracking, in that they are technical in nature. A technology company must therefore provide a mechanism for customers to contact the company on technical matters.

Customers with many product issues, especially corporate customers with a large installed base of products from a company, expect a certain level of management attention from the vendor. In fact, it behooves a technology company to understand how a customer uses its products, and to keep track of product issues reported by a customer. By providing a means for customers to contact the company on technical issues, and by tracking customer usage and issues, a company furthers its relationship with its customers. In the days when most sales were large and made directly by a company to its customers, the company's sales staff established and managed the customer relationship. In these days of smaller sales and multiple channels, it falls upon the Technical Support Organization to provide this *account management* role.

Nonproduct Revenue Role

Hardware-only companies have always charged their customers for hardware maintenance. Software companies, on the other hand, often provided technical support at no charge, or charged license fees for the usage of their product and covered technical support costs with these fees. As product prices have come down, product complexity has gone up; and as computing power has increased and penetrated new markets, the costs of providing support to customers have gone up. What used to be just another cost of doing business buried in operating costs has became a significant line item in a company's financial statement, and it is getting increased scrutiny from company executives. Product sales alone can no longer cover the costs of providing support. To offset support costs, therefore, an increasing number of companies are charging for technical support. As the practice becomes widespread, more and more companies are finding that customers are willing to pay also for value-added services, such as consulting and application design. Technical support fees and charges for value-added services are therefore providing an increasingly important revenue stream for technology companies. This is the *nonproduct revenue* role of the Technical Support Organization.

Competitive Differentiator Role

The fifth major role of a Technical Support Organization is that of *competitive differentiator*. Even though technology is changing rapidly, few companies can maintain competitiveness solely on the basis of a technological lead. This is especially true in such technology segments as software, where barriers to entry are typically low. Competitors appear almost overnight, the technology becomes commonplace, and the lead disappears. Cost advantages diminish, and it becomes increasingly difficult to differentiate products from those of other companies. One way to achieve differentiation from the competition is to provide a higher level and value of technical support. This may be through easier access to services, a broader range of services, or better execution of services provided. The Technical Support Organization can therefore play an important part in product differentiation, and so contribute to product sales.

Internal and External Roles

The actual delivery of support by a Technical Support Organization is concentrated in the first three roles described previously: consulting and training, service, and account management. The other two roles are internal to the company, in support of the company's profitability. The extent to which a Technical Support Organization plays these roles affects its positioning within a company. Broadly speaking, Technical Support Organizations that focus primarily on the traditional service functions tend to be positioned as *product support* organizations, regardless of whether they charge for support. Managers of such support organizations will in general have a more difficult time demonstrating their strategic value to the company. On the other hand, Technical Support Organizations that provide value-added consulting and training, and perform account management services, tend to be positioned as *customer support* organizations. Managers of such organizations can enlist the support of customers to demonstrate their strategic value to the company, as well as more clearly demonstrate the effect of the Technical Support Organization on company revenues.

ECONOMICS OF TECHNICAL SUPPORT

Company executives in many but not all technology companies view technical support as a necessary evil, and a place where costs must be incurred. In these companies the Technical Support Organization is treated as a cost center; money spent on technical support is treated as a cost of doing business. There are historical reasons for this. In the days when software was sold by big hardware companies, the hardware service part of the business was far more profitable than the software support part, so companies could afford to subsidize the software support with money from hardware services. As hardware got more reliable and competition and technology made computer systems cheaper, hardware service became increasingly less profitable. At the same time, as software became increasingly more complex and users less sophisticated, software support costs went up—to a point where the hardware service business was unable to subsidize software support.

Software-only companies went through a similar progression. Software companies were initially able to subsidize technical support with product revenues. Introduction of cheaper hardware, dramatic increases in the user base, and competition from many startup software companies drove product prices down and support costs up—this time to a point where product sales could no longer carry technical support.

As a result, almost all technology companies now charge for technical support. We will discuss fee services in a later chapter; the remainder of this section discusses the economics of a Technical Support Organization within the context of a company, and how a support manager can position the Technical Support Organization. Should a Technical Support Organization be positioned as a cost center or a profit center? How can the economic effect of a Technical Support Organization be measured? We answer these questions by examining the three support delivery roles described previously: consulting and training, service, and account management.

Consulting and training are value-added services. They help the customer use the company's products more effectively; in other words, they enhance the value the customer realizes from the products. For this reason we believe that consulting and training should be measured as profit activities. Support management should be able to package and offer value-added services to customers, realize revenues for the delivery of these services, and incur costs associated with them. The entire operation is wholly contained within the Technical Support Organization, and so should the business measures.

The traditional service function is a cost activity. As technology products get more complex, there is a greater potential for product defects, and for customers to experience problems with installation and operation. A case can be made that a quality product should have no defects, self-install, and be intuitively obvious to use. The industry is not quite there yet, so the need for the service role of the Technical Support Organization can be attributed entirely to product quality. For this reason, the costs associated with the service role of the Technical Support Organization should be funded by the organizations that make the products, and treated as a cost of producing the product. Doing so gives company management better visibility into product profitability, since products with poor quality will generally incur higher support costs. This method of allocating service costs back to the product development organization provides a tangible measure of the effects of product quality, and an incentive to improve quality. However, as the paymaster, the product development organization can (and should) have visibility into support delivery operations and the opportunity to examine support costs for this activity.

Account management in a Technical Support Organization is a cost activity but should be measured as a profit activity. The costs incurred in this role are usually buried in other costs; but to the extent they can be separated, these costs should be those associated with issue escalations, customer visits and calls, problem management activities, sales support, and customer information tracking. These costs should be offset by all revenues realized from the installed customer base and from sales situations in which the technical support made a significant contribution, because the primary purpose of account management is to satisfy and retain customers by moving them to the content and loyal quadrant of the satisfaction/loyalty matrix. This methodology does not provide an actual statement of profit or loss; rather it is a way for support management to highlight its contribution to product revenues.

INDUSTRY TRENDS

There are four major industry trends that have had, and are continuing to have, a significant impact on technical support:

- Lower cost of computing platforms
- Increasing complexity on platforms
- Growth of platform networks
- Changes in the selling model

Lower Cost of Computing Platforms

The cost of computing platforms has been decreasing steadily since the early days of computers. This has led to the rapid proliferation of computers in all market segments. Although recent data suggest that the growth in the proliferation of computers is slowing down in the United States, growth is strong in other markets all around the world. In addition to the decrease in cost of computing platforms, there has been an increase in hardware reliability. This is true at all levels of computing power, from portable to desktop to mainframe. The combination of these two factors means that more reliable and less expensive computing power is available to more and more people, who may not always be familiar with the technology or its applications. Second, as computing costs have come down, more businesses and individual consumers have come to rely on computers for everyday tasks. In many cases their usage of computers is *mission-critical*; that is, the availability of the computing resource is essential to them. For example, many businesses, small and large, rely on computers to do everything from managing finances to designing new products.

Increasing Complexity on Platforms

This is an important point, because along with lower costs of platforms has come an increase in the quantity and complexity of software that runs on these platforms. It used to be that there were only a few hardware vendors, and fewer independent software vendors. All the software that ran on a platform came from no more than a handful of different vendors, and the complexity of the software on the platform was low. Software was generally custom written for a few specific applications. Now as more customers use computers for many more tasks, the amount of software available to do tasks has increased. Competitive pressures mean that a lot of software applications must be sold in quantity to be profitable, so software is mass produced. To sell into a mass market, however, the software must have features that appeal to as many customers as possible; the result of this is applications that have a lot more features than any one customer would normally use, but the features are included because some other customers may need them. This tendency to add features to software increases product complexity.

Another contributor to complexity on a platform is the sheer volume of available software that can be, and often is, installed on a single computer. This book was prepared with word-processing software that ran on a platform with printer and video drivers, graphics packages, Web browers, spreadsheet programs, utility programs, and many other applications, some of which were running at the same time. The interactions between the programs on a single platform, whether by design or not, can significantly affect the complexity on a platform. Furthermore, many applications are produced by different vendors who have varying levels of appreciation of interactions with, and the effects on and of, other applications on the same platform. This can lead to conflicts between applications, and can cause issues in unpredictable ways.

Growth of Platform Networks

Not only has there been an increase in the complexity on a platform, but there has also been an increase in the complexity of a platform's environment. As described previously, lower costs of computing platforms have meant that computing platforms are within the reach of more people, and so are widely scattered. In the days of mainframes, computers were often centralized in a computer installation. To use a computer you would either have to go to the installation itself or to a *remote job entry* facility. The development of computer terminals allowed users to connect to the central location and use the computer from a remote location; however, the computing capability of the terminal itself was limited. With the advent of minicomputers, computing capability started to be distributed in departments, and these departmental computers were often connected to the central computer installation. Users could then access the central computer through departmental computers, but the minicomputers were in a hierarchical relationship with the main computer. As user needs changed and the power and capabilities of minicomputers increased, networks of computers became common. In these networks, more and more minicomputers were interconnected in a *peer-to-peer* manner, with no single computer controlling the entire network. The development of Local Area Networks (LANs) did the same for desktop computers, and soon LANs were connected to other LANs through Wide Area Networks (WANs). More recently the popularity of the Internet, which is really a network of networks, has meant that many computing platforms are close to and can easily be connected to a network.

The complexity of networks means that applications on a platform can have interactions not only with other applications on the platform itself, but also with the network, and with other applications on other platforms in other networks. This interconnectivity means that there is a greater potential for issues arising from network connections (see Figure 2.2).

Changes in the Selling Model

The way in which computer products are sold, the *selling model*, has also been changing. In the days of proprietary systems, computer vendors would have effective control of all the systems software that ran on a system, and so could focus on the sale of the hardware. The customer's business needs were usually met by developing new applications, often with the vendor's help because of the technical complexity of working with proprietary systems.

As prices started falling and software for business applications became generally available, customers started basing hard-

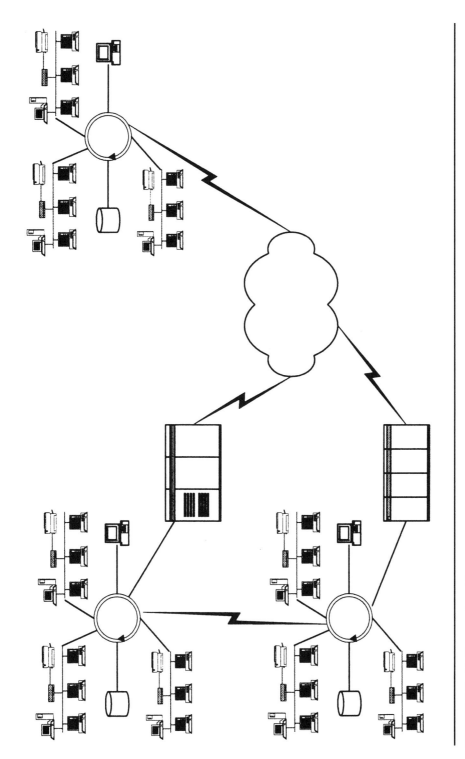

FIGURE 2.2 Platform networking.

ware purchase decisions on the amount of software available for each hardware platform. Hardware vendors therefore had an incentive to recruit software vendors to develop applications for their platforms, to make the hardware more appealing to a broader base of customers. Customers would then first select the software that met their needs, and then shop for hardware based on the software purchase decision.

This was sometimes a time-consuming process. Rapid technological changes, cost pressures, and the effects of corporate downsizing resulted in opportunities for systems integrators. These integrators would bring together hardware and software technologies to address business needs, and sell the package as a solution. More recently many hardware vendors have also entered the system integration business.

At a consumer level, many hardware vendors are selling platforms with preinstalled software. Low margins mean that each system cannot be cost-effectively configured with software to meet a customer's specific needs, so many vendors sell systems that contain a representative sample of software suitable for the consumer market. Almost all systems are sold with an operating system, some productivity software like word processors and spreadsheets, some multimedia applications, and increasingly some applications to access online services and the Internet.

In general, vendors of systems are nowadays selling more than products they manufacture, and customers of those vendors often look to the vendor for technical support.

IMPLICATIONS FOR TECHNICAL SUPPORT

The trends described in the previous section combine to have some effects on the Technical Support industry. The main effects are:

- Business consulting
- Knowledge management
- Value-added services
- Globalization

Business Consulting

The lower cost of computing platforms and the rapid pace of technological change mean that new products are entering the marketplace at a rate which often overwhelms the capability of customers to effectively utilize the products. Adopting and deploying a new technology can take some time, and even technologically savvy customers need help learning the technology. This is an even bigger problem for corporate customers, because changing a technology often impacts employees with a wide range of technical skills.

To be successful, a technology company must help its customers effectively use its products, and to do so requires that technical support personnel understand not only the products and their applications, but also the customer's business environment and processes. For example, almost all vendors of database servers offer product support and technology training, but many also offer consulting services that focus on assisting customers to use the database products in the customer's business environment. These database vendors have support personnel who are specialists in business environments, such as manufacturing or finance, as well as the vendor's products.

Knowledge Management

Another major effect of trends in the computer industry on technical support is the vast amount of product knowledge that needs to be created and managed. Rapid product and platform changes mean that many versions of a product may be running on many versions of different platforms, and each customer's implementation of a product interacts with other products on the customer's platform and network. As more customers use a product in new ways and generate support requests if necessary, product knowledge is created in the Technical Support Organization. Efficiently managing and disseminating this product knowledge is a critical success factor for the Technical Support Organization. In fact, we believe that a major part of technical support is *knowledge brokering*; that is, the acquisition, management, and dissemination of product knowledge.

Value-Added Services

Improvement in product quality and reliability in most markets, including technology markets, has trained customers to expect technology products to work right, first time and every time. In many technology market segments customers are reluctant to pay for defects in the vendor's products. They are, however, generally willing to pay for other services.

The pervasiveness of computer technology in businesses and the home means that support needs are changing. In addition to the traditional service and training roles described earlier, and the business consulting role mentioned previously, Technical Support Organizations are being called upon to perform additional services. In some business segments, more and more customers want to *single-source* their support needs; in addition to traditional technical support, this includes such functions as asset management, platform migration, and systems and network management. In the home market, customers are looking for one vendor to provide support on all installed products. As a result, the Technical Support Organizations of many technology vendors are now entering the multivendor and site services marketplace.

Globalization

Another effect of low cost computing, and networking, is the increasing globalization of technical support needs. Technology penetration is increasing in many markets around the world, and all these new customers also need technical support. Many technology companies are based in the United States, and they are having to learn how to deliver technical support in different business cultures.

In addition to supporting existing products that may have been translated to address the needs of foreign markets, a Technical Support Organization may also have to support products specifically developed for foreign markets.

TRENDS IN SUPPORT DELIVERY

All the factors previously described are affecting technical support, and we see the following trends as a result of those factors:

- Centralization and automation
- Electronic support services
- Fee-based value-added services

Centralization and Automation

Cost pressures arising from increased competition and lower margins are forcing many Technical Support Organizations to centralize operations in a few support centers, and so cut costs by realizing economies of scale. As product margins get smaller, the cost structure of most vendors cannot sustain decentralized support resources. By consolidating support resources into one or a few support centers, vendors can support a greater number of customers with the same number of people.

Technical support is increasingly relying on automation to help reduce support costs. Automation is being used to make customers self-sufficient, and also in the daily operations of the support center. In the past, support was delivered in person, with the vendor's support representative working with the customer at the customer site. Nowadays that situation is rare. Customers are expected to play a greater part in the support cycle, and may be provided such tools as Internet access, voice response units (VRUs), or fax-back systems to help them find answers to their support requests. Similarly, vendors have installed sophisticated tools to track customer support requests, and other tools to enable support personnel to quickly determine and resolve customer issues.

The dynamics between the cost pressure to centralize and the market pressure to globalize are forcing companies to develop innovative solutions to globalization. Some companies have placed support centers in geographic locations such that at any given time one or two support centers are always open. The centers concentrate their support on local customers, but are available to handle after-hours support from the other centers.

Other companies have only one main support center, and a few support personnel in key locations around the world who can access information from the main support center. As telecommunications costs come down, yet other companies are experimenting with one worldwide support center.

Electronic Support Services

An increasing number of companies are delivering support by electronic means, such as e-mail, bulletin boards, discussion forums on online services, USENET discussion groups on the Internet, and the World Wide Web. This trend is only partly fueled by expectations of a reduction in support delivery costs. The major forces driving this trend are the increased network connectivity and self-reliance of customers, and the benefits of round-the-clock and *asynchronous communications* with technical support personnel.

A major advantage of electronic support received by customers through public forums, in addition to low cost, is that a single request for help may result in many different solutions to the issue provided by other customers. The problem, of course, is that some of the solutions may not be accurate, and support personnel have no control over what gets disseminated.

Support delivered through private communications is much like support delivery over other media. An advantage of this approach over the other methods is that programs and other attachments can be exchanged with the customer, and a bug fix delivered rapidly.

Fee-Based Value-Added Services

The third major trend in the technical support industry is that of an increasing use of fee-based support services. In the past, customers paid license fees to the vendor, and support was expected on the licensed products. Vendors generally funded their support efforts from the license fees, which they could because of the high margins. As computer products became more of a commodity, prices and margins dropped, and vendors found it difficult to fund support centers from license revenues. More and more vendors therefore started charging customers for support.

There is, however, resistance from customers to paying for support unless they can see a tangible value. It is difficult for a company to show value for the traditional service functions, such as creation and delivery of bug fixes, but it is easy to make the case for value-added services such as consulting and training. This is because value-added services help customers realize value from the products they have purchased, so they are generally willing to pay for them.

Process and Infrastructure

No matter how a Technical Support Organization is structured or physically distributed, the major part of all work done in such an organization is the delivery of support to customers. This chapter will talk about the activities that are performed to deliver support from the time a request for support is received to the time it is satisfied, and the flow of these activities. It will focus on that work that involves some human involvement: entirely automated, or nonattendant, support delivery will be discussed in Chapter 7, "Products and Tools." We will also talk about escalations, account management, and the infrastructure necessary to facilitate the workflow.

As the products and technologies you support change, or as your market changes, you will want to look at how you are organized. A framework is presented to help you evaluate and restructure your organizational model.

REQUESTS, ISSUES, AND RESOLUTIONS

Terminology

As mentioned earlier, a support center exists to deliver support on product-related issues reported by its customers. To receive support a customer will contact the support center, explain the symptoms of a product-related issue for which support is needed, and request a resolution to the issue. The customer has then initiated a *support request*, which we define as a report of a particular *issue* with a product or products supported by the Technical Support Center, and a request for assistance and/or information to address the issue, the *resolution*. Some support centers refer to support requests as calls, cases, incidents, problem reports, or even escalations; we prefer the term *support request* because it more accurately describes the nature of the transaction, and does not imply the means by which the request is presented to the support center. Support requests are just that: a request for some assistance, and they arrive in any one of a number of different ways.

Linkage between Requests, Issues, and Resolutions

Many different customers may experience and report the same issue with a product, and so create many support requests in a support center. However, the underlying issue is the same for all these support requests, and the same resolution may resolve all or most of the support requests (see Figure 3.1). For example, many customers may run into a problem changing font sizes in a particular word-processing product because of a bug in the product. Even though there is one support request for each customer that requests assistance, there is only one underlying issue: the bug in the product. A resolution to the issue may be for each customer to reinstall the product with a different setup configuration. In some cases there may be multiple resolutions for the same issue; for example, the preceding resolution requires the customer to make a minor configuration change, while another resolution to the same issue may require the customer to obtain and install a fix to the product bug.

In some cases, an issue may be identified by a Technical Support Representative (TSR) even if it has not been reported by a customer. The TSR may then develop a resolution to that issue so that it is available for use by other TSRs in the event a support request about that issue comes into the support center.

We prefer this way of looking at the relationships between support requests, issues, and resolutions, because it makes ap-

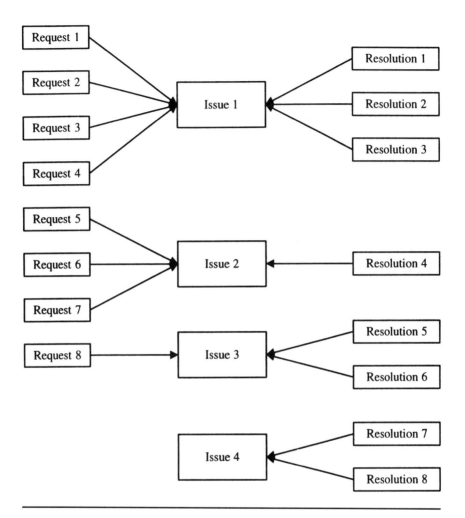

FIGURE 3.1 Requests, issues, and resolutions.

parent the differences between the three things. Readers familiar with database concepts will see that our approach represents
a normalized view of the three logically distinct things. A benefit
of making the logical distinction between a customer's specific experience of an issue (described in a support request) and the support center's knowledge about the underlying product issue and
its associated resolutions is that the distinction gives insight into

the impact of a product issue on the customer base. If a particular issue is encountered by many customers, then it may be a likely candidate for some proactive action by the support center, such as a documentation or product change. An issue that is reported by only a few support requests may not warrant the same amount of attention.

CATEGORIES OF SUPPORT WORK

There are four main categories of support requests that are initiated by customers: questions, reports of suspected defects in the products, feature requests, and requests for consulting assistance on the usage of the company's products in the customer's particular situation (see Table 3.1). A support center sometimes also gets requests for assistance that are better handled by other parts of the company. For example, many support centers receive requests for assistance with shipping or billing inquiries. Such requests should be routed to the Customer Service department. Any contact made by a customer is important, so a support center should have procedures on what to do with requests that are beyond the product-related charter of the center but still need attention by the appropriate company department. A cus-

TABLE 3.1 Categories of Support Requests

Category	Subcategory
Questions	Usage
	Installation
	Interface
Suspected Defects	
Feature Requests	
Consulting Design	Application
	Business
Consulting	

tomer who has contacted a company should always be served, even if the initial contact is not made with the right person. In some companies the support center may be responsible for all customer requests for assistance, and should implement procedures to handle all the different types of requests. In this book, however, we will confine our discussion to those product-related support requests that are within the purview of the Technical Support Center.

Questions

Questions on products generally make up the bulk of work for most support centers; for some products, questions make up 90 percent or more of the support work done on that product. Questions generally fall into three broad subcategories: usage, installation, and interfaces. Usage questions occur when a customer wants to do something with a product and cannot determine how to do it. So, in our preceding word-processing product example, if we wanted to change the layout of the text so that it appeared in three columns instead of one block, we may have requested support from the vendor. Of course, we could also have looked it up in the user documentation, but that's a separate matter! In this book, we will also classify issues with product operations as usage questions; for example, if for some reason one of the documents we produced using the word-processing package was corrupted and could no longer be opened by the word-processing package. We may have called the support center to see if we could get assistance to recover our document even though the corruption may have been caused by another product.

Installation questions arise when the customer has difficulty in installing the product. This may have happened, for example, if we tried to install the word-processing product on our computer and there was already a file in existence that the word-processing product needed to create before completing the installation. If the product installation procedures did not handle this situation, and there was no guidance available to us on how to work around this issue, we may have called the vendor for support.

Interface questions, while similar to installation questions, have to do with connecting the product to other products. For example, we decided to purchase a high-speed printer to use with our already installed word-processing software, but despite following the instructions to the letter we could not get the printer to work with the software. At this point we may have had to call the vendor to ask how to interface the printer to the word-processing software. There may also be interface issues between software products. For example, customers may have questions on how to use an Application Programming Interface (API).

Suspected Defects

Reports of suspected defects on products make up a smaller but still significant portion of support requests reported by support customers. By *suspected defect* we are referring to those situations when the product does not conform to published specifications or behave as expected. In the software industry, defects are commonly called *bugs*. If our word-processing package was designed to let us have up to four columns per page, but for some reason did not allow us to create pages with exactly three columns, we would suspect a product defect. Defects are often reported first as questions; in researching the issue in a support request a TSR may determine that the issue is in fact the result of a product defect.

Many product defects are usually detected and corrected prior to product release, but some defects make it out to customers and may result in work for the support center. A case may be made that most product-related questions are really defects, if not in the product itself then in the accompanying documentation. For example, if we need to call for support with a question on how to perform a certain function in our word-processing package even after reading the available documentation, one may argue that there is a defect in the manual or online help. In this book we will stay with the definition of defect as a nonconformance to published specifications.

Feature Requests

A customer may have an issue with a lack of functionality in a product. These types of issues may result in feature requests being reported to the support center. A feature request may be for additional functionality on an existing feature, such as asking for the word-processing product to permit up to six columns per page, up from four. Or a feature request may be for new functionality, such as adding a Table of Contents feature to the product. Feature requests are normally collected by the support center and passed on to the appropriate group in the company that will address the feature request.

Consulting Assistance

Finally, customers may initiate support requests that are really requests for consulting assistance on the usage of the company's products in the customer's particular circumstance. For example, we needed some help to develop a layout for our draft manuscripts. Rather than getting help from our editor, we could have contacted the vendor to help us design a layout. Consulting services can cover a wide range of activities, all the way from using products to actual business consulting. Consulting requests often come in under the guise of usage questions; the distinction between the consulting requests and usage questions depends on the service policies and offerings of the Technical Support Center. Service offerings are discussed in Chapter 8.

MIX OF SUPPORT REQUESTS

It is important to understand the mix of the different types of support requests that come in to a support center. The amount of work and the skill level required to answer each type of support request is generally different, so the mix of support requests can affect both the design and the staffing and scheduling requirements of a support center. Take a simple case of a support center that handles only two types of support requests: questions and product defect reports. Questions generally take less time to address than product defect reports; if a question takes an average of 10 minutes of work, and a product defect 30 minutes, then the total workload for 100 support requests can vary from as little as 1,000 minutes if all support requests are questions, to as many as 3,000 minutes if all support requests are product defect reports. This is shown graphically in Figure 3.2.

The mix of support requests could also affect the skill level that is required of Technical Support Representatives (TSRs) in the support center, and their training needs. Many questions may mean that the TSRs should be skilled in using the products; many product defect reports may point to a need for TSRs that have excellent diagnosis and analysis skills. Similarly, the way you organize your support center can be affected by the mix of your workload. More on this in the later section on organization.

Understanding the mix can help you decide where to apply scarce resources. Many support requests for installation help can point to a need for better installation guides shipped with the product. If you can estimate how many support requests can be avoided by improving the installation questions, then it may make economic sense to create the guide.

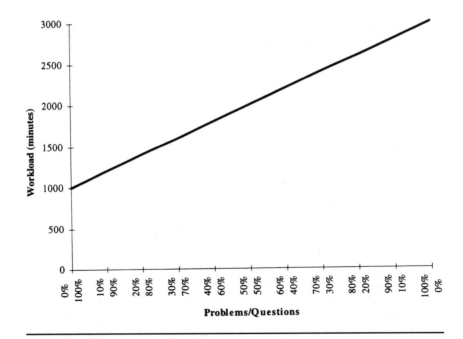

FIGURE 3.2 Workload variation.

Factors Affecting Support Request Mix

While it is easy to measure the mix of the types of support requests you receive in your support center, it is not so easy to determine why the mix is the way it is. There are many factors that go into creating the mix, but we believe that five factors are the main contributors: the market segments of the products, product and environment complexity, the quality and completeness of the products, the point in the product's life cycle, and the sophistication of the user community.

The markets into which the supported product are sold significantly affect the mix of support requests a customer may initiate. Commodity products, such as games and personal software, sold to the mass markets may generate mostly installation and usage questions, and almost no defect reports or feature requests. Business products, such as a small business accounting package, sold to business customers may result in a higher percentage of usage questions and requests for consulting assistance. Products used in a mission-critical environment, such as enterprise database servers sold to large organizations with significant technical expertise, may result in more defect reports and feature requests, and fewer usage questions.

The complexity of the supported products and the environment in which they operate also affect the mix of support requests. Simple products with few bells and whistles may result in relatively fewer usage questions than a complex product even if they are sold into the same market. For example, a solitaire game with one screen is more likely to generate installation questions than a fast-moving computer action adventure game with multiple controls and screens—the latter game may result in many more usage questions. The complexity of the environment in which a product operates can also affect the mix of support requests. For example, a single-user file server product may cause fewer usage questions and defect reports than a network file server with many users. Similarly, the usage of the product in the customer's environment can also affect the support request mix. If a customer is developing an application that makes use of the network file server, then the mix of support requests will change from mostly installation and application consulting at the beginning and during the customer's application development cycle, to usage and defect reports when the customer's application is put into production.

A product that has few defects and has good documentation is less likely to generate usage questions and defect reports than a product with poor quality and documentation. So too is a product that is easy to install and use, when compared to a product that requires a complex installation process and is difficult to use, even for technologically sophisticated users.

Products early in their life cycle are likely to cause more installation questions and product defect reports, relative to other types of support requests. Over time, as customers find most of the defects not fixed prior to product release, and your company fixes those defects, the relative number of defect reports will decrease. Similarly, as the user community at large gains familiarity with the product, installation questions will be driven by sales to new customers, and there will be a relative increase in the number of usage and perhaps consulting questions.

Finally, the sophistication of the user community relative to the product and its associated technology will affect the mix of support requests. The product or its associated technology may be so different from anything the user community has experienced that the support center may get a lot of usage questions and requests for consulting assistance. This often happens when new technologies are introduced to an existing market, or existing technologies introduced to a new market. On the other hand, the introduction of even complex products may not result in more usage questions or requests for consulting assistance if the user community is technology savvy and understands the uses to which the product may be put.

In addition to understanding the demographics of the support customer community, it is important to understand the markets into which support products are sold, the complexity of the products, the quality and completeness of products, and the sophistication of the user community. These factors affect the mix of support request types, and can give the support manager guidance in planning operations.

OVERVIEW OF SUPPORT PROCESSES

A *business process* is the execution of a series of activities that together produce a product or service required by an organization to fulfill its goals. In a well-designed process each activity builds on work done in the preceding activities, and contributes to the overall product or service being produced. Implicit in this definition of a business processes is the assumption that the activities performed and the circumstances under which each activity is performed are consistent and repeatable. In other words, the same things are done in the same way under the same circumstances.

How does this apply to technical support? A key operating goal of a support center is to resolve product-related issues reported by customers. The primary service produced in this case is the delivery of product issue resolutions to customers, and the activities taken to provide these resolutions make up business processes that fulfill the goal of the support center.

Three Key Support Processes

In the technical support environment a support request typically goes through three distinct processes on its way to being resolved for a customer. The customer is first validated and a support request accepted, then information is collected about the issue being reported, and the reported issue is researched and analyzed. If an existing resolution will address the reported issue, the resolution is delivered to the customer. Otherwise a resolution to the issue must be created and made available for delivery to the customer. The actions taken to validate the customer and accept the support request make up the *Validation Process*. The actions taken to collect information, research and analyze the issue and deliver the resolution to the customer's issue collectively make up the *Support Delivery Process*. To research an issue reported by a customer the TSR must search through a collection of resolutions to previously reported issues, and technical documentation on products that may be available to customers. We refer to the activities undertaken to create and maintain the information used by TSRs in the resolution of customer issues as the *Knowledge Process* (see Figure 3.3).

The three processes—Validation, Support Delivery, and Knowledge—together form the core business processes of a Technical Support Organization. There are many other activities that must be performed in a support center, but the activities performed in the three core processes are the most important, because these activities most directly bear upon the key goal of any support organization. These processes provide the operational capability to execute the mission of the organization. All other processes are executed to support the core processes. For example, the main purpose of the support sales process is to create and maintain customers for the core processes; the main purpose of planning and budgeting processes is to identify and obtain resources for these processes.

The execution of support processes is usually but not always sequential. Sometimes data collection and research and even

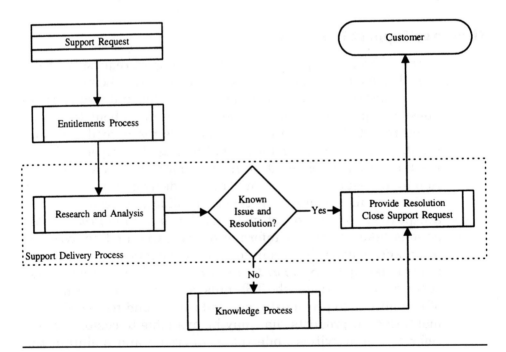

FIGURE 3.3   Overview of support processes.

knowledge creation proceed in parallel. A TSR may collect some data by asking a few questions, research existing information based on the data collected, and ask more questions using the results of the research. This is a common technique used in diagnosing a problem, and is the basis for many search systems that guide the TSR through a series of questions.

Analysis of data collected can also require further data collection. For example, a TSR may obtain a description of an issue from a customer, but the data collected in this interaction may prove to be insufficient as the issue is analyzed. The TSR may need more descriptive information, such as a series of steps to follow to reproduce the reported issue or even some sample code to reproduce the problem if the problem cannot be reproduced by the TSR using the data already collected.

Process Independence from Automation

Notice that in our preceding discussion we did not once mention any automation tools; the processes that are followed are independent of any automation tools used to implement or facilitate the process. In a support center with no automation tools whatsoever, the validation process may require going over to a file cabinet to look up a customer's folder to verify entitlement for service. The support delivery process may involve exchanging faxes with the customer, and sending a bug fix in the mail. The knowledge process may be entirely in the head of a TSR, and the knowledge base itself may be on various scraps of paper, or it may even be organized in folders and manuals stored in a central location. In fact, it is our experience that while the most effective TSRs appear to know everything necessary to support a product, they actually have a very good understanding of what knowledge exists in the support center, and how to find it. The specific steps in a support process, their invocation, and their sequencing are specific to a support center, and no two support organizations will perform work in the same way. This is one of the reasons that you should understand your workflow and map the support processes you want to implement before you make any automation investments.

While a detailed examination of the support processes in different companies may show differences in how each process is performed, who performs it, and the extent of its automation, the overall conceptual support processes are essentially the same in all Technical Support Centers. Our approach breaks out the core processes into logically separate sets of activities.

GOALS OF SUPPORT PROCESSES

By implementing and standardizing the three core processes, a support center achieves four goals:

- Deliver support only to valid customers
- Provide quick and accurate resolution
- Provide consistent look, feel, and performance to customers
- Enhance account management and issue escalation

Only valid customers are able to initiate support delivery, thereby ensuring that support is delivered to the expected customer base for which resources have been allocated. The number of customers being supported often drives the workload received by a support center. These support centers base their workload forecasts on this driver, and allocate resources accordingly. By providing support only to valid customers, one element of uncertainty in the workload forecast is eliminated. Support centers that are funded by support revenues and measured by their financial contribution to the company can ensure that resources are applied to customers that have purchased support services. On the other hand, some support centers may choose to support *all* customers, regardless of whether they have purchased the product or a support offering. It is important therefore to decide who is a valid user of the support center, and the extent of services offered to customers.

Support processes result in the quick and accurate resolution of customer issues. The support delivery process permits a TSR to rapidly collect information necessary to resolve an issue, minimizes the need for internal transfers of issue ownership, and facilitates the analysis of issue information collected by a TSR. The knowledge process ensures that resolutions to previously reported issues, and other information useful in the resolution of support requests, is organized and readily available to TSRs.

Standard processes provide a consistent look and feel to both internal and external users of the processes. Studies by market research companies and much anecdotal evidence have shown that support customer expectations are set in part by their experiences in the past; if a customer is used to a certain look and feel and level of performance from a support center, then a change in the support delivery could significantly alter the customer's satisfaction. If the change is positive (for example, a significantly better level of performance than usual), then a customer may start expecting a higher level of support delivery; if that expectation is not met, then the customer may have a very negative opinion of the support center. Conversely, a customer may be forgiving if the change is negative; but if the customer sees a constant deterioration in service, then the customer's satisfaction will decrease. Customers who purchase a given support offering should experience the same interfaces and performance for all issues.

Last, the support processes promote the systematic gathering of customer and product information, and can and should make that information available to users of the processes and other interested parties. This information can be used to enhance customer satisfaction through account management, and improve product quality through product issue escalation. For example, some support centers analyze the support transactions of key customers, and initiate management or sales contacts if the transactions point to problems at the customer's site. Similarly, many Research and Development organizations take great interest in the volumes and type of support requests for the products they have produced; even cursory analysis of these data can point to potential problem areas.

VALIDATION PROCESS

No matter how a request comes into a support center, both the request and the customer must first be validated and accepted for processing by the center. Most support centers implement procedures to first establish that a support request is in fact for a service provided by the center, and transfer or reject the support request if the center cannot help the customer. For example, customers often contact a support center and ask to buy a product sold by the company; if the support center does not handle product sales, then it must have procedures to transfer the request to the sales department of the company. Similarly, support requests are sometimes even made to the wrong company; this is becoming more prevalent as increases in both the number and complexity of products being sold and supported make it difficult to always identify the offending product or the vendor.

As more and more high-technology companies move away from free support offerings to fee-based support services, it is increasingly common to authenticate the identity of the customer initiating the support request, and verify the customer's entitlement for the support service being requested (see Figure 3.4). Some support centers require validation even for free support because they wish to provide support only to registered users. This lets them build up a database of registered users, which can be extremely beneficial for future marketing purposes. In some markets, the only direct interaction the company has with end-user customers is through the support center. Information collected about these end users can be used by the sales and marketing departments of the company to sell upgrades and new products and services. The information can be used by Technical Support Organizations to design and sell support offerings. We will discuss this more in subsequent chapters.

A number of different schemes are used to authenticate the identity of customers and verify entitlements. A simple method used by many vendors of consumer products is to have the customer provide a product serial number, which is often marked on the product itself. The product serial number is checked against a database of entitlements, and the customer is allowed to proceed for technical support if so entitled. If, on the other hand, the product has not been registered, or if the entitlement for support has lapsed, then the customer is routed to company personnel who can register the user or sell more support offerings. A common variation of this process is to assign each registered cus-

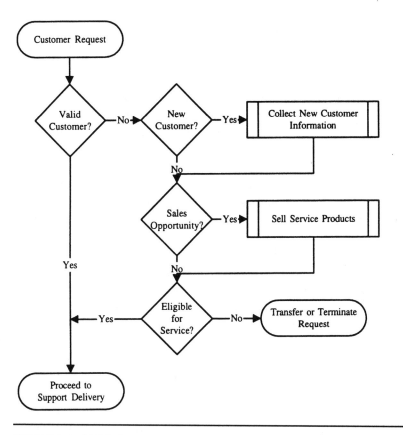

FIGURE 3.4 Validation process.

tomer a *personal identification number* (PIN) or contract number. Each such number is then associated in a database with products that are covered for support, and the type of support entitlement for each product. This scheme is widely used by companies that may sell many products to the same customer.

SUPPORT DELIVERY PROCESS

Once a support request has been validated, the next step is to gather enough information about the request to resolve it to the customer's satisfaction. Information collected in this step includes a detailed description of the symptoms of the issue, the customer's specific request for assistance or information, details on the product and version, and a description of the environment in which the issue arises. In some situations, the customer may also provide examples of program code or other information to reproduce the reported issue. Depending on the policies and practices of the support center, information may also be collected on some characteristics of the support request, such as the customer's perceived severity and priority of the issue, the classification of the support request, and the desired resolution date (see Table 3.2). These characteristics often affect the subsequent treatment of the support request.

The description of the symptoms described by the customer is used to search a database of previously reported issues and their resolutions. If a match is found to an issue that had been resolved earlier, the resolution to that issue is given to the customer as an *interim resolution*. The customer may then test the resolution and accept it as a *final resolution* if it resolves the issue to the customer's satisfaction. In some situations, a support request will describe an issue that has been reported earlier by another customer, but for which the resolution is not yet ready for delivery. In these situations, the support request is put on hold until the resolution has been identified. If the issue in the support request is sufficiently severe, a customer may want an interim resolution until the final resolution is available (see Figure 3.5). Support requests of this nature are often escalated to a TSR who can develop an interim resolution.

If no match is found to a previously reported issue, or if a resolution in a previously reported issue is not acceptable or applicable to the customer, then the information in the support request is analyzed, additional information collected if necessary, and the database researched again. The purpose of analysis in this cycle is to refine the information collected so as to better search the knowledge base. This may take the form of additional questions asked by the TSR, or the development of the environment that consistently reproduces the problem. The data collection, research, and analysis cycle continues until the TSR determines

TABLE 3.2 Contents of a Support Request

Customer Information	Customer Name
	Customer Address
	Customer Phone Numbers
	Other Contact Information
Product Information	Product Name
	Product Number
	Product Serial Number
	Product Version
	Product Environment
	Other Product Information
Issue Information	Brief Description
	Symptoms/Detailed Description
	Instructions to Reproduce Issue
	Workarounds Attempted
	Other Issue Information
Support Request Attributes	Customer Perceived Severity
	Customer Priority
	Desired Resolution Date
	Category/Subcategory
Tracking Information	Tracking Number
	Date/Time Created
	Current Status
	Current Owner
	Date/Time of Next Action
	Date/Time Closed
	Resolution Code
	Cause Code
	Customer Satisfaction Rating
Working Notes and Logs	

that the symptoms either describe a new issue, or the interim resolutions available for likely matches do not address the issue to the customer's satisfaction. In both cases, the knowledge process is invoked. When a resolution becomes available through the knowledge process, the customer is given the resolution.

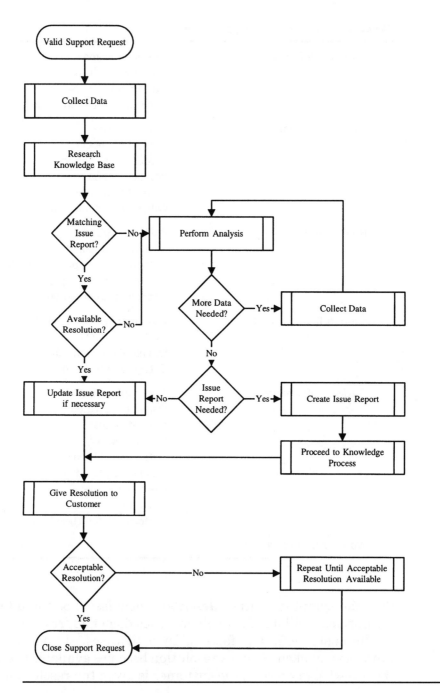

FIGURE 3.5 Support delivery process.

KNOWLEDGE PROCESS

The purpose of the *knowledge process* is to create and maintain knowledge about products for customers of technical support. By *knowledge* we mean that information about products and product behavior that is valuable to customers, and necessary for a TSR to perform support delivery. We refer to the totality of knowledge in a Technical Support Center as the *knowledge base*. In many support environments a large number of support requests are on issues that have already been reported by other customers, and resolved by support personnel. As described earlier, if each issue can be isolated, described, resolved, and the issue and resolutions made available to all TSRs, then a support organization can minimize the duplication of work in the center. In fact, a key measure of success of the knowledge process is its efficiency in avoiding the duplication of work for issues already reported and resolved.

We use the concept of an *issue report* to describe a distinct issue in the knowledge base. An issue report contains a brief description, or headline, that summarizes the main symptoms of the issue, and a detailed description of the circumstances under which the issue may occur and all the known symptoms of the issue. An issue report may also contain examples of program code that isolates the issue and demonstrates its effects. Last, an issue report either contains or indexes all known resolutions that are available for that issue. The contents of a sample issue report are shown in Table 3.3.

Problem resolution systems (see Chapter 7) use the concept of an issue report; when a TSR is searching through a knowledge base of known issues and their resolutions, a search is typically being made using keywords in the brief and detailed descriptions of the issue reports of known issues. If the search is successful, then the customer is given one of the resolutions described in the issue report. The TSR has in this situation minimized the amount of work that needed to be done to resolve the customer's issue, by using the work already done by another TSR for another customer.

An issue report is generally initiated by a TSR when a support request reports an issue not previously reported. An issue report may also be initiated by a TSR if the TSR finds an issue that

TABLE 3.3 Contents of an Issue Report

Issue Information	Brief Description
	Symptoms/Detailed Description
	Instructions to Reproduce Issue
	Other Issue Information
Tracking Information	Tracking Number
	Date/Time Created
	Issue Creator
Working Notes and Logs	

Product information exists for every product for which this is a known issue.

Product Information	Product Name
	Product Number
	Product Serial Number
	Product Version
	Product Environment
	Other Product Information

Resolution information exists for every known resolution to this issue.

Resolution Information	Resolution Type
	Resolution Description
	Resolution Attachments
	Category/Subcategory
	Resolution Creator/Owner
	Date/Time Created

is likely to come up in a support request, even if a support request has not yet raised that issue. For example, a TSR may have identified a new bug that occurs in some rare circumstances, and developed some ways to work around the bug. The TSR could then use the knowledge process to create an issue report and ensure that a description of the product issue (the bug) and the resolutions available to work around the issue are available to all other TSRs in the event that the bug is reported by a customer. A typical example of this is a *known bugs* database that is kept in most support centers. This database contains the equivalent of issue reports that describe bugs that are known to have shipped with a product, and generally describes what the TSR should do if a customer should report an encounter with the bug.

Issue reports may describe questions, documentation issues, feature requests, product defects, and so on. In short, any distinct issue on which a customer may call the Technical Support Organization is a candidate for an issue report. Issue reports are not the same as bug reports, because they are reports about any distinct *issue*, which may not always be a bug. For example, there may have been an omission in the user documentation on how to change font sizes in a word-processing product. After the first report of the issue, an issue report may have documented the symptoms of the issue (e.g., User cannot change font size), and a resolution that describes the proper way to change font size. Readers whose organizations create and disseminate Tech Tips or Support Notes will recognize these as variations of issue reports. Another example of issue reports is the solutions found in commercially available knowledge bases.

A TSR may sometimes invoke the knowledge process if a change or update is needed to an issue report. For example, a new support request may have reported some new and different symptoms for an existing issue that has already been documented in the knowledge process. In this example, the description of the issue report must be changed to reflect the new symptoms. At other times, a new resolution may be developed for an existing issue. In these situations, the issue report must be updated to contain or point to this new resolution.

In the knowledge process, as shown in Figure 3.6, all new issues and interim resolutions may be further analyzed and researched; and if product changes are necessary to resolve the issue, then a *product change request* may be initiated and forwarded to the appropriate department in the company, usually the Engineering or Research and Development organization. If and when product changes are made to resolve the issue, they provide a final resolution to the issue reported in the support request. Some examples of product change request include: a request to fix a suspected defect in the product; a feature request; a request to correct the documentation that accompanies the product; or a request to change the packaging of a product.

Each issue report describes a distinct issue. This is impor-

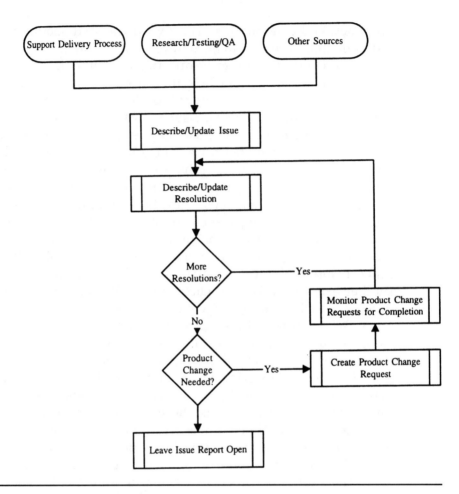

FIGURE 3.6 Knowledge process.

tant for two reasons: ease of search, and metrics. By limiting each issue report to one issue only, issue reports are easier to index and organize, and so easier to find. The other important reason is that each distinct issue report represents a measure of the knowledge process, and the frequency of usage of each issue report provides valuable information about the incidence of the issue in the customer base.

Some support centers use the term *solution*, or *resolution*, to refer to an issue report; we prefer to use *issue report* because it more closely describes the nature of the entity. An issue report is more than just a solution, because it also contains a description of the underlying issue, as well as (potentially) multiple resolutions available to resolve one issue.

INBOUND AND OUTBOUND SYSTEMS

By definition, every support center receives its core work from outside the organization, and in response to its customers disseminates knowledge in the form of resolutions. How the work comes into the center is important for the simple reason that it is the point at which your customers first come in touch with your organization, and their perceptions (and hence customer satisfaction) will be influenced by their experiences. The way work comes in also has implications on how it is distributed within your center and how efficiently it can be processed. We will refer to the mechanisms used to funnel support requests from customers as *inbound systems*. Similarly, the mechanisms that are used to deliver support to customers are called *outbound systems*.

Factors to consider when deciding on inbound and outbound systems include:

- Ease of use for the customer
- Cost to implement
- Common market segment practice
- Available staffing levels

As is the case with most management decisions, these factors are not always coincident, so you must make some trade-offs to determine the best mix for your support center.

First and foremost, the systems must be easy for the customer to use. It should be easy to report a problem or ask a question. *Easy* is a term relative to your market segment. If your market segment is relatively narrow and customers have a common level of technical understanding and knowledge, then you may be able to offer only one or two systems. If, however, your market is broad based and your center supports many different products in many market segments, the technical expertise of your customers will vary widely, so you should provide inbound systems that are appropriate to many technical skill levels. For example, in a narrow market segment with a small customer base you may need to provide only a means for customers to receive support by telephone. For a widely knowledgeable customer base, you may have to provide telephone support and perhaps bulletin boards and other systems, such as World Wide Web access on the Internet.

The cost to implement your systems is obviously a constraining factor on the systems you select. When considering costs, you should consider not only equipment costs, but also costs (and benefits) that may not be obvious at first glance but clearly must be incurred to operate the system. For example, many support centers allow customers to fax in a support request. The benefit may be that the fax system allows users to send in requests at any time without having to wait in a telephone queue, and to receive support in the same way. The cost analysis must, however, include the costs of distributing the incoming faxes to support personnel, and perhaps even of transcribing the support request into a problem resolution system, and then faxing back a resolution.

Vendors providing technical support in most market segments tend to have similar offerings and characteristics, so there is an expectation in the minds of customers that all vendors have a similar range of systems. So, if the common practice is for customers to report problems via e-mail, then customers in that market segment will expect new entrants to provide an e-mail inbound system. If you decide to go with inbound systems that are not common to that market segment, then you must be prepared to overcome some resistance and undertake some customer training.

Another important factor to consider when selecting systems is the level of staffing available to support those systems. If your analysis shows that you need to provide a telephone inbound system (a common situation), and customers in that market segment expect to talk to a support representative in a relatively short time frame, then you must ensure that you have adequate staffing to meet customer expectations, or you may reduce customer satisfaction with your support organization. In general, the greater the interactivity the market segment expects, the higher the staffing level you will have to provide to support that degree of interactivity.

INBOUND AND OUTBOUND SYSTEMS TECHNOLOGIES

Support is delivered by most support centers over the telephone system, but sometimes also via e-mail, direct electronic access and over the Internet, fax, and postal mail. Some of these technologies are discussed at length in Chapter 7, but we briefly compare them here for completeness.

Almost all support centers have some kind of telephone inbound system. It may range from something as simple as an answering machine for customers to leave a message, to a single telephone number staffed by a company receptionist, to a sophisticated Automatic Call Distributor (ACD) that routes calls to the next available TSR in any support center in the world. In most countries telephone systems are fast and convenient, and it is generally easy for a customer to place a call to a support center. Telephone technology is sophisticated, and offers both the company and the customer many options. However, the convenience and sophistication of telephone systems means that it is sometimes easier for a customer to pick up the telephone and request support from the company than it is to do some self-diagnosis. This can lead to high volumes of essentially trivial questions that can overwhelm a support center. Another problem with telephone inbound systems is that sizing and staffing can be quite challenging due to the variations in call volume during the day. We will discuss scheduling issues in a later chapter. Telephone systems work well in *immediate support* situations that require a low *talk time* for each support transaction, the time a TSR actually spends on the telephone with the customer. Support delivery is also often done over the telephone, but clearly the telephone system does not provide for transfer of hard media.

E-mail-based systems are also quite common. In these systems a customer sends an electronic mail version of a support request, either in free text or filled out in an online form, and receives support in the same way. An advantage of e-mail-based systems is that they allow asynchronous communications between the customers and the TSR. This is useful if both parties are not in the same time zone, or cannot easily communicate via telephone. On the other hand, e-mail systems do not provide the high degree of interactivity provided by a telephone system. Another advantage of e-mail systems is that (like telephone systems) some logging, validation, and routing can be automated. A major problem with e-mail systems is that it is difficult to ensure that the intended recipient has in fact received a message.

Direct customer access to the Problem Resolution System is increasingly common; customers access the system either by direct dial-in, or over some network, such as the Internet. Customers can log in their support requests, check on the status of requests they made in the past, and receive resolutions to issues that have been resolved. An important advantage of such a system is that it allows customers to browse through a database of known issues, and resolve issues on their own without requesting help from a TSR.

Fax systems provide a written record of communications, and allow asynchronous communications, which may be desirable when time zones or other reasons do not permit telephone conversations. Fax systems also allow work to arrive at any time—the upside being that customers can report problems at their convenience; the downside that there may be an expectation of service from the time the fax was sent, and not the time the fax was first received. Centers that use fax systems for reporting problems also need an efficient document management and tracking system, as well as some way to efficiently transfer fax information onto electronic media.

Postal mail-based systems are like fax and e-mail systems, albeit slower but with the advantage that communications can be certified. In general, you would not want to use postal mail systems with anything more than very low volumes.

WORKLOAD CONSIDERATIONS FOR ORGANIZATION

In this section we talk about workload implications on organizing a group, using a simple model of support work to examine the relationship between the variability of the work, and its complexity. Consider the variability of work in your support center. By *variability* we mean how many different types of work your support center handles. This is usually determined by the types of products you support and the services you offer. Workload in a support center that supports only a few stable products and provides no value-added services will likely have many similar support requests; in other words, there will be low variability in the support workload and the work will be routine. A support center that supports many products that work on a number of different platforms and have many interfaces will probably have many different kinds of support requests; there is a high degree of variability in the workload. Another way to think of variability is as the number of exceptions to the norm.

The other dimension to consider is the complexity of the workload. By *complexity* we mean how well the support requests are defined and understood. Low complexity workload means that the support requests report issues that are known and easily understood, so the work is simple; high complexity means that the support requests are new or require a degree of analysis before they can be understood. Low complexity workload usually arises when the supported products, and the environments in which they operate, are relatively stable. Common issues are known and well understood, and the few new issues that come up are easily identified as new issues. High complexity workloads usually arise when products or technologies are new, or environments are so complex that a fair amount of work is required to understand the issue.

The relationship between support workload variability and complexity is shown in Figure 3.7.

Routine and simple support workload suggests an organization that relies heavily on automation, and does not require a high degree of training. Work is quite repetitive, and since the support requests are easy to understand and analyze, the support transaction is usually short. This type of work is analogous to mass production of a few items in a factory. You can realize significant cost advantages if you can automate this kind of work.

Varied but simple workload also suggests the advantages of a high degree of automation; however, the skill level required of

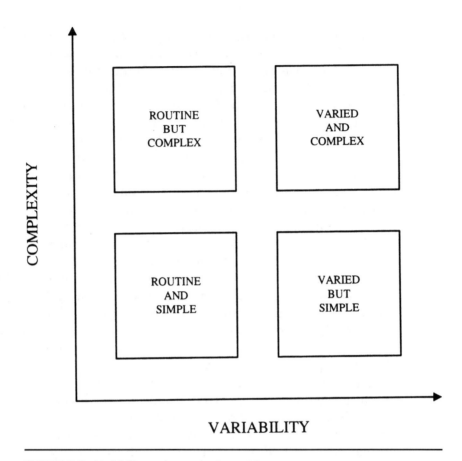

FIGURE 3.7 Variability and complexity matrix.

support personnel (especially in diagnosis skills) is higher, as they must be able to quickly identify the nature of the support request. The work is still simple but there are more types of work. The length of the support transaction in these situations is affected mostly by the amount of time it takes to define and understand the support request; once the support request is clarified, a resolution is generally available. The analogy here is to mass production of many items in a factory.

Routine but complex workload means that the workload is not so variable, but support requests take longer to understand because of their complexity. In these situations the resolution for the issue reported in the support request often has to be created. This suggests that this kind of workload will not realize a lot of benefit from automation, since most of the time is spent in analysis and knowledge creation. Personnel in these groups tend to be highly skilled and specialized. Support transactions are typically an order of magnitude higher. Routine but complex work is analogous to customized production in a factory.

Varied and complex workload is an increasing part of the workload of support centers, as more and more Technical Support Organizations offer value-added services such as consulting and design assistance. Those functions by their very nature are unpredictable and highly complex. This kind of workload suggests marginal benefits of support automation, and support transactions tend to be very long. Varied and complex workload is analogous to design and "one-off" production in a factory.

The organizational implications of this model are clear: If most of your work falls in the *simple* range, then you should organize your TSRs into large pools with roughly similar skills, and implement as much support automation as possible. Simple work that is highly variable benefits from a team approach if a high degree of automation is not possible, so that TSRs can discuss support requests to identify the issue being reported.

If most work falls into the *complex* range, then TSRs will not benefit much from support automation, and the actual organization of the TSRs is more dependent on other factors in your organization.

COMMON ORGANIZATIONAL MODELS

Organizing support personnel into groups in a way that makes sense is an art, not a science. As the Technical Support Organization grows, the usual approach in most support centers is to group along product lines and put a manager in charge of TSRs in each product area. When each product group grows beyond a certain size, it may be broken up into smaller product groups, with specialties within the product line; or into similar groups for the entire product line. Another way of organizing groups is by geography, with each group responsible for a certain geographic area or time zone. Yet another way is to organize by customer type, with each group supporting a certain type of customer. In larger organizations, groups may be created for combinations of the preceding reasons.

There are a few organization models that are commonly implemented in support centers; after all, how many ways can you organize a few different groups? This section discusses some of the models from a process viewpoint, and the considerations in deploying that model.

The simplest organizational model is the *one pool* model as shown in Figure 3.8. In this model all support requests are routed to a pool of TSRs, and an available TSR handles the next request. All TSRs may be physically co-located, or in remote locations.

This model works well when the support requests exhibit broadly similar variability and complexity (regardless of the quadrant of the variability/complexity matrix into which they fall), and TSRs all have roughly similar skill levels. This model

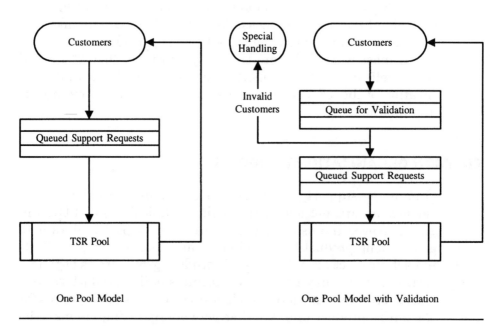

FIGURE 3.8 One pool organizational model.

is a good candidate for support automation if complexity is low and volumes are sufficiently high. A large pool offers the best solution to telephone wait times if telephones are the main inbound system. One problem with this model is that if there is a need for customer validation, then TSRs have to perform the validation. This takes them away from support delivery functions, and could have an impact on service levels. A variation on the one pool model is to add on a validation function, possibly automated, prior to the support request reaching the pool of TSRs. The organizational impact of adding on the validation function could be that support requests may be delayed in the validation function if it is not properly implemented, and may be delayed again when they reach the TSR pool. In the models discussed later we assume that the validation function can be added on if necessary, so we will not show it as an option.

If the variability of support requests is so high that a TSR may not be able to handle any support request that comes in, then the large pool of TSRs may be structured into smaller pools of TSRs that each handle support requests with a smaller range of variability. We call this a *multiple pool* organizational model, as shown in Figure 3.9. A common way to do this is by product: If each TSR in one large pool cannot handle support requests on all products, then TSRs may be grouped into *product groups*. Another common way of doing this is by support request type: Some TSRs may handle only installation questions on all products, others may handle only usage questions, and so on.

A problem with this model is that it reduces the size of the pools, and so can have an effect on service levels in an immediate-support model. This is discussed in some depth in Chapter 6. From an organizational viewpoint, we recommend that support managers try to keep the size of the pools that handle support requests as large as possible. The three main ways to do this are by support automation (making it easier to handle more types of support requests), product changes (making products so that they produce information that reduces the variability in the support request), and by training support personnel in as many products as possible.

If the complexity of most of the support requests is low but the complexity of some is sufficiently high that handling them re-

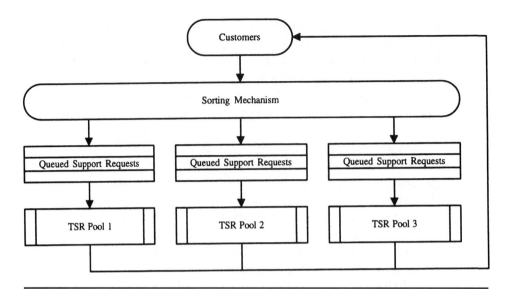

FIGURE 3.9 Multiple pool organizational model.

quires specialized skills, then a *multilevel* model may be indicated. An example of a multilevel model with two levels is shown in Figure 3.10.

In this model a pool of TSRs handles the majority of support requests, but the requests requiring specialized skills are packaged and sent on to a pool of people at another organizational level, with those skills. Of the processes described earlier, the support delivery process would map onto the first level, the knowledge process to the second. The second level is normally organized into multiple pools, for the same reasons as given previously. This arrangement can actually improve overall service levels, since those requests that require skills not available in the first level are transferred to the second level, where more specialized skills are available. The extent of the impact is determined largely by the speed and accuracy with which a TSR at the first level can identify the need to send the support request to a second level. As before, support automation is of value to TSRs at the first level; automation at the second level is often of marginal benefit.

There are three major problems with the multilevel model:

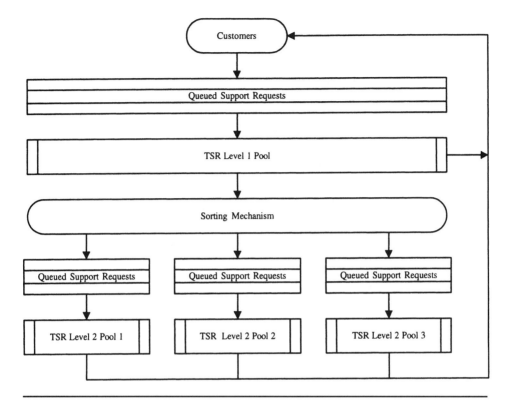

FIGURE 3.10 Two-level multilevel organizational models.

context capture, work standards, and morale. For sufficiently complex issues, the first level may not always capture all the data needed by the second (and subsequent levels); ways to address this include training and product instrumentation. Second, unless quality is rigorously monitored there can be a tendency on the part of the first level to send on support requests to the second level without fully investigating the issue; the effect of this is to expend more expensive resources on the increased likelihood of rediscovering previously reported issues. The third major problem is one of morale: There is definitely a pecking order in the support hierarchy, and first-level personnel may require reward and recognition programs to keep them satisfied and effective.

DISTRIBUTION OF WORK

Once work has arrived in your support center, you need to route it within your organization. The goal of any such work distribution scheme should be to quickly get the work to an individual who is most likely to meet service and quality goals for that work. So, in a telephone inbound system, the call should be directed in real time to a support representative able and ready to take that call. In a fax inbound system, the fax message must be routed appropriately.

While the goal sounds simple, it is not always easy to implement. The implications of this goal are that the work should be handled by as few individuals as possible, and that each individual be ready and able to add value to the work. The actual routing of the work depends on the structural organization of the work group relative to the type of work being routed, the customer-perceived severity of the work (where applicable), and the availability of individuals capable of handling the work.

If work must be transferred within a center, it is important to minimize the number of times it is transferred, because every transfer introduces a delay in processing and may require an element of relearning on the part of the individual who receives the work. Another guiding principle is that work should be transferred only to individuals that are going to add significant value. If you have a process in which work is transferred between individuals, you can minimize the transfer delay by designing a distribution system such that work is directed to individuals that are ready to receive the work. In a telephone call distribution system, this may mean that calls are transferred in round-robin fashion to the next available individual logged into the system; you will have to institute controls to ensure that a sufficient number of people are logged on.

The number of transfers that must be effected depends in large part on the structure of your support group, and the responsibilities of each level in that structure. Many support centers have only one or two levels of support, and therefore transfers are somewhat limited. A first level may serve to log support requests, perform initial screening, and route the support request to more technical TSRs. A second level, which may be organized by product specialty, may process most support requests and escalate a small percentage to the Development or Engineering organization. Some centers may choose to combine the functions previously described into one level of support, and use technology and customer input to perform some tasks, such as initial screening and routing.

As mentioned earlier, a distribution system depends on having staff available to handle support requests. In general, the more specific and narrow the skill set of your support personnel, the more difficult it is to route calls to the proper individuals. In other words, the bigger the pool of people that can handle a support request, the easier it is to implement an efficient distribution system.

HOW WORK IS PERFORMED

A lot of support work is repetitive; most support requests will fall into one of a few distinct categories. The processing of these support requests generally requires that the same steps are followed; formalization of these steps can provide a way of standardizing support work.

Should support work be standardized? Yes. Due to the repetitive nature of the work it makes a lot of sense to standardize support procedures. The benefits include cost savings through reduced training costs; customer satisfaction through common look and feel, no matter who is handling the support request; efficiencies realized through repetition; and metrics that relate directly to the work performed. This does not mean that there is no room for creativity; the standards must always be subject to review and improvement, and you will find that your support personnel will not be hesitant in offering suggestions.

Developing a good standard will take some time. You can start with procedures based on your own experiences, or better still, the collective experience of your staff. In most support centers, you will find that your senior people have developed methodologies that work very well for them, and may work well for the whole organization.

Improve existing process using any one of the numerous Continuous Quality Improvement methodologies (these may be found in books on Re-engineering or Quality Methods). You will be surprised at how many steps are taken and how many actions are performed in the processing of a support request. Discuss with your staff how many steps actually add value (in the context of your organization's mission), and which steps are absolutely necessary. Then look at who does these steps, and determine the right resource to apply to each step.

Ask selected customers for help: They are often a good source of information on how to improve your support processes, as they are the primary users and recipients of the results. If your improved process requires customer action, test the waters with these select customers and confirm that customers will accept the changes you are making.

When you have finalized your standard processes, you must communicate the standard to *both* your staff and your customers. Standard processing must be made a part of the training given to all support personnel.

Any good standard process is useless if it is not used, or used improperly when it is used. Included in your standard processes must be an indication of how you will measure compliance. If your standard processes are not being used, you must know and you must find out why. If they are being used, then you must know how effective they are. As in any continuous improvement scheme, you monitor performance and provide feedback to your support personnel. The metrics may well identify further opportunities for improvement.

PRIORITIES AND SEVERITIES

If your center supports many products, especially those sold into business markets, you may find it necessary to implement a priority and severity scheme to ensure that your resources are effectively applied to customer issues. Not all issues that customers encounter are equally important, even to customers, and not all issues have the same impact on the customer. It is common, therefore, to classify support requests in terms of both priority and severity. Priority and severity schemes are necessary only when work will be deferred and there is the potential for conflict with other work. If your support center operates on a first-come, first-served model, and a TSR works on each support request until it is resolved, then a priority and severity scheme is not necessary.

The *priority* of a support request determines responsiveness to a support request. Highest priority support requests typically get attention before support requests with a lower priority. The focus with high priority requests is on getting an interim resolution to the customer. If an interim resolution is acceptable, then the priority of the request may be lowered.

The *severity* indicated in a support request provides information to the TSR and Support Management on the impact the reported issue has on the customer. Severities are typically used in conjunction with priorities, sometimes as tiebreakers, in determining the responsiveness to a support request. Higher severity support requests typically get more attention than lower severity support requests, for a given priority.

It is possible to have high-priority support requests with low severities, and low-priority support requests with high severities. An example of the former may be a support request for some information that a customer needs by a certain deadline; the impact to the customer's business may be minimal but the need is urgent. An example of the latter may be a support request that reports a problem that only happens once a year, but when it happens it causes data corruption on the customer's system. The priority may be low, because your support center has up to a year to resolve the issue, but the impact is very high. Priorities and severities can change over time for some support requests on the same issue, as deadlines approach or as more information becomes available. For example, if your product is used by customers to prepare tax returns, then the priority of support requests may increase as the filing deadline approaches, and the severity of a support request may increase as more and more customers encounter the issue.

An example of a priority and severity scheme is shown in Table 3.4.

If you implement a priority and severity scheme, you must make the scheme very clear to both customers and TSRs. A good

TABLE 3.4 Sample Priority and Severity Scheme

	Priority	Responsiveness Guideline
	1	Interim Resolution in 30 minutes
	2	Interim Resolution in 4 hours
	3	Interim Resolution in 1 day
	4	Interim Resolution in 1 week

Severity	Definition	Examples
Critical	Customer unable to conduct business	System Failure Data Corruption Network Outage
High	Customer business impaired	Recoverable failures Unable to back up data Degraded system or network performance
Routine	Customer business affected	Compiler error Intermittent noncritical bug

strategy is to publicize the scheme in support marketing material, as well as train TSRs to negotiate the priority of a support request with the customer (only the customer can specify the severity), and then deliver on the negotiated promise.

SERVICE LEVEL AGREEMENTS

A *service level agreement* is essentially a contract between a Technical Support Organization and a customer. It has its origins in hardware service contracts, and now is also called a *support contract*. A service level agreement will typically spell out the roles and responsibilities of both the customer and the TSO, as well as expectations of the type and quality of service the customer may expect. Some service level agreements spell out the amount and type of work a customer is expected to do prior to making a support request, and make the performance of the TSO contingent on the customer's participation. Most service contracts also spell out the hours of availability of support for the customer.

In immediate-support models a service level agreement may also spell out the service level a customer may expect. For example, a service level agreement may guarantee contact with a TSR within 30 minutes of initial contact.

ESCALATION

Depending on the type of center you have and the nature of the products your center supports, your support personnel may occasionally need to escalate support requests to other personnel. There are essentially two types of escalation: routine and exception. Routine escalations occur when all the work that can be done by the person handling a support request is complete, but there is still more work to be done. Typical examples of routine escalation are passing on complex support requests to another level of support, or sending a new bug report to the Engineering group.

Exception escalations occur when the support request must be treated differently from the routine process. Typical examples of exception escalations are the customer demands to speak to a manager; or the customer's business is significantly affected by the problems being reported, and the customer needs a greater amount of support than can be provided by the person handling the support request.

Is escalation necessary? Clear, well-defined escalation paths are absolutely necessary in every support center that has more than one level of support and/or management, for both routine and exception escalations. Your support personnel, and your customers, should understand when a support request will be escalated, and what must be prepared by each level of support prior to handing off a support request.

Most routine escalation schemes depend on some division of responsibilities between levels of support. For example, in a two-level support center it may be the responsibility of the first level to receive support requests, validate the caller, and close all support requests that relate to previously answered questions and previously reported problems. The second level may be responsible for logging new support requests, researching new questions and problems, and handing off new bug reports to the Engineering group. Quite often, the division of responsibilities between the first and second levels can be formalized via internal service level agreements as shown in Table 3.5.

Some companies have also experimented with routine escalation based on both a division of responsibilities and a timer. When a support request is open beyond some preset time limit, the support request is escalated to the next level of support. The advantage of such a scheme is that it often improves overall responsiveness to customers; the disadvantage is that higher levels of support end up handling a large volume of simple support requests and therefore cannot spend time on their own mission.

Exception escalations may occur for one of two categories of reasons: complaints, or demands for immediate technical attention. No matter how well trained your personnel are, you will always get customer complaints. Your support personnel should be taught to recognize when a customer wants to speak to a manager, and must know how to reach the appropriate manager. Most larger centers have duty managers that are on call to handle customer complaints.

With the increasing use of software to run many businesses, exception escalations due to demands for immediate technical attention are on the rise. If the products you support are key to a customer's business (so called *mission-critical* products), then you have a responsibility to restore a customer's business to an operational state as soon as possible. Very often this type of support request requires a skill set that you may not have available in the first level of support, so many support centers have a *crisis center* or a *response team* that handles such support requests. When a customer reports a critical problem, then the first level of support routes the call to the special group. When the customer's application is restored the customer is handed back to the first level for any additional support that may be required.

Setting the customer's expectations is very important in managing escalations. It makes good sense to document your escalation processes and procedures, and to convey them to your customer base. If they understand how their problems will be

TABLE 3.5 Internal Service Level Agreement

Activity	Level 1 Responsibilities	Level 2 Responsibilities
Support Request Creation and Maintenance	• Ensure quality of customer information • Ensure that support request accurately states customer's issue • Verify priority and severity information • Manage relationship with customer	• None
Issue Research	• Search all known issues for possible matches • Document results of search • Provide interim/final resolution to customer • Close support requests that can be resolved by research	• Verify search results for escalated support request
Issue Analysis	• Collect additional information from customer as necessary • Verify and reproduce issue described in support request • Identify product(s) and version(s) exhibiting issue • Document all analysis activities • Escalate new issues to Level 2	• Analyze support request to identify specific issue • Create and maintain new issue report if appropriate • Create interim and final resolutions as appropriate • Identify other version(s) of the product(s) that exhibit this issue • Escalate issue to Engineering if appropriate • Manage relationship with Engineering

handled, they are more likely to follow the process, and not demand to speak to a *support guru* on every support request they make. Of course, you must adhere to the processes and meet expectations you set if you are to gain the confidence of your customers.

ACCOUNT MANAGEMENT

Account management in a Technical Support Organization is about managing your company's relationship with the customer, above and beyond the product-related support requests initiated by a customer. Although we use the term *account management*, which may imply that only Technical Support Organizations with large *accounts* need to manage the relationship, the discussion in this section applies equally to your relationship with individual customers.

Account management is an essential task in a Technical Support Organization, because your effectiveness in this task goes a long way toward affecting the satisfaction of the customer. As we discussed in Chapter 2, customer satisfaction is linked to loyalty, and loyalty to profits. Good account management can also provide an opportunity for you to sell additional products to a customer.

Account management, like escalation, may be on an exception basis, or performed routinely. Account management in exception situations means handling customer complaints and managing the escalations due to a need for immediate technical attention. In these situations, the main concern of the customer (account) is to get the immediate complaint or technical issue resolved. Good account management means that you resolve the issue, and follow up with the customer at a later time to discuss the situation and how you could improve your support delivery.

Routine account management means keeping in frequent contact with customers, even if they do not call in. In the days of mainframes, the sales representative for the account, or the local service or support manager, was the designated account manager. This account manager would periodically have a meeting with the customer to discuss all open issues. The value in account management lies in building a relationship with the customer. In a centralized, remote support model, you can still maintain contact with your customers by telephone, electronic mail, or even periodic site visits and discuss all their open issues. In Table 3.6 we show a list of discussion points for the meeting.

By keeping in touch with the account, you can learn of changes to the accounts current usage of your products, or planned new usage. You may also learn of areas of potential customer dissatisfaction, and try to address those before issues escalate. Last, frequent contact with the customer can reveal new sales opportunities, either for your company's products or for your support offerings.

Routine account management can be time-consuming and expensive, so many Technical Support Organizations provide account management services only for key or strategic accounts, or as a value-added service on a fee basis.

HOURS OF SUPPORT AVAILABILITY

The hours of operation of your support center, and the availability of support, are of great interest to your customers. Most support centers publish their standard operating hours, and often commit to those hours in writing as part of a support contract.

TABLE 3.6 Account Management Meeting Discussion Points

General	Greeting
	Review of current environment
	Gauge customer satisfaction
	Any other customer issues
Update	Review support requests closed since last meeting
	Review all open support requests
	Identify training needs
Future	Discuss planned changes in customer's environment
	Discuss applications to be deployed/retired
	Identify future training needs
	Assess impact on support center

The actual hours of operation of your support center are determined primarily by two factors: the geographic distribution of your customer base, and the market segment into which your product is sold.

The geographic distribution of your customer base gives you an idea of who may contact you with a support request, and where they are. If your customer base is located primarily in one time zone, then you do not have to make special arrangements for time-zone differences. If, on the other hand, your customer base spans many time zones, then the support center must be available to customers in each time zone during the hours they may reasonably be expected to call.

The market segment into which your products are sold affects the times at which your customers may normally want to contact you. Support centers that sell products primarily into the home consumer market may reasonably expect customers to want support in the evenings and on weekends. Similarly, business customers will want support mostly during the business day.

If your company sells products that are used in mission-critical applications, then you will need to provide a way for your customers to contact you at any time in case of a critical situation that impacts your customer's business. If your support center is normally closed at certain times, then you must provide a means for customers to reach a TSR who is on call for emergencies. This is normally done with paging services, cellular telephones, and personal communicators.

4

People and Culture

People are your greatest asset. They are the brains and brawn that give your organization life. Together they are your organization's personality, reputation, ambition, and energy. The environment in which they work is your culture.

Consider your organization. Every area is likely to be humming with activity on any given work day. It may even be chaotic at times. Now imagine walking into your company at 2 a.m. or on a major holiday. Most departments will be quiet. Even your technical support department, which is available to field customers' support needs 24 hours a day, seven days a week, is likely to be slower and quieter than the frenetic pace of a typical Tuesday afternoon. The lights still work, the hum of the systems will be there, but the entity—people—which moves your business forward every day will be missing . . . or at least obviously diminished.

Who those people are and the culture they create has tremendous impact on how successful your organization will be. They look different, think differently, believe in different things, and generally are unique. So how do you bring a group of people together who can effectively act as one to create a successful business? You hire the appropriate people; educate them on your products, policies, and processes; provide systems; and create a culture that encourages them to act in ways that achieve the desired business results.

CREATING A CULTURE

Culture is the result of the ideas, arts, customs, skills, refined thoughts, acts, and communications of a given people in a given period. It is influenced by the ability to trust and feel trusted. A culture is created as a result of every action taken by the people within the organization. An organization's culture also shapes the actions of the people within it. So where does an organization's culture come from and how can you influence it to be what you want?

Typically, culture is most strongly influenced by the people holding the highest level positions within the organization. This is due to their stature in the organization, their perceived power, and their visibility. Yet we all know situations where a respected and powerful influencer is someone other than one of the top brass. There are many types of people in an organization. Some are people who go by the books to complete their responsibilities. Others take more of a renegade approach in completing assignments and objectives. Both contribute to the overall success of the organization, and either type can become an influence.

Anyone who acts in a leadership manner will exert significant influence over the culture of the organization. The best way to create the desired culture is by consistently and enthusiastically walking the talk. Actions speak louder than words, and in a leadership role what you do tells others within the organization more about how they should think, act, and communicate than any words you might say. However, while a leader's conduct is inherent in shaping the organization's culture, there are other components that should also be defined. Examples of these tools include a mission, philosophy, and shared values.

A mission is the special task or purpose for which an organization is destined. A mission should be a succinct statement of what the group will strive to do and how it will do so. It should clearly support the mission for the company and be broad enough to acknowledge and provide guidance to every person in the organization.

> **Examples of Mission Statements**
>
> • To assure customer satisfaction through consistently anticipating, meeting, and exceeding customer expectations
> • To make technology transparent to the user
> • To produce delighted customers every time

A philosophy generally reflects the fundamental principles upon which the organization is to grow. Principles to consider include meeting defined financial objectives; being better than the competition at what is important to customers; pursuing long-term win/win relationships with employees, customers, partners, and vendors; being passionate about people, products, process, and continuous improvement; and adopting a mission and shared values widely understood within the organization and at the core of decision making.

An organization's shared values or tenets are guidelines for the way in which the people within the organization will conduct business. Suggested shared values include:

- Achieving and supporting the organization's and company's financial objectives
- Striving to understand the needs and experiences of customers
- Defining and meeting high-quality standards
- Practicing *kaizen* (a Japanese term meaning continuous improvement)
- Sharing responsibility for creating the desired company culture
- Sharing responsibility for developing their own careers
- Supporting the desired business style and ethics

Shared values such as these reflect the various facets of business and serve to create a balanced foundation and environment which acknowledge and guide the day-to-day contributions and impact of people (employees, vendors, customers, and partners), finances, quality, responsibility, approach toward improvement, and business ethics.

Examples of Shared Values or Tenets

- Hire the best, then trust them.
- Change the rules.
- We are all sales and support people.
- We will treat each other with respect.
- Do it right the first time.
- Be passionate about people, products, quality, and improvement.
- Do the impossible with small teams.
- Be better than the competition at what is important to customers.

If the mission, philosophy, and shared values are not written and well communicated, identify and work with other influencers to document and communicate them. Every organization has these elements in some form. Documenting them provides a means of sharing and discussing them with the people within the organization in a way that ensures their knowledge, understanding, and support of them. Then use these elements in all your technical support business decision-making efforts and ensuing actions, and encourage your team members to do the same.

Enhancing your role as an influencer and leader will help to position yourself to better complete your responsibilities and add value to the organization. By consistently supporting the mission of the organization in a manner that reflects the organization's philosophy and shared values, you will more effectively and efficiently persuade your team members to consider new ideas. And new ideas, developed with creativity and fiscal responsibility, are the lifeblood of any healthy organization. On the other hand, if team members are unsure of the mission or shared values of their organization, objectives may be achieved but at greater cost to the organization, the employees, and your customers. Investing in developing a culture with the help of a mission, shared values, and philosophy will increase the chances that your team members will be satisfied with their jobs, which in turn will increase customer satisfaction, which will result in significant positive contributions to the bottom line. There is a casual, yet strong, relationship between employee satisfaction, customer satisfaction, and positive impact on the company's bottom line, which should not be forgotten or taken lightly.

There are many ways to communicate and bring your organization's mission, philosophy, and shared values or tenets to life. One company put the mission statement, shared values, and company logo on the top of a letter-size sheet of brightly colored orange paper. The orange was part of the company's logo color. It was professionally formatted and cost-effectively done by someone in the Human Resources department. Each sheet was also personalized for every employee, with their name, their own department's mission statement, and a fill-in-the-blank section that began with "I contribute to this by . . ." on the lower half. At department staff meetings these were handed out and everyone was asked to fill in the remainder of that sentence. Some departments asked employees to share them with the rest of the team; all asked the employees to post the paper somewhere in their work space. And it made a difference; every time employees saw one of those orange sheets it reminded them of two things. One was what they had written on their own sheet, and how they contributed to achieving the company and department mission. The second was a reminder of what others in the company do to support that same company mission.

A different company took its tenets or shared values and also printed them on brightly colored paper reflecting the company's logo. These were put in inexpensive plastic sheet protectors and taped to the middle of all of the conference tables. It was interesting to see how frequently, especially when discussions became heated or were off track, someone would point to those tenets, bringing the meeting and decision making back on track with the premises outlined within them.

Still another company prints its tenets on the back sides of every employee's business cards. This reminds not only the employees of the mission and tenets of the company, but also any potential customers and partners, influencers, and even competitors of the company's values and expectations of how each employee will do business.

Due to the fast-moving pace of many Technical Support Organizations, the ability to have confidence in the honesty, integrity, and reliability of other people within the organization is a tremendous asset. This confidence, more often referred to as trust, is what allows an organization to move forward faster and more efficiently, accomplish more complex and difficult objectives, and make a greater contribution to the organization's overall goals. The more you are able to trust and be trusted, the more time you can spend on moving the business forward, rather than on the inefficient tasks of checking other people's work.

Creating an environment of trust is a key and sometimes difficult element to embrace within a company culture. Especially with all of the upheaval, rightsizing, and economic challenges businesses and employees are going through today. Many organizations address this today by including statements of trust in their shared values. (Note the shared value: Hire the best, then trust them.) The reality too often is, in this fast-paced business world, management teams have good intentions that aren't always fulfilled. The management of one company, concerned about this from previous personal experience, was so dedicated to its desire to have trust as a fundamental part of the company culture, that in addition to stating it as one of the company's tenets, *Get out of jail free* cards were created and distributed to all employees. It was an effort by the management team, who acknowledged that they might unintentionally slip and act contrary to the tenet without intending to. The result was a culture that embraced an *act now and ask forgiveness later* environment, which encouraged employees to take risks in the pursuit of doing the right thing. It provided a reality that employees were empowered to do what they thought was right for the customer and the company without having to first obtain permission.

Creating a culture is an ongoing activity. It happens every time an employee or customer does work on behalf of or interacts with the company. It happens regardless of whether management is paying attention. It can be set as a goal with specific objectives. However, simply achieving the objectives set will not necessarily achieve the goal as intended. A culture will develop, but if the tasks, projects, and programs developed and held to promote a specific culture are not done with complete trust and sincerity, then a culture that achieves goals without trust or sincerity will be the result. Once again a well-worn phrase is true: Company leaders, formal and informal, must walk the talk through consistent behavior when it comes to creating culture. For example, scheduling an event to recognize employees for their efforts is a great step toward developing a culture in which employees feel appreciated and are motivated to take the extra step. If the task undertaken causes employees additional time away from their families (e.g., significant travel beyond the normal job requirement, numerous late nights or weekends working), inviting spouses or significant others, or even the entire family, may be a nice touch and appropriate for the event. There may even be great food and enjoyable entertainment. However, if the leaders show up late, leave early, or don't engage with employees while they're at the event, small, meaningful messages about the importance of the party, or lack of importance, will be sent. On the other hand, leaders who arrive on time, sincerely participate in the conversation and evening activities, and take time to sincerely thank the party planners for a wonderful event (and the employees for their efforts and accomplishments to achieve objectives so that celebration events such as the party could be held) will send another message entirely. To use a common cliché, it's not what you say that matters, it's what you do that will define the culture of an organization.

STAFFING AND HIRING

Staffing and hiring is taking the time to define positions, determine the criteria of people you'd like to have in your organization, carefully selecting them through a rigorous interview process, and recruiting them to be a contributing member of the team. Hiring is often a tedious project, but time invested here can significantly reduce time spent on individual personnel issues in the future. A careful selection process can also save substantial dollars later. By hiring people well suited to the job, you can minimize the time and fees involved in recording, implementing, and defending any disciplinary actions that might need to be taken with an unproductive or mismatched employee.

Adding or replacing staff for any reason is an excellent time to reevaluate your needs for a particular position. Reviewing and defining position descriptions should be done on a regular basis, as well as a first step in the hiring process. Invest the time to update position descriptions to reflect the current and near-future needs and plans of the organization. Define what criteria you believe are required of a person to successfully do the job. What are the educational requirements? What previous work experience is needed? What special skills are needed? Talk with people in similar positions, people who work closely with the open position and, if possible, the person vacating the position. Add those perspectives to your own to create and prepare a document of the criteria you seek. For each criteria, note if it is a requirement or an unnecessary but beneficial trait. Also give each criterion an *importance weight,* which will make it easier to select candidates to interview.

Suggested criteria include specifying the minimum education or the acceptable experience equivalent required, customer service experience (any type), applicable product experience, applicable work experience, and applicable technology experience. In addition, look at the candidate's history as a team player. This could take the form of high school or college sports, community volunteering, or involvement in community theater. Ask the candidate what role they played, if they liked the team activity, and what they didn't like about it and why. Also ask how the role they played was important to the team. These questions will tell you a lot about what people think of themselves, how they value others, and the roles they may play in your organization. This is important because most Technical Support Organizations are actually teams, or groups of people working in a coordinated effort. As a result it is important that the individuals who make up the Technical Support Organization understand that they can achieve greater success if they are willing to do what's right and necessary for the team to succeed, sometimes at the potentially perceived immediate cost to them as an individual contributor. Team players who understand the exponential benefits of a team effort compared with the benefits achieved by numerous individuals will help achieve organizational goals more efficiently, just like the old adage: The whole is greater than the sum of its parts.

Look for demonstrated problem-solving skills. Questions that help uncover this aspect of the candidate include: What's the most challenging problem you ever faced? How did you handle it? Why? What would you do differently if faced with the same situation today? Questions like these will help uncover how risk-adverse candidates are, how they respond to and work with authority decisions, and if and how they break the rules.

Similarly, questions about specific business experience, class schedules, and what they do with their nonwork or school time provide an indication of the candidate's demonstrated ability to handle stress and multiple tasks. Specific examples might be candidates who worked two jobs and have strong recommendations from both employers, or candidates who worked while going to college without letting their grades drop.

Another area to explore is the candidate's degree to which they are driven with a desire to provide service to customers. Suggested questions to identify this trait might include: What's the most difficult customer situation you ever handled? What did you do? Why? What was the result? What would you do differently next time?

If you're looking for candidates who will do more than simply follow the rules, look for a demonstrated ability to take risks for justifiable reasons. Questions that ascertain this ability might include: What was the biggest risk you've ever taken? Why? What was the result? Have you ever challenged your boss? Why? How did you go about it? What was the result? What did you learn?

Other fundamental skills required for a strong technical support candidate include being motivated with a desire to achieve objectives, demonstrating excellent written and verbal communication skills, and demonstrating a desire to learn and grow.

If you are hiring a number of people for the same position, also determine what mix of skill strengths you are looking for. For example, a support center may give high weight levels to a computer science degree. However, if you're hiring five people, you may decide all candidates must meet the minimum criteria for all areas, while two will contribute superior technology skills based on applicable experience, one might provide experience from the customer's perspective, one might have significant research skills, and another might be considered to have exceptional communication skills. Determine these needs ahead of time by looking at your current organization and identifying what areas will provide you with the most comprehensive skill set as an entire organization.

Finally, look for specific behaviors and a track record of performance which indicates an attitude that displays a strong desire to work with customers, conveys a sincere concern for high levels of customer satisfaction, and will do what's right for the customer. Remember, in most cases, such how to's as technology, responses, processes, and so on, can be taught at a reasonable cost. Attitude is expensive and often impossible to teach, so hire what you can't efficiently teach and invest in training to provide the rest.

Choose your interviewing team carefully. Obtaining the perspectives of a variety of people increases the chances that the desired skill set will be reviewed from numerous points of view, increasing the chances of making a good hiring. However, the person who will be responsible for managing the new employee is almost always the person who will still make the final decision.

In a younger or smaller company, the interviewing team often consists of the immediate supervisor, manager, a person who would be a peer, a member of Human Resources, anyone who will likely work closely with the new employee, and the President/CEO. In a more mature company the interviewing team frequently includes the immediate supervisor, manager, a person who would be a peer, a member of Human Resources, and one person outside the immediate organization who will likely work closely with the new employee. An interview team, consisting of employees who represent various areas of the company and will likely work with the new hiree, will provide different perspectives on how the candidate may contribute and fit into the multiple situations an employee is liable encounter while in the position.

Provide the interviewing team with a current position description, the weighted desired criteria, and a list of topics upon which each interviewer will be asked to focus. Most topics should be covered by more than one interviewer, yet each interviewer should be looking to identify or confirm particular traits. Each interviewer may also be given a piece of information that should be communicated. For example, the Human Resource person might be responsible for looking for company fit and long-term contribution potential, while also being responsible for communicating general employee benefit information, such as time-off policy, health care plans, dress code, and so on.

As soon as the staffing need is known, begin working backward from the *must have* date to know when the process must be initiated. For example, if you know a major upgrade is going to be released the end of the second quarter, back your way out to determine when your staffing process must begin. Be sure to give yourself ample time for finding the person, the transition time from their current position, and training.

Determine and Allocate Time for Staffing

- Placing ads, contact recruiting sources, and attending recruiting events
- Receiving applications
- Reviewing applications and narrowing the candidate pool
- First-round interviews
- Second-round interview
- Third, fourth, and fifth interviews, as necessary
- Making the offer and giving the candidate time to consider the offer
- Two weeks for the candidate to disengage from current commitments
- However long it takes to complete the initial training program

Working backward to set your hiring processes timeline can be a wonderful tool when time permits. In those cases when it does not, keep in mind that you will have to make trade-offs in your process. Trade-offs aren't necessarily bad, especially if they are made with consideration of what the impact will be. In most hiring processes that have less time than desired, the trade-off is speed and efficiency vs. effectiveness. As in all efforts there is a point of diminishing return, so review your desired process and eliminate or minimize steps carefully.

When you find yourself caught up with your hiring plan, don't stop looking. Build a résumé pool so that if an employee leaves suddenly you're not starting at the beginning to fill the position. Take the time to review and modify the position to be filled: experience, skill, area of expertise. However, if a résumé pool has been developed, the time to find and hire a person to replace the departing employee can be significantly shortened, minimizing the negative impact on the Technical Support Organization.

Another way to build a résumé pool is through part-time staff, or through consultants. The Technical Support Organization at Taco Bell headquarters in Irvine, CA, has developed an interesting way to staff its organization. About 45 percent of the team are Coopers & Lybrand consultants. Those Coopers & Lybrand consultants selected and hired to work on the Taco Bell account go through additional training on the products supported and tools used to deliver support by the support organization. They then work in the Technical Support Organization as technical support representatives for 18 to 24 months. At the end of that time they are offered full-time jobs with either Coopers & Lybrand or Taco Bell. This arrangement allows the Taco Bell technical support management team to focus on developing and implementing strategies around systems, processes, and people, rather than spending time recruiting staff. It also creates an opportunity to staff the organization with more highly qualified and committed personnel, and offer them a wider variety of long-term career opportunities.

A large, billion-dollar software company with an enviable reputation for customer service and achieving consistently high levels of customer satisfaction used another variation to staff. This company invited candidates to go through a two-week training program before deciding whether they would make the candidate an employment offer. The candidate attended the training program without pay, and at the end of the two-week period, hiring managers would select candidates to go through a short interview process and then determine to whom they would make offers. Of course, the trainer was a highly sought source of information regarding the candidates fit for the job. In most cases the hiring managers attended, without participating, some part of the two-week session to actually see the candidates in action. In some cases candidates left before finishing the program, and some others were asked to leave by the trainer if the trainer did not believe the candidate to be a good fit for the technical support representative position. Again, everyone was a winner. Candidates were able to try the job and the company before committing themselves. The hiring managers knew more about the candidates before hiring them than is normally obtained in a series of 30-minute interviews. The company reduced the time and money spent on managing poor performers out of the company, and a pool of candidates was always being developed.

RECRUITING

The better your recruiting sources, the more efficient your staffing and hiring processes. Develop a broad repertoire of recruiting sources. Enlist Human Resources if they are available for this purpose to help run ads, attend career days, recruit through college placement centers, and create an employee referral program. Engage a recruiter if your budget permits. Talk with your industry and service professional contacts. Look for candidates at competitors, companies that have the potential to be your customers, and under certain circumstances even at your customers. For example, if you were supporting software designed for insurance companies, include insurance agents in your recruiting target. If you are supporting drafting tools, consider including draftspersons or artists in your recruiting efforts. They may not have a superior understanding of the technology, but they may be better suited than a technology wizard to helping your customers use the product.

If you hire recruiters, select them carefully. They will be representing you and your company and significant time and dollars can be lost with a recruiter who doesn't really know your business. If possible, find a recruiter who has experience either in a job similar to yours, similar to the position you are hiring for, or at a minimum, in your industry. An ideal recruiter will have a successful track record for recruiting the type of position you are filling. Ask for and check references, and if feasible participate in the first few interviews the recruiter conducts. By participating in the early interviews you will be able to ascertain the recruiter's interview technique and understanding of the position, giving you the opportunity to add to or correct the information used by the recruiter to screen candidates.

Develop your recruiting sources as you would any other strategic relationships by keeping in contact, providing updates on successes and changes within the organization, and sending an appreciative note or gift if a referenced person is hired. Also create a candidate pool so that whenever an opening occurs you will have a head start on the process. This is especially effective for organizations that know they will have openings in a few months due to a new release, anticipated loss of staff, or another projected business need. An example of this is a company that knew four months ahead of time that its technical support needs would increase. After attaining hiring approval, the company interviewed and made offers to candidates to start at the appropriate time, which was often two to three months away. By doing so, the hiring team was able to take the time needed to make good selections, and the chosen candidates had a couple of months to wind up current jobs and take some time off before starting the new job. It was a win-win situation for everyone involved. Just be sure to keep in contact with your new hirees to reaffirm that you are looking forward to working with them and are anxious for the day they will join you.

TRAINING

Train, train, train, and train some more! Unless you're working in the ice age, developing and providing ongoing comprehensive training programs to employees is critical to keep their knowledge current on issues customers will be asking about. Training might be more structured in a more mature organization than in a young organization. However, all organizations must be constantly improving their content, curriculum, and methodology to keep up with the needs of a growing Technical Support Organization and fast-moving customer base.

Regardless of size, a formal training program should be developed. The five main components to be included in a quality comprehensive training program include a company orientation, product training, training on marketing programs, how to use support tools, and communication and interpersonal skills training.

Company orientation should be designed as the employee's first formal introduction to company expectations, origin, culture, mission, shared values, products and programs, target markets, competitors, partners, distribution channels, and processes. It provides the foundation from which the employee begins to understand the role the company is playing in the industry, the role the company is working toward playing in the industry, what the market segment is like, what it's like at the company, and generally how to get work done.

The best product training takes many forms: lecture, hands-on, watching while someone else does, doing with someone else listening, and eventually training. Lecture and hands-on training are two of the most common types. Developing these aspects of product training with input from senior service members and product designers increases the chances of a content-rich program. Once trainees have received the lecture and hands-on part of the training, it is important to let them try their new knowledge in a low-stress situation. The first phase might be to provide an opportunity to role-play answering calls, fielding questions, and using support tools to find solutions. The second step might be simply to let trainees listen to some more tenured team members take actual calls. Having them listen to more than one other specialist gives the opportunity to observe different communication styles, so they can develop their own. This also gives trainees a chance to hear answers to questions, pick up phrases used, and see the organization's support tools being actively used. The third step would be to have trainees take calls, with a buddy or more tenured person listening, providing assistance during the call, and reviewing the strengths and areas of improvement after the call has ended. Product training should cover peripheral products or those not produced, distributed, or even formally supported by the company, but those which the supported products interface with regularly. Product training may be tied to knowledge-based proficiency tests discussed later in this chapter, and should be offered on a regular schedule for both new and review training sessions.

Technical Support Representatives often have more customer contact per day than any other organization in the company. Yet, too often they're not kept up to date on the marketing programs in which the company is investing significant amounts of money. Therefore, teaching technical support personnel about the active marketing programs being offered by the company is also important. Personnel who provide service to people who receive any of the company's marketing messages should be informed about programs before they are communicated to anyone outside the company. Making this investment increases the ability for the company to speak to its current and potential customers and partners in a consistent manner. It increases customer satisfaction by making sure the support representative knows of a problem, special offer, or company change when a customer asks about it. Providing this training also decreases technical support persons' stress by giving them the information and tools to be knowledgeable company representatives when communicating with customers. There are few things more frustrating from a customer's perspective than when they know more than the Technical Support Representative (TSR) they're contacting, maybe even paying, for help. It's equally difficult and stressful for the TSR. Training for marketing programs is most often best developed and delivered by marketing, or by a marketing liaison from within the Technical Support Organization, with the assistance of marketing personnel. The content should include review of product collateral, programs, special offerings, and positioning. These training sessions should be held before making any communications to the market or channel and copies of materials should be provided to service personnel whenever possible. Instead of providing actual pieces of all collateral to every support representative, creating libraries of information for groups of Technical Support Representatives is often enough. As long as the library is current, comprehensive, and easily accessible, and the support representatives know what's in the library, costs of providing this information can be kept to a minimum.

Support personnel need to know a lot of information to do their jobs well. In fact, so much information in many instances that it's too much for even the most talented Technical Support Representative to remember. In addition, most support organizations are working to capture and leverage the cumulative knowledge of the group by capturing it in knowledge bases, customer information management systems, and other tools. Once those investments in such support tools as knowledge bases, customer information systems, e-mail tools, fax servers, and so on are made, Technical Support Representatives are expected to use those tools to increase the quality and efficiencies with which they complete their tasks. Providing support representatives with training on the reasons for the tools, and how to use them, will enhance their ability to do their tasks more effectively and efficiently. It will also increase the return on the investment made to purchase and deploy the chosen support tools.

Words and tone of voice are the elements that make up a telephone communication. Words and writing skills are the elements that make up written communications. Therefore, the last but not least important of the five main training components is communication and interpersonal skills training. This element of a comprehensive training program focuses on developing an employee's skills in the areas of handling disgruntled customers; taking and maintaining control of telephone conversations; writing directions, letters, and e-mail responses; and how to teach users to prevent situations as well as how to solve them. Often referred to as *soft skills training*, it should cover such topics as how to problem-solve by stating the problem, gathering facts, restating the problem, gathering solutions, looking at the options and risks of each, providing a solution, evaluating results, and following up. It also teaches technical support personnel which phrases are better than others. For example, asking the caller, "Would you mind . . ." instead of saying, "You must . . . ." Additionally, many also teach skills in reducing and relieving stress, which a person in a service role might experience.

The Six Parts to a Technical Support Transaction

1. Establish rapport.
2. Identify the customer's situation.
3. Restate the customer's situation to confirm understanding.
4. Provide the solution, explaining why it occurred and how to prevent it.
5. Close by thanking the customer.
6. Follow up.

Five Basic Customer Needs

1. To be understood
2. To be welcome
3. To feel important
4. To get resolution of issues
5. To be reassured

In addition to regularly scheduled training, it is essential to provide personnel with product training before a product release. Providing training to the employees who will field calls from customers on the product before it is released is one of the most beneficial activities that can be done. Before the fact, training increases the employee's product knowledge and confidence, which increases callers' success and satisfaction with the product. The results are fewer disgruntled customers, more effective and efficient employees, and lower service and support costs related to the product.

Employees demonstrating leadership skills should be given the opportunity to enhance their abilities by attending workshops and conferences that help develop those skills. Additionally, speakers from outside the organization should be brought in on a regular basis to increase awareness of the trends, issues, and developments occurring in the broader environment in which the supported product is involved. For example, employees supporting personal finance software that includes an investment management function may benefit from hearing speakers talk about current investment options, methods, and concerns. Finally, every trainee should expect to be tomorrow's trainer.

The benefits of training are numerous and are most often realized through lower minutes per call, increased success in first call resolution rates, and increased Technical Support Representative confidence levels and lower stress levels. The amount of training provided for Technical Support Representatives varies based on products supported and skill level of the support person. New Technical Support Representatives are often given two to four weeks of initial training before beginning to assist customers on their own. Additional ongoing training is commonly provided four to eight weeks throughout the year, again depending upon the products being supported and the skill sets of the Technical Support Representative. The averages should only be considered as industry average data points. You'll need to determine the quantity and degree of difficulty of the material a Technical Support Representative needs to know to do his or her job well from the customer's perspective. Remember knowledge, in the form of solutions to requests, is why a customer is contacting your support organization in the first place.

SETTING GOALS

People tend to do, and pay attention to, what gets measured. Goals are an object or an end that one strives to attain. For those reasons, goal setting and measuring are important parts of the people and culture components within your support organization.

To make them effective, goals must be measurable and written. A well-written goal usually includes a statement of what is to be achieved, in what time frame, and to what degree. Sometimes goals may also indicate how a goal is to be achieved (by which process, utilizing which tools, involving which individuals). Whenever possible individual goals and organizational goals should be linked, with individual goals being subsets of the organizational goals.

Goals are often most effective when created with the persons who will be held responsible for achieving the goal. By involving them in the goal setting, they are more likely to understand why the goal is considered important, who is impacted by it, who depends on its completion, and the degree to which work must be completed to meet or possibly exceed the goal. Once goals are created and written they should be reviewed regularly to determine if they are still appropriate, to determine if they will be met, and if not, what needs to be done to assure achievement.

At the end of the goal period, the goal should be reviewed to determine if it was met. If it was not met a conversation should be held to clearly identify why. Possible causes could be any combination of lower than expected quality of work, quality of result, late delivery, or quantity not met. Although this introspection may not necessarily help this goal, it will help the attainment of future goals by improving goal-writing skills that will help clearly communicate expectations of future goals.

Even if the goal is met, reviewing the goal is a good investment. It provides an opportunity to show appreciation for achievement. It also provides an occasion for understanding what made the goal attainable, and how similar goals might be exceeded in the future.

MOTIVATION

Motivation is a key component to building a successful Technical Support Organization. It is the force or forces which incite or impel people to certain behaviors and decision-making patterns. It has also been defined as the result of inspiration and envy. Motivation is based on some inner drive, impulse, or intention that causes a person to do something in a certain way. Our job is to identify as best we can what the forces are that influence our service personnel, and to identify the underlying issues that cause TSRs to be demotivated, or lacking the drive to do what the organization needs. By doing so we can design programs that control the making of their decisions. This is not unlike what is done through advertising and marketing campaigns. The biggest difference is that we don't want people to buy something as a result of our programs, rather we want them to behave in a particular way.

There are three main elements to motivating service personnel. All three must be considered in conjunction to assure the programs achieve the desired results. Each should be reviewed and revised as needed to achieve the desired results. The first of the three elements is *compensation,* which includes many components. The second is the act of *acknowledging* and showing appreciation for efforts made and achievements accomplished. The third centers around *involving* technical support personnel in understanding, proposing, and implementing processes, business rules, and other decisions that impact their professional lives.

Compensation will typically include a base salary, health benefits, stock options, profit sharing, and any other benefits offered by your company such as reimbursement for continued education. The compensation package offered to your service personnel will depend upon your company policy regarding stock options and profit sharing. It will also depend upon whether your service personnel are rated as exempt or nonexempt employees. Consult the Human Relations organization within your company to be sure your team members are correctly identified as exempt or nonexempt according to local legal requirements.

Regardless of which type of employees with whom you work—exempt or nonexempt, leader or follower, renegade or supporter—it is important to create compensation plans that motivate them while simultaneously staying within your company's guidelines and budget. Ways to do this include:

Starting Salaries

Differentiate starting salaries based on different skill sets and experience levels. More than likely a fundamental skill set must be met to be considered for the job, such as a demonstrated ability to speak clearly in the language in which support is delivered, a basic understanding of technical terms, and the ability to regularly be at the work site at the designated time. Those might be considered basic needs that a person must have to be an eligible candidate. However, if, for example, you are servicing financial software, you may create a gradated scale that gives credit for certain types of service experience, software use experience, software support experience, financial experience, professional accreditation (such as a CPA), computer science experience, or a computer science degree.

Sample Model for Differentiating Starting Salaries

Years Experience	Indirect Experience without Special Degree	Direct Experience without Special Degree	Indirect Experience with Special Degree	Direct Experience with Special Degree	Indirect Experience with Special Accreditation	Direct Experience with Special Accreditation
Under 1	$25,000	$25,000	$26,000	$26,000	$26,500	$26,500
1–2	$25,500	$25,700	$26,500	$26,700	$27,000	$27,200
2–3	$25,750	$26,050	$26,750	$27,050	$27,250	$27,550
3–4	$26,000	$26,400	$27,000	$27,400	$27,500	$27,900
4–5	$26,250	$26,750	$27,250	$27,750	$27,750	$28,250

Direct: More than 50 percent of time involved in tasks directly related to responsibilities of Technical Support Representative.

Indirect: Business experience with tasks not directly related to responsibilities of a Technical Support Representative.

For example, using the previous Sample Model a financial software company may consider a Finance, Accounting, or Computer Science degree to be a desired "Special Degree." They may go further and value a person with a CPA (Certified Public Accounting) certificate even more as a "Special Accreditation." To further illustrate this, a person just out of school with a degree in Physical Education and no previous Technical Support Representative experience would be offered a starting salary of $25,000, while a person with the same degree but with two and a half years of technical support experience would be offered a starting salary of $26,050. Similarly, a person with a Computer Science degree with two and half years technical support experience would be offered a starting salary of $27,050, while an accredited CPA with an Accounting degree with three and a half years previous experience would be offered $27,900.

These salary categories, salary amounts, and variances between salary amounts are examples only and are for purposes of illustrating a consistent, yet flexible starting salary model. Competitive salary information is compiled and can often be obtained from a number of sources. Your Human Resources department will have lists of market research companies that complete and provide comprehensive compensation studies.

Salary Reviews

Salary reviews should be tied to performance reviews that include the following three elements.

Ongoing Responsibilities Ongoing responsibilities are those responsibilities documented on the employee's position description. The position description should be written in such a way that all responsibilities are covered in as measurable a way as possible. Position descriptions should also be written to clearly indicate what experience, accomplishments, and education are required to move to the next level, and also what the responsibilities of the next level are.

Quarterly Objectives Each employee should, together with their immediate supervisor, set and review four to six quarterly goals, depending upon the magnitude of the goal. The goals should be written in a way that is easy for both parties to interpret and measure. All goals should be based on completing projects or attaining skills that are needed by the organization. At least one goal should also focus on developing a skill the employee has identified as an area he or she would like to grow. Quarterly goals are recommended since they are the most common frequency for setting goals and most often consistent with corporate goal setting and review patterns. However, this can be done more or less often than quarterly. Four to six goals are recommended since the intention of setting goals is to give support representatives additional personal goals beyond their ongoing responsibilities. More than six is often too many to be achievable, while fewer than four is often not challenging enough; however, the number of goals should really be determined by the scope of each goal, the interest of each Technical Support Representative, and the projects/skills needed by the organization. Whichever way you do it, goals should be set and reviewed often enough to ensure the Technical Support Representative is continuing to expand their knowledge, skill, and contribution level on a regular basis.

Shared Values and Tenets Each person should be evaluated regarding their adherence and contribution to the stated shared values or tenets of the organization, as defined previously within the discussion on creating a culture.

Whenever a representative is given a less than perfect score, suggestions should be provided on how the individual could improve performance. Salary reviews should then be based on the evaluation of the three elements over the period the salary review covers. For example, an annual salary review would take into consideration the last four quarterly goal results, the annual review of the Technical Support Representative's ongoing responsibilities, and a review of the support person's support of the company's shared values.

Knowledge Level Testing Programs

A knowledge measurement program, designed to provide base salary increases to successful participants, allows individuals to control the speed at which they move forward in the early stages of their technical support careers within your organization. This program encourages personnel to motivate themselves to participate in training offerings, which results in increased control over how quickly they increase their compensation, contribute to the organization, and positively impact customer satisfaction levels.

A complete program includes training, tests, review programs, and compensation programs on product knowledge, customer service skills, marketing programs (when they are a responsibility of the employee), and support system usage. For example, an employee would need to take a class and pass a test on a given curriculum in order to attain the associated compensation. A peer evaluation of the employee's performance in support, demonstrated consistent and accurate usage of support systems, and customer satisfaction survey ratings by employee may also be contributing factors. The entire Technical Support Organization benefits from increased confidence in an employee's knowledge level, and from having a program that can be marketed to customers to increase their confidence and respect of the quality of technical support services offered. Employees benefit by being reassured of their knowledge in a particular area and through increased compensation. Unsuccessful candidates should participate in a curriculum review session before signing up to retest.

To be most comprehensive, the tests often include a True/False section, a multiple choice section, and case studies. Supporting resources identical to those available on the job, such as manuals and knowledge bases, are often allowed and encouraged in the case study section. In addition, segments are typically time limited.

When peer evaluations, support system usage, and the results of customer satisfaction ratings are included in the program, systems must be designed and implemented that accurately measure these factors. Employees must trust that the systems provide dependable and accurate information for all participants. Creating these programs provides the added benefit of more clearly defining and measuring the achievement of the organization's goals by group and individual employee. The effectiveness and efficiencies of the organization often benefit significantly as a result.

Incentive Plans

In some environments it is also practical to create incentive plans to encourage certain activities by technical support personnel. Providing incentives for signing callers on certain service plans, for selling support tools (CD knowledge base, annual newsletter, training, etc.), or for attaining certain call and quality standards should also be considered. This is especially effective when personnel are already responsible for selling these offerings, or when organizations hold cross-functional responsibilities. Incentive plans can also be used to increase adoption rates of new programs.

For example, one Technical Support Organization had just invested in a comprehensive customer information system. Yet after many requests and stated requirements the number of calls actually being recorded into the system was nowhere near the 100 percent goal. In an effort to encourage the Technical Support Representatives to take the initiative to enter all of their calls into this customer information system, an incentive plan was designed. The plan was based on number of calls handled per day, number of calls recorded into the customer information system per day, and customer satisfaction rating per day. The components were weighted according to the behavior desired, and the top incentive value was annualized at approximately 10 percent of the each technical support person's annual salary. How it worked was simple: The representatives took calls with the intent of achieving high customer satisfaction balanced with meeting a call goal of a certain number of calls per day, averaged over a week's period. Systems and a process did the rest. The ACD, or automated call distribution system, tracked the number of calls taken by each support specialist per day (internal calls and personal calls were not included). That number was compared to the number of calls logged into the customer information system for the same day for that specialist. If the ACD reported more calls than the customer information system, the representative was not meeting the goal of logging 100 percent of all calls. If the number was higher, the customer information system could quickly be searched to identify the reason for the calls logged that day, and the reason for the overage identified. In addition, an effort to measure customer satisfaction, which was already underway, was also utilized. The customer satisfaction measurement effort already in place consisted of a telephone survey conducted by a small team of people staffed specifically for this purpose. Utilizing the call information recorded in the customer information management system, this survey team would call customers within a week after the customer received service from the Technical Support Representative. Originally designed as a program to better understand and measure customer satisfaction, the calls were also used as a component of this incentive program.

The calculation for the incentive plan was based on the number of calls taken per technician as recorded by the ACD system, weighted according to the customer satisfaction survey information for that same support representative. The factor determining whether the incentive was paid depended solely on the technician's demonstrated effort to record all calls in the customer information system. In summary, the call productivity coupled with their own customer satisfaction rating determined the value of the incentive. However, the technician's actual attainment of the goal to record all calls in the customer information system is the factor that determined if the technician would get the incentive. Within two weeks the technical support team's behavior had changed to record all calls into the new customer information system.

Incentives can be monetary in nature but many are not. Some incentives may be designed for individual efforts, while others might be group-focused. For example, successful attainment of a certain program, sales goal, or adoption of a new process might earn an individual the right to leave early or arrive late on a prearranged day; a coveted parking spot reserved for them for a week, month, or quarter; or the ability to participate in a popular project. On the other hand, successful attainment of a goal might earn the group a new computer, modem, or other business tool.

Different things motivate different people. To help increase the chances that your incentives will truly impel employees to the desired behavior, you may want to ask them what they would want. To set expectations, let them know what the program is, why you want their ideas on incentives, and that their ideas are all welcome but may not all be used. You may also narrow down the responses by defining the parameters of suggestions (i.e., incentive value may not exceed $100 per successful person, or $1,000 for the group). You may receive some extreme (or at least over budget) ideas, but by asking they become involved in the design of the program, which often increases their participation. For example, one person indicated that a luxurious recliner, in place of his office chair, would motivate him to really stretch to help the organization achieve a very challenging goal. After considering that the person had high energy, was unlikely to take naps in this recliner, and his performance warranted it, and after restating that all awards (this and those that other support representatives selected) would be limited to a value of $75, the chair was agreed upon for this employee. The employee achieved his goal. The organization, to everyone's great pleasure, met the challenge and exceeded the overall goal—and the employee got his chair. It was an old chair that became his trademark and added a sense of character to that area of the organization. In reality he quickly sought to get his old office chair back, keeping the recliner oddly tucked in a corner of his office. In addition, the support organization had a great story to tell new employees. That story told more about company culture and the willingness to break the rules for the right reasons, that employees are important and are listened to, that it's okay to take risks, and that rewards come in all shapes and sizes—even worn-out, herringbone brown—than any poster we could have put on the wall or all the training we could have provided.

The purpose of rewards and recognition is to reinforce desired behavior. They may be something given in acknowledgment, recognition, or gratitude for a good deed. Most people want to be successful, so when they join an organization like your technical support staff they attempt to identify the successful employees and emulate their behavior. Rather than making new employees guess what behavior will help them be successful, recognize personnel who demonstrate traits that you'd like others to develop. This reinforces the behavior of the person you recognize, and clearly identifies the skills and behavior valued in the organization. Additionally, technical support personnel often hear what's wrong with the product, the company, and the marketing piece. Technical support management must make sure that negative information is balanced with acknowledgment and appreciation of efforts and achievements, and updates on how product plans, marketing plans, and company objectives are being met.

Acknowledgments and appreciation can take many forms and be provided often. They should also always take a tone of celebration. Rewards can be provided to individuals, groups, or an entire division or company. Sometimes they can be used to thank employees for an extra effort by giving them something they can do outside of work with their friends or family. They can also be used to enhance teamwork. Providing acknowledgments of appreciation can but does not have to be extravagant.

An example of this is a software company in Silicon Valley that is growing very fast. The technical support, training, and consulting teams had just completed an excruciating year and really pulled together to exceed some pretty lofty goals. To show their thanks, the management teams for these organizations decided to have a Customer Service week, during which the team was honored. One day during the week the team went bowling, the next to a park for a picnic that had been prepared entirely by the management staff. Not only did the team have a great time, as the pictures clearly showed, but the management did also. It was hard to tell if the management team had more fun the night before preparing the picnic meal, or at the event itself. Another day, the team members were given the opportunity to select the manager's clothing for the day. They did, and one male manager spent the day wearing a very elegant evening gown. The vice president of the team, a good-natured man, spent the day in leotards and a tutu. A third day, the management spent the day outside washing the cars for the entire staff. A fourth day, an old, valueless car, with the names of the company's competitors painted on it, was brought to the parking lot just in front of the main entrance. Customer service personnel were then invited to join in the fun of bashing it with sledge hammers. Even the CEO got involved in this event.

It's easy to imagine how energized this team was after such a week of appreciation. It didn't cost a lot yet built a lot of team work and appreciation, in great part because the organization's leaders *did* the activities—in some cases, even allowing themselves to be a little embarrassed for a day. Everyone had a good time, everyone felt a little more appreciated, enthusiasm within the organization went up a few more notches, and the team was recognized throughout the company as one that could work hard to achieve results, then take a little time to savor the success. Later on this same company, as part of a thank-you to all employees for an outstanding year, allocated a certain amount of money per person in each department for that department to spend as it wished. One team got everyone great leather jackets and flew to Anaheim, CA, to enjoy Disneyland for a day. A second team flew to Burbank, CA, for a weekend to explore Universal Studios, with a privately hosted back-lot tour, and a crazy day riding roller coasters at the nearby Six Flags. A third department rented limousines and went to the wine country for a couple of days, while a fourth took all the team members and their significant others on a train to Reno, NV, for a weekend of fun and entertainment.

As team building activities, these events were a huge success. As culture building events they were even more successful. They created stories that will be passed on to new employees to help describe what the company culture is really like, in addition to what the mission and tenets say the culture should be.

Ideas for Acknowledging and Appreciating a Job Well Done

• Hold a weekly wine and cheese event for the department. Invite one other department every other week.

• Give an employee a handwritten thank you with a couple of movie tickets, bottle of champagne, passes to a local theater or amusement park, or a gift certificate to a nice restaurant for a job especially well done or for a project which kept them away from friends and family.

• Hold a department picnic.

• Hold a department holiday party. Get the CEO, CFO, or GM to dress up as Santa and hand out small gifts.

• Hold an annual awards event based on a theme chosen by the support personnel. Provide certificates of achievement like Most Improved, Most Valuable, Biggest Single Contribution, Biggest Team Effort, Best Resource, and so on. Invite the CEO or General Manager to come and say a few words. If possible allow employees to invite a guest.

• At times when you're expecting large call volumes, plan to bring lunch in one day: banana splits one day and a goofy, stress-reliever toy another.

• After an especially large call volume or project (such as after a new product release) hold a We Did It! party. Give a gift of beach towels, water bottles, or whatever item is interesting to your group, imprinted with the achievement, date, and a thank-you message.

• Celebrate milestones with t-shirts, milkshakes, or pizza.

- Thank other departments for assistance they've given, or to acknowledge a job well done. It's amazing what good will a milk-shake and thank-you will do to build rapport with the personnel in the Engineering and Marketing organizations.
- Provide opportunities to attend skill-building sessions.
- Read positive customer letters aloud at department and company meetings.
- Create a *pride wall* in a high-traffic area by hanging framed customer thank-you letters.
- Nominate your employees for company-wide excellence awards. If a company-wide excellence program has not been created, help to get one started.
- Send an employee to a big customer appreciation event, user group, sales meeting, and so on, with the responsibility of being an ambassador for your group and providing a short presentation of the event at the next department meeting.

Recognition is one of the easiest ways to show appreciation and motivate team members. There are three keys to giving recognition for it to be most effective. The first is to give the recognition publicly whenever possible. The ultimate is to give the recognition with the recipient's family and friends present. When that's not feasible, doing so in front of a group at a company or team meeting is also very powerful. When the thanks does not necessarily warrant a big public moment, presenting the appreciation within the work environment after first getting the attention of a few team members whose offices are close by is also effective. Even a simple personalized thank-you note, or verbal thank-you can be very effective.

Second, make the appreciation appropriate to the accomplishment. People quickly see when a thank-you is given as a perfunctory task instead of from the heart, and when that happens it is just as powerful in sending the exact opposite message. Whenever possible provide people with something they can keep, such as a copy of a letter from a customer complimenting them. If you can, ask the CEO or division manager to write a small note of appreciation on the letter before giving it to the representative. Many employees keep a file of these reminders, share them with family members, and even post them in their workspace as a reminder to themselves that what they do makes a difference.

The third key to providing sincere, effective appreciation is for it to be timely. Saying thanks as soon after the achievement has occurred is another easy way to show how important the achievement of the task was, and how sincere you are in your appreciation for the effort and accomplishment.

A simple tool used by a company to encourage the giving of appreciation in a timely manner is a card called a *Gotcha* card. These cards are the size of business cards with the word *Gotcha* printed on front. Any manager or employee could give them to anyone else in the company; all they need to do is write a short message on the back about why they were giving it to a particular person, along with the date. It was a very informal program, which made it very easy to acknowledge and thank people for a job well done. Many recipients arranged them in the work space, similar to the way a football player puts stickers on the back of his helmet for every tackle made. One department designed a program to turn them in for company gifts, such as t-shirts, mugs, and so on, with different numbers of cards being redeemable for different gifts. The employees kept the cards they were redeeming; they were just stamped with the date of redemption, so they could display them and keep them as reminders of how they were appreciated. In addition, the CEO of this company began making a habit of walking through the technical support department on a regular basis to read the cards and thank the employees in person for the efforts they made which won them their Gotcha cards. This was just one more simple, cost-effective way to make others aware of the technical support team's daily contributions to the success of the company, and an easy way for a CEO to better understand and thank these team members for their daily efforts and accomplishments.

For the most part, rewards and recognition have a very positive influence on an organization. However, poorly designed or overdone programs can have little or even a negative effect. We've all been in or heard of situations where everyone knows who will receive the monthly award just because he or she is the only person in the organization yet to receive it. However, taking care to offer and deliver meaningful rewards and recognition for desired results will significantly increase your organization's ability and desire to meet and exceed goals.

Involving technical support personnel in understanding, proposing, and implementing processes, business rules, and other decisions that impact their professional lives is very important. Technical support personnel are one of the company's main contacts with customers on a daily basis. To do their jobs well they need basic information and skills, such as product knowledge and understanding of the tools available to do their jobs, and enough information to know when to question or break the rules to do the right thing. This understanding can be developed in numerous ways. One is to involve team members in the planning for annual or quarterly goals. Ask them, even the newest members, to submit ideas on what the team needs to do in the next quarter or year to be better than the competition at what is important to customers. Ask them to submit their ideas in writing and to be prepared to explain the idea at the next staff meeting that is dedicated to the planning process. Let them know that the reason they are being asked for their ideas is because they are the closest to the job itself. Remind them that there are no bad ideas. Also let them know that there is no guarantee that the idea will be able to be utilized, but that all ideas will be considered. Before the meeting, go through the ideas to categorize them. Do not reject or leave any out. At the meeting remind the team that the purpose of the meeting is to share the ideas with the group without judging them. Outline the method that was used to categorize them and go through them individually, briefly describing what you understand them to be. Allow the contributors to clarify their ideas for the group. After all the ideas have been discussed, ask for their input on which ideas they believe will most benefit the customer, the company, and themselves. Reinforce their thinking on items you also agree on. Take time to discuss items that you've prioritized differently than they did. Ask them to explain the reason they placed it high on the list. Explain to them why you placed it lower on yours.

This sharing of thinking is almost always a very valuable learning exercise for all involved. It gives you, the manager, a perspective from the team's point of view and it gives you new knowledge, insight, or ideas you might not have considered before. It also gives you the opportunity to explain more about the big picture of the company, its objectives, view of the market and the future, the role the technical support plays in that future, and what is feasible for the company for the period being planned for. On the other hand, the employees get the opportunity to contribute to the planning process and to learn more about the company's goals, challenges, and constraints. Too often managers think that just because their team members have heard the company strategies and goals at a company meeting, their team members understand what those strategies and goals mean and how each team member, as an individual, can contribute to achieving them. This process involves employees in activities and thinking that benefit the business and create opportunities for greater understanding of the big picture. Equally important, a process like this gives the team a sense of ownership in goal setting, giving them increased desire and accountability for achievement. Be sure to thank everyone for their ideas and participation, keep them informed of and involved in, whenever possible, goals selected and why. Remember to give credit to the individuals who contributed ideas that became goals, and if feasible encourage those individuals to take an active role in designing and implementing the tasks needed to achieve the goal.

CAREER PATHS

Technical support personnel want to perform their responsibilities well for various reasons. Some personnel do it simply so they can keep their job and take home a paycheck. Others have additional ambitions, such as wanting to get ahead, learn something new, or assume new responsibilities. People, for the most part, do not want to become bored and stagnant within their positions. Even people who are happy with the job they have want the choice to try new responsibilities. Providing employees with opportunities to try new tasks, then helping them to complete them successfully, is a strong management tool to building employee confidence. This confidence is a powerful catalyst to building a stronger team and a stronger organization, resulting in greater contributions to the company.

As a manager it is your responsibility to work with your team members to identify what their career ambitions are, then to create challenge and growth opportunities for them to work toward achieving their goals in conjunction with your organization's needs. This can be done by introducing employees to new ideas and regularly informing them of the big picture by regularly sharing the company's overall goals, objectives, plans, and competitive position. It can also be done by giving employees challenging objectives with guidance on how to successfully complete them, or by providing opportunities to try new jobs before a permanent transfer.

Career paths can be offered within the Technical Support Organization in many ways. One way is to create different levels of responsibility within a particular job area. This might be done by varying the number of calls a technical support specialist is required to handle, or the number of contributions they are required to make to a centralized knowledge base. Another level might require and acknowledge a person for attaining and demonstrating a superior level of proficiency in a particular product, operating system, or programming skill. A third level might provide opportunities for personnel to spend a portion of their time on responsibilities requiring project management, writing, or technical skills. Additionally there should always be a path leading to supervisory roles.

Career paths outside of the organization can and should also be proactively developed as well (see Figure 4.1). Technical support personnel with presentation skills should be encouraged to consider training, sales engineering, consulting, or sales positions. Personnel with writing skills should be encouraged to consider technical documentation or marketing as career opportunities. Those employees with strong analytic skills might consider competitive analysis, finance, or engineering. Or an employee with a well-developed sense of the proficiency and interpersonal skills required of technical support personnel may find a career within Human Resources rewarding.

In all cases, whether the potential career move is within or outside of the Technical Support Organization, providing an op-

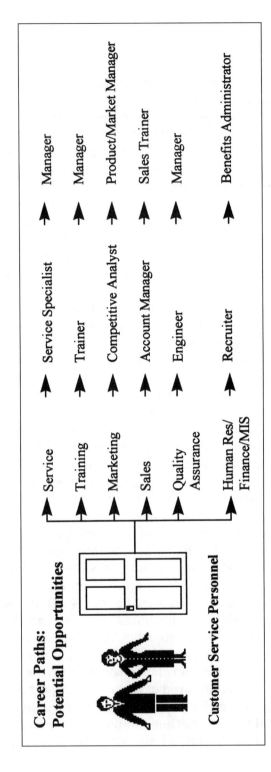

FIGURE 4.1 Examples of potential career paths for TSRs.

portunity to try new jobs before a permanent transfer increases the chance of success by decreasing the risk incurred by the employee and the new department. These forays can be provided by giving someone interested in technical writing the responsibility of working with technical writing on all technical-fix information before it is shipped. It may also be accomplished by giving someone interested in a marketing career the responsibility for being a liaison to Marketing, working with Marketing on behalf of technical support, and reporting back to tech support what is happening within the Marketing department. Additionally, some responsibilities might become shared as a position within itself. For example, some of your most knowledgeable technical support personnel might have the potential to be excellent trainers, but they will be reluctant to apply due to the amount of travel required. At the same time the training department may be struggling with the challenge of keeping product trainers up to date on the most recent product issues when they're out of the office so much. However, by creating a position that includes the responsibilities of a technical support specialist two-thirds of the time with a traveling trainer position one-third of the time, you may generate interest from candidates who would otherwise not even apply. There will be other benefits as well. The training department would have access to personnel who are up to date on the most recent product issues, who are also excited to travel and be face to face with customers. The support department wins by having staff members take a break from only having interactions with customers over the telephone while bringing back stories and reminders to the rest of the staff that those voices are real people. The customer wins by having a trainer who has current product knowledge, and who may even earn immediate credibility with the class by being able to introduce themselves as someone who may have helped them with a recent technical support issue. Employees win by increasing their skill set, broadening their job, and broadening their overall experience. It's a win-win-win-win-win situation with five parties (training, technical support, the customer, the employee, and the company) benefiting. This scenario can be done with Marketing, Quality Assurance or Engineering projects, or special sales programs. The added benefit is that by developing these multitask positions you are able to infuse other departments within the company with a stronger sense of customer issues, while also broadening your employees' experiences and enhancing their career opportunities. An effort such as this requires solid scheduling techniques and coordination between departments. The result is a stronger cross-company capability that benefits the company, customers, and employees.

5

Performance
and Measurement

As described in other chapters, there are many activities that are conducted in the operation of a Technical Support Organization. How do you keep track of everything that's going on, and how do you know how well you're doing? You could rely on informal methods, such as having occasional conversations with employees and customers, and handle issues as they come up. You could have a systematic way of collecting information about your organization and its activities, and a way of interpreting the data you collect so as to assess how well you're doing and what actions you need to take to avoid problems in the future. Or you could have some combination of both methods, the extent of each being set by the size of your organization and your personal preferences.

The information you collect about activities in your organization, the way you go about collecting that information, and how you use that information is important, because it is this information you are going to use to manage your organization and make decisions that affect not only the Technical Support Organization, but also your customers, people, and other company departments.

This chapter talks about performance and measurement in Technical Support. We will go over what performance and measurement really mean, different ways to assess performance and track operations, and how to use the performance information and other measures to manage your organization.

WHAT IS PERFORMANCE?

The word *performance* has many different definitions, the one we prefer is, *operation or functioning with regard to effectiveness.* Performance in a Technical Support Organization is about the effectiveness of the operations and functions carried out in the organization. Effectiveness in this context is about the ability of the organization to bring about a desired result in a particular operation or function, or in the organization as a whole. To be able to assess performance, therefore, we must know the results we want, the standards, and have a way of measuring the operations and functions that are being assessed. Measurements in themselves contain little information, because they just report the quantities or dimensions of things. It is when we apply standards and interpretation to the measurement data that we get useful information. It is this information that is called performance, because it gives us an idea of the effectiveness of the operation or function. Take an example from sports. If someone told you a male athlete ran 100 meters in 10.0 seconds, it would be just a fact. If you apply the standard of the world record to that fact you would have some performance information about the speed of the athlete, and you may say that this was a very good performance by that athlete.

Additional measurements, and the application of different standards to those measurements, can lead to more performance information about the same operation. If you are now told that our athlete came in last in a field of eight runners, you might change your assessment of his performance, and think that even though the athlete ran the race in 10.0 seconds he was not very good compared to the competition. More measurement data may further change your assessment. You find out the runner had not run a race faster than 10.1 seconds in the last 12 months. By having this historical data, you now know that the runner has improved his time, so your assessment of his performance is now favorable. You are able to make more assessments about performance as more data about the same event become available. The implication of this is that the amount of data available can affect the assessment of performance.

Different standards or evaluation criteria may be applied to the same data, and these may result in different performance assessments. Even though you may think that our athlete performed well, unknown to you he may have been trying to break the world record for that distance. Judging the 10.0-second time by his standard, this was not a good performance. The point here is that performance is assessed by the standards of the person making the evaluation. In a Technical Support Organization you have a number of different constituencies, and members of each constituency apply a different sets of standards to measurements to draw conclusions about performance. What you may think is good performance may not be the same as what your customers or employees think. You may think you're not doing well, but your organizational superiors think you're doing a great job. Conversely, you may think your organization is doing very well, but your employees hear otherwise from your customers.

MANAGING PERFORMANCE ASSESSMENT

How can you manage how your organization's performance is assessed? One way would be to tightly control all measures of and within your organization, and to release performance information interpreted the way you want to present the facts. Make available only those measures you think are absolutely necessary for your constituents, and tell them what those measures mean and how the measures affect them. This method may be effective in a small organization, but eventually facts leak out and the greater the perceived secrecy, the greater the likelihood that constituents will make incorrect and unpredictable and hence unmanageable performance assessments. Even if you are able to control the information, you run the risk of being judged on anecdotal evidence.

Who Measures Your Performance?

Another approach would be for you to understand how your constituencies may assess your performance, and provide to those constituencies the measures that they want. We think this is a far superior approach, and being open in this way gives you the opportunity to set the expectations your constituents have. The expectations of some of your constituents are easily determined. For example, your company's management will have set goals for the Technical Support Organization. These goals give you a good idea of which performance assessments are important to your management, and which measures are necessary to make those assessment. One of the goals set by your management may be: Improve the Technical Support Organization's contribution to the company's bottom line by 10 percent this year. You know last year's contribution, and now you know what you have to do this year. Your management has told you what will be assessed, and the standard that will be used to make that assessment.

Hierarchy of Goals

You in turn can take this organizational goal and assign goals to individuals or departments or even processes in your organization. To meet your margin contribution goal, you may decide that your revenues need to increase by 30 percent in the period. This in turn becomes the performance standard for the people and departments responsible for generating support revenues. On the cost side, you may be able to afford a cost increase of 10 percent in certain departments. That is then the goal for the those departments. Managers of those departments may translate that goal into plans to reduce hiring growth, and set a support delivery process goal to reduce the time to resolve customer issues by 20 percent. You now have a hierarchy of goals and measures, and clear indications of how performance will be assessed at the end of the year (see Figure 5.1).

Setting Expectations

You may not always be able to break down your goals into a hierarchy of specific departmental, individual, or process goals; be-

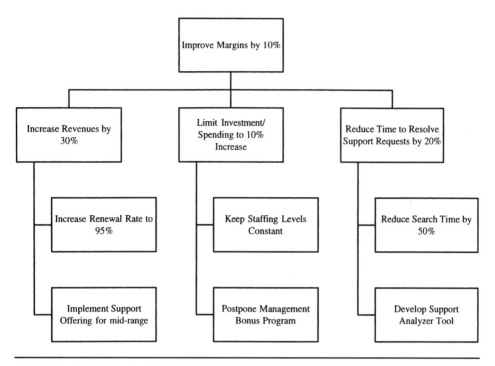

FIGURE 5.1 Sample hierarchy of goals.

cause some assessments are made in a complex and qualitative way. In these situations there are multiple assessment criteria that are interdependent, and the extent of the interdependence is not always constant, predictable, or objective. You are sometimes not even able to determine the assessment criteria, let alone how much weight is placed on each criterion when making the assessment. A typical example of this is customer satisfaction. Customers and employees make assessments about you and your organization without always telling you how or why they have made that assessment. In some cases you may be able to survey your customers and employees and determine how you will be measured by them, but there is no assurance that they will actually use those criteria. We have experienced many situations in which a customer's assessment of satisfaction is heavily influenced by one bad (or good) experience with the Technical

Support Organization, and not by the quality of support that the customer has received over an extended period of time.

In these situations you may have to define and publicize your goals, and report measures against those goals. By deriving measurement standards from published goals, you are in effect managing how your performance is assessed, because you have set the expectations of the assessor. Ultimately you cannot control how you are assessed, but you can influence the assessment by publicizing your standards when reporting measures. This does not let you off the hook to deliver on your commitments, but rather makes it clear to you and your constituents what you are doing and how you are measuring your performance. It also provides a means for you to demonstrate some consistency in your services.

OTHER CATEGORIES OF MEASUREMENTS

Measures of Effectiveness

So far we have been talking mostly about performance measures, or measures of how well you perform against a standard. In addition to these *measures of effectiveness*, we define two other categories of measurements: operations and finance. If you cover all three categories of measurement for each area of measurement, then you will have a comprehensive metrics system to help you manage all areas of your business.

Measures of effectiveness are those measures that provide an indication of how well the measured entity performed; they are usually taken after the event. The information provided by these measures cannot be used to adjust execution while in pursuit of a goal. For this we need some intermediate measures. In our example of the athlete, we know that he ran the 100-meter race in 10.0 seconds, and that he did not achieve his desired goal of breaking the world record. An athlete of that caliber may have decomposed the race into segments, and set intermediate goals to help him achieve the desired end result. He knows he has to make a good start, reach full speed within 25 meters, and put on a surge at 90 meters. During the race he takes measures of each of these points, and makes changes to his execution of the race based on this performance at each intermediate point. A poor start may force him to start his surge at 80 meters rather than 90. An excellent start may have allowed him to reach full speed at 20 meters, and reduced a need for a surge at the end.

Measures of Operations

We call these intermediate measures used to monitor execution while working toward an end-result *measures of operations*. They differ from measures of effectiveness, or performance measures, in that performance measures benchmark the end result against the desired standard, whereas measures of operations are taken during execution, and help managers either make adjustments to execution so that the goal can be achieved, or have sufficient warning ahead of time that a goal will not be met. If our athlete made a terrible start, he would know very early on that there was a very low probability of achieving his goal.

Measures of operations are also used to monitor the assumptions that are made in planning execution; if these assumptions no longer hold true, then performance will be affected. We gave an example earlier of setting a support delivery process goal to reduce the time taken to resolve customer issues by 20 percent. As managers of the support delivery process, we may have put plans in place to achieve this goal after making some assumptions about the expected volume of support requests, say 35-percent growth over the previous year. Two measures of operations in this example would be the total number of support requests received, and the time to resolve support requests (see Table 5.1). Current measures tell us the total number of support requests are higher than the expected volumes by approximately 10 percent, and the time needed to resolve customer issues has increased beyond acceptable levels. At this point we may be able to make some adjustments to staffing levels, or alert our management to the possibility of not meeting the desired goal because of the incorrect assumption of volume.

Measures of Finance

An essential part of any support business is tracking and managing revenues and investments. This gives us the third category

TABLE 5.1 Measures of Operations

Period Ending	# Support Requests	Expected Volume	Over/Under %	Average Resolution Time (minutes)	Goal	Over/Under %
4-20-96	5,390	4,889	9.30%	18.90	18.80	0.53%
4-27-96	5,558	4,974	10.50%	19.03	18.80	1.22%
5-4-96	5,568	4,993	10.33%	19.30	18.80	2.66%
5-11-96	5,756	5,194	9.76%	19.17	18.80	1.97%

of measures, *measures of finance*. Accounting measures of finance, such as total revenues and investments, are usually easy to identify and monitor. Most companies have accounting systems in place that give managers periodic reports on revenues and expenses. These measures are usually available at an organizational level, and also at department levels. The procedures for collecting and reporting these accounting measures are usually standardized and outside the control of support managers. In their financial accounting form, measures of finance are of marginal use to support managers in the day-to-day running of the business.

Of far greater interest to support managers are measures of finance in their *managerial accounting* form, because these measures are more useful in the planning, control, and decision making of support operations. Managerial accounting became popular in the early 1960s as more and more businesses found that they needed better ways to measure and control investments associated with operating a business than were afforded by financial accounting measures. There are two key differences between financial accounting measures and managerial accounting measures. First, financial accounting measures are generally intended for audiences external to the company, and are required by law to be collected and reported in certain ways; managerial accounting measures, on the other hand, are intended for use by internal audiences, and their creation, interpretation, and usage are entirely up to their users. The second difference is in the hierarchy in which the measures fit: Financial accounting measures generally report along organizational hierarchies, whereas managerial accounting measures report on activities, processes, and products and so may roll up along hierarchies that may not be the same as organizational hierarchies. To illustrate the example, consider a support process for three products that spans two departments, Call Reception and Support Delivery. Each department works on all support requests (and only on support requests), and is able to identify all costs it incurs in supporting all the requests. This is shown in Figure 5.2.

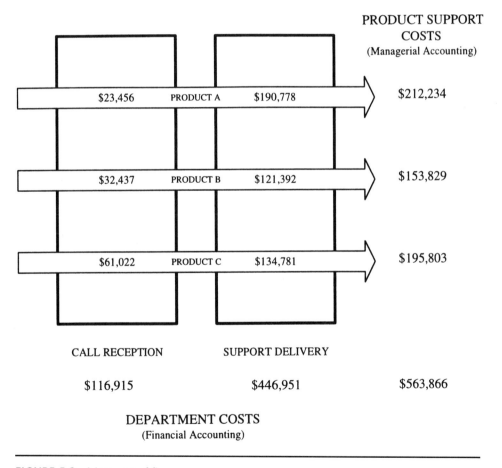

FIGURE 5.2 Measures of finance.

The financial accounting measures of finance give us information along departmental lines, whereas the managerial accounting measures give us information of how much it cost the organization to support each of the three products. Notice that the sum of the costs is the same for both measures of finance; we have *allocated* the departmental costs across the three products.

This book talks mostly about managerial accounting measures of finance, and how you can use this information. Typical measures of finance in a support environment include direct and burdened costs per employee, support revenues and costs by support offering line, and such unit costs as cost per support request or cost of supporting a particular customer.

SEGMENTATION OF MEASURES

We gave an example earlier of the growth in support requests being higher than anticipated. In that example looking at the growth in the total volumes may not be enough to make decisions about how to make adjustments to performance to get back on track. We may want additional information about the reasons that support request growth was higher than predicted. One way to do this would be to break out the total volume in a number of different ways, and match that against the assumptions. For example, we may have projected workloads for each product line based on sales assumptions of product sales. We could now break out the total volumes by product line and see that almost all the extra volume is coming from just one of the product lines, possibly due to higher sales than anticipated (see Table 5.2). We could then examine the resolution times for this product line, and see if they are contributing to the overall increase in resolution times. We find they are, and so decide to look at types of support requests that this product line is generating. This breakout shows that not only are volumes higher than anticipated, but there is also a higher proportion of defect reports than questions. We finally see that the time to resolve defect reports is substantially higher than the time to resolve questions, and that is the real reason overall resolution times are going up. We are now in a better position to address the situation either by adding more

TABLE 5.2 Different Breakouts of Support Request Volumes

Period Ending	# Support Requests	Expected Volume	Over/Under %	Product A Volume	Expected Volume	Over/Under %	Product B Volume	Expected Volume	Over/Under %	Product C Volume	Expected Volume	Over/Under %
4-20-96	5,390	4,889	9.30%	2,458	1,955	25.70%	1.137	1.124	1.12%	1.795	1.809	(0.76%)
4-27-96	5,558	4,974	10.50%	2,640	1,990	32.68%	1.130	1.144	(3.59%)	1.815	1.841	(1.39%)
5-4-96	5,568	4,993	10.33%	2,616	1,997	30.99%	1,092	1,148	(4.91%)	1,860	1,847	0.69%
5-11-96	5,756	5.194	9.76%	2,660	2,078	28.03%	1,203	1,195	0.70%	1.893	1,922	(1.50%)

Period Ending	Overall Time	Goal	Over/Under %	Product A Time	Goal	Over/Under %	Product B Time	Goal	Over/Under %	Product C Time	Goal	Over/Under %
4-20-96	18.90	18.80	0.53%	16.21	15.20	6.65%	17.61	17.50	0.63%	23.40	23.50	(0.43%)
4-27-96	19.03	18.80	1.22%	16.77	15.20	10.33%	17.33	17.50	(0.97%)	23.35	23.50	(0.64%)
5-4-96	19.30	18.80	2.66%	17.56	15.20	15.55%	16.85	17.50	(3.71%)	23.18	23.50	(1.36%)
5-11-96	19.17	18.80	1.97%	17.06	15.20	12.23%	17.45	17.50	(0.29%)	23.23	23.50	(1.15%)

Period Ending	Product A Volume	Expected Volume	Over/Under %	Questions Volume	Expected Volume	Over/Under %	Defects Volume	Expected Volume	Over/Under %
4-20-96	2,458	1,955	25.70%	1.913	1,564	22.28%	545	391	39.35%
4-27-96	2,640	1,990	32.68%	1,974	1,592	24.01%	666	398	67.36%
5-4-96	2,616	1,997	30.99%	2,003	1,598	25.37%	613	399	53.47%
5-11-96	2,660	2,078	28.03%	2,058	1,662	23.82%	602	416	44.87%

Period Ending	Product A Time	Goal	Over/Under %	Questions Time	Goal	Over/Under %	Defects Time	Goal	Over/Under %
4-20-96	16.21	15.20	6.65%	10.13	10.25	(1.17%)	37.55	35.00	7.30%
4-27-96	16.77	15.20	10.33%	9.87	10.25	(3.71%)	37.22	35.00	6.35%
5-4-96	17.56	15.20	15.55%	9.72	10.25	(5.17%)	43.19	35.00	23.41%
5-11-96	17.06	15.20	12.23%	9.54	10.25	(6.93%)	42.76	35.00	22.18%

staff to that product line, or having the development group release some product fixes.

Breaking up a measure of operation into subsidiary measures of the component parts gives valuable information to managers; we call this information the *segmentation* of a measure. By definition we must have a *dimension of segmentation*, which tells us how the larger measure is broken out. Most segmentations give you insight into the parts of the segmentation dimension that are the major contributors to a larger measure, and to the extent that data are available you can develop successive dimensions along which to segment your measures. In our earlier examples, we segmented total support request volumes over different product lines, then for a particular product line we segmented the support request volumes over the different support request types, and finally segmented resolution times over the different support request types.

Segmentation over Time

Time is a very commonly used dimension of segmentation on measures of operation and finance. Almost every measure is recorded and reported over some period of time. It is useful to segment a measure over time because the segmentation gives the manager a sense of the variations in the measured entity and a possible indication of a trend or exception. For example, support request volumes may be reported over a period of months, and we may see a gradual increase in the volume each month. If there is a sudden change in the volume, then the manager may want to investigate the change. Consider the chart found in Figure 5.3.

In this chart we see that support request volumes have been increasing quite regularly except for a few big decreases (in October and December 1994, and February 1995), and a large increase in August 1994. To investigate the decreases you may segment the support request volumes by week instead of by month, and see that the decrease in December can be attributed to a reduced number of calls over the Christmas week, and the decrease in February to the lower number of days in the month and a national holiday in the United States. The increase in

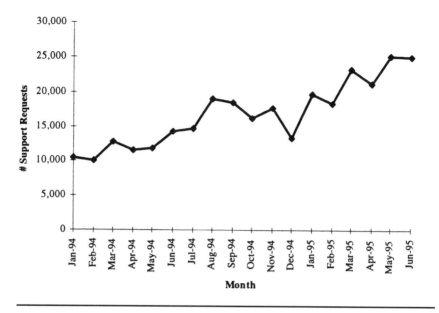

FIGURE 5.3 Support request volumes by month.

August 1994 may have been due to the shipment of a new product or version, and the decrease in October 1994 just due to the tapering off of the initial surge of support requests on the new product. This is shown in Figure 5.4.

LOCATION AND DISPERSION

Central Location

When looking at measures that have many data values, it is common to report the *mean* value of the measure. The mean gives managers some idea about the central location of all the data values, and is a convenient way to summarize the data values. In this book we will use the terms *mean* and *average* interchangeably. Many measures in a Technical Support Organization are reported as means: average time to resolve, average call length, average handling time, mean wait time, mean time between fail-

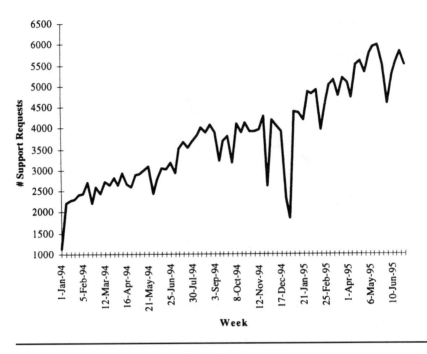

FIGURE 5.4 Support request volumes by week.

ures, and so on. If you actually plot each data value for these measures, however, you will see that they form a distribution over the unit of measurement. An example of the actual distribution of call length for an average call length of 21.7 minutes is represented in Figure 5.5. The figure shows the percentage of calls resolved in each minute, up to a maximum of 100 minutes. Approximately 14 percent of calls took between six and seven minutes to resolve, and about one percent took approximately 78 minutes to resolve.

The mean is a very useful measure. By virtue of its representation of the central location of a set of data values, it gives you a sense of what is being measured, and can provide a basis for comparison over time. On the other hand, the mean will be influenced by a few unusually high or unusually low data values. For example, a few exceptionally long telephone calls can dramatically increase the average call length time, so the average value will not give an accurate indication of the central location of the call length of all calls. The distribution in Figure 5.5 shows

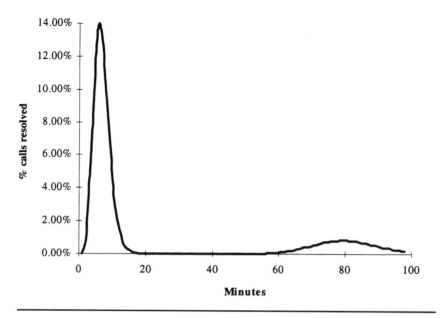

FIGURE 5.5 Distribution of call length.

that a majority of calls is in fact resolved in less than 21.7 minutes; it is a few exceptionally long calls that have increased the average resolution time.

For this reason it is useful to look also at the *median* value of all the data values. This is the value of the middle data value when all the data values are arranged in ascending or descending order (for an even number of data values, it is the average value of the two middle data values). This method reduces the effect of the unusual high and/or low points, and provides a better measure of the center of the distribution. If the mean and median values are significantly different, that is a good indication that the mean has been affected by some unusual extreme values. In these situations the median value is a better representation of the central location of the data values.

Understanding Distributions

The mean and median values together give an indication of the central location of all the data values, but do not give much insight into the distribution of the data values. Common sense says that if the median value is less than the mean value, then there must be some unusually high values that have caused the mean to be higher than the median. But you still do not have much visibility into how the data values are actually distributed. Clearly the simplest but possibly time-consuming way to get an idea of the distribution would be to plot each data value and see a graphical representation of the distribution. A quicker way is to report some *percentile* values of the measurement data. As their name implies, percentile values are those values below which a certain percentage of data values fall. The median, which is the middle point of all the data values, is the 50th percentile because 50 percent of the data values are below this point. Similarly the 25th percentile is that value below which 25 percent of all the data values fall, and so on. Percentile values are often used in expressing service levels. For example, a service level expressed as "95 percent of all calls will be answered within one minute" is making the statement that the 95th percentile of hold times will be one minute. Percentile values are useful to support managers because they provide an indication of the percentage of the measured entity covered by the value. Customer satisfaction is often affected by extremes in service, so managers need to track not only the mean, but also the distribution of service. As an example, if the mean time to resolve a customer issue is 21.7 minutes but the median time is 6.9 minutes, then we know that a few customer issues are taking quite long to resolve. A percentile measure can give us an idea of how long; in our example we find that the 95th percentile for the time to resolve is 86.5 minutes. This means that 50 percent of all issues are resolved within 6.9 minutes, but the next 45 percent take between 6.9 and 86.5 minutes. Figure 5.6 shows the same distribution, with the mean, median, and 95th percentile marked in.

Understanding Dispersion

But what is the longest time it takes to resolve a customer issue? Another useful concept in performance measurement is the *range* of a measurement. The range of a measurement is a statistical term that indicates the dispersion of a particular measure along one dimension by giving the difference between the highest and

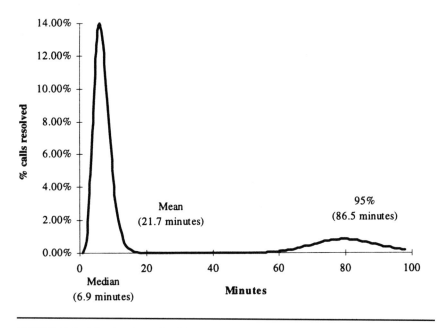

FIGURE 5.6 Distribution of call length.

lowest data values. For example, the time to resolve a customer issue may be 21.7 minutes on average, but it may vary from a low of one minute to a high of 115 minutes, giving us a range of 114 minutes. The range of a measure is useful to know, because it gives us an idea of the consistency or reliability of the measured entity. A range of 114 minutes tells us that there was close to a two-hour difference between the time taken to resolve customer issues. In our example the mean time to resolve a customer issue is 21.7 minutes, but what the range says is that at least one customer issue took over five times as long to resolve. Whether this is acceptable depends on the support organization and the expectations of customers. At a minimum, a wide range merits further investigation because it may be an indication of process, product, or training issues.

Effects of Segmentation

When a measure is segmented along a dimension, the range of the data in each part of the segmentation may be and usually is

TABLE 5.3 Segmentation Effects on Distributions

Call Type	# Requests	Mean Time to Resolve (Minutes)	Median Time to Resolve (Minutes)	95th Percentile (Minutes)	Lowest Time (Minutes)	Highest Time (Minutes)	Range (Minutes)
All Types	2134	21.7	6.9	86.5	1	115	114
Questions	1702	8.0	6.2	10.9	1	36	35
Defects	432	67.1	79.3	96.8	15	115	100

different from the range of the total measure. In Table 5.3, if we break out the time to resolve customer issues along a dimension of call type, then the range of the resolution time will be different for each type. Question-type calls may range from 1 to 36 minutes, giving a range of 35 minutes. Defect-type support requests may range from 15 to 115 minutes, giving a range of 100 minutes.

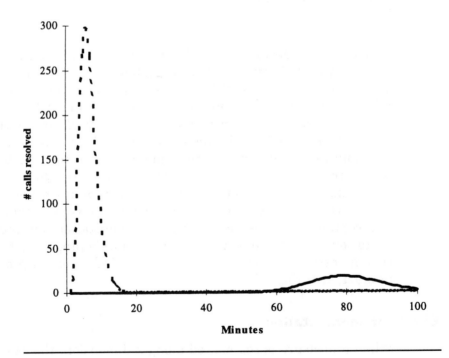

FIGURE 5.7 Segmentation effects on distributions.

Figure 5.7 shows the distributions for questions-type calls (dotted line) and defect-type calls (solid line). These two distributions together make up the distribution shown earlier.

The practical implication of the separate distributions is that if you look only at an average value, then you do not get a full picture of the situation. By first looking at the distribution of call lengths, then breaking out that distribution into its constituent distributions, we see that defect-type calls have a significant effect on the average call length, and distort our actual performance on question-type calls. To reduce our overall time to resolve customer issues, we would have a greater effect if we focused our efforts on the defect-type calls.

We recommend that whenever possible you measure not only the mean of a set of data values, but also the median, the 95th percentile, and the high value. This set of measurements, while not exhaustive, gives you a much better picture of the distribution of the data values, and allows you to take corrective action when necessary.

AVERAGING GENERALIZATION

As mentioned earlier, the mean is useful in locating the central point of a set of data values. It can be a good basis for comparing one set of data to another, and in fact some means are often used to measure changes in performance. For example, we gave an example earlier in which we wanted to reduce the time to resolve a support request by 20 percent. To do this we would normally use the mean, but as discussed in the preceding section the median may be a more reliable indicator of actual performance, so the performance improvement should be measured by tracking the median time to resolve support requests.

Assumptions in Averaging

An assumption implicit in the use of averages is that the thing we are averaging exhibits the same behavior, or pattern of behavior, all the time. This is often not the case. In the examples in the preceding section the overall mean time to resolve a call was actually determined by the mean times of two separate distributions (the time to resolve questions, and the time to resolve defects), and their relative contributions to the overall call volume. Question-type calls made up 80 percent of the total call volume, defects made up 20 percent, and that is why the overall mean time came out to 21.7 minutes. But what if the mix of call volumes changes? If questions go up to 90 percent and defects down to 10 percent, the mean time to resolve calls will decrease from 21.7 minutes, because the overall mix is now more weighted by the low-time-to-resolve questions than the high-time-to-resolve defects. Our overall mean time to resolve improves even if our support delivery performance does not change!

We call this the danger of *averaging generalization*, the tendency to assume that the characteristics of and relationship between the numerator and the denominator remain the same. In our case, if we use the mean time to resolve a call to track performance improvement we are making an assumption that calls, and their relative mix, will remain the same over time.

Effects on Common Averages

Averaging generalization is pervasive. Consider a simple metric that is used in many Technical Support Organizations: calls/employee. This is an interesting number and certainly can be used to track performance, but only if there is an apples-to-apples comparison.

Consider the example in Table 5.4. In the first part of the table, the overall call processing rate is 71.1 calls/employee. If we look at the breakout by call type, we may find that the call rate for question-type calls is 85.1, and that for defect-type calls 43.2. Does this mean that the employees who work on questions are twice as productive as those who handle defects? Probably not, since we expect defect calls to take longer. By some coincidence, we receive exactly the same number of calls in the second month. This is shown in the second part of Table 5.4. The difference is that we receive more questions than defects in that month. The effect of this is that the call rate for questions went up by 6.6 percent, but the call rate for defects went down by almost 26 percent. Does this mean that the employees handling defects suddenly be-

TABLE 5.4 Averaging Generalization Example

Call Type	# Calls	Employees	Calls per Employee
All Types	2,134	30	71.1
Questions	1,702	20	85.1
Defects	432	10	43.2

Call Type	# Calls	# Employees	Calls per Employee	% Change
All Types	2,134	30	71.1	0.0%
Questions	1,814	20	90.7	6.6%
Defects	320	10	32.0	(25.9%)

came less productive, and those employees handling questions suddenly more productive? No, because the mix of calls changed and the generalization in the averaging masks that change.

A similar analysis can be done on cost/call, another common measure. Very few of the costs in a Technical Support Organization are variable, since most of the costs are associated with personnel. Once you hire someone, that person's costs will be incurred regardless of whether that person actually works on calls. So if the number of calls coming into your Support Center changes, your cost/call number will change even though your actual costs may not. An example of this is shown in Table 5.5.

TABLE 5.5 Calls/Employee and Cost/Call

	January	February	March	April	May	June
# Calls	910	975	1,040	1,105	1,170	1,115
# Employees	8	8	8	9	9	10
Calls/Employee	5.17	6.09	6.19	5.85	5.91	5.31
Total Cost	$55,000	$55,000	$55,000	$59,167	$59,167	$63,333
Cost/Call	$60.44	$56.41	$52.88	$53.54	$50.57	$56.80

In the first three months the number of employees has remained constant, as has the total cost, but both the calls/employee and cost/call have changed because the number of calls coming in changed. In later months the number of calls, number of employees, and the total costs all change. In no two months are the calls/employee and cost/call the same, so using any of the rates for planning would give unreliable estimates.

The important point here is that while averages can be useful in giving you a sense of the data values, you should understand how the average has been computed, and the assumptions made in the averaging technique, before you use the average in future calculations.

USING MEASURES

Many support organizations keep and report performance and other measures, but managers are often unclear on exactly why they have all this information. They are therefore unable to effectively use the measures to manage the day-to-day operations of their organization. In other support organizations, especially those in small companies, there are no measures in place, and management has no visibility into the current state of support operations. A *metrics system* is an absolutely essential tool for support managers, because it produces measures that provide an objective basis for decision making. This is not to say that decisions are always, or even should be, made based solely on measures: The extent to which decisions are based on quantitative information is influenced by a manager's preferences and the prevailing organizational culture. We assert that quantitative information should be an important factor in the decision-making process, regardless of whether it supports the final decision.

Context of Measures

Quantitative information about an operation may be used in isolation or in the larger context of the interrelationship of that operation with others. For example, a set of measures could provide data on the number of support requests that come into a support organization, and give you a basis on which to forecast workload and scheduling requirements for your support organization. Another set of measures could report on the segmentation of support request by request type; you may use these data together with the first set to change your workload and scheduling forecasts. In both examples, the data from the measures are used in isolation from other parts of your operation.

But measures can also give you insight into the interrelationship between different parts of your business. Why is this important? As any technical support manager (in fact, any operating manager) will tell you, management is the art of striking the right balance between conflicting forces. Most technical support managers are called upon to increase revenues, cut investments, and improve employee morale and customer satisfaction. These goals can pull you in opposite directions; you could increase your revenues and cut your investments at the risk of reduced employee morale and customer satisfaction. Conversely you could dramatically improve customer satisfaction if you had unlimited money to spend and no revenues to worry about. But the world isn't perfect, and you have to make some compromises. Goals are often at odds with each other, and together form a set of constraints on the actions you take in running your organization. To do this, you must have a sound understanding of the dynamics of different parts of your business.

Understanding Interrelationships

A good metrics system can give you some insight into the relationship between many operational and strategic factors of your business. You should be able to draw on data that show you what happened in the past, as well as develop quantifiable linkages between parts of your operations. You may find, for example, when you had ten people on your telephone system and the workload was 50 calls per hour, the average wait time experienced by callers was approximately 30 seconds. Further investigation may show that there was hardly any improvement in the average wait time when you had 12 people on the telephones, for the same workload. But you may have noticed more recently that calls on a newly released product have increased beyond expectations, and even though the overall call volumes have remained steady, the average wait time experienced by callers has been creeping upwards. All these observations may lead you to some conclusions between product releases, call mix, average wait times, and staffing levels.

Intersecting Measures

A well-designed metrics system will also give you many measures of the same thing. Each measure provides additional information, and gives you a basis for a greater understanding of the thing being measured. Such measures are called *intersecting* measures. For example, one measure of calls is *call volumes*, which tells you how many calls you receive. Another measure of calls is *average wait time*, which tells you how long a call had to wait on average. A third measure of calls is *call quality*, which tells you how the customer rated the service provided by your organization. Each measure individually gives you information about calls; the three measures together give you a better understanding of calls, because you may observe a relationship between call volumes, call hold time, and call quality.

CHARACTERISTICS OF A GOOD METRICS SYSTEM

A good metrics system should produce information that is:

- Timely
- Accessible
- Reliable
- Relevant

Timeliness

If the information provided by your metrics system comes too late to help in making a decision, you may as well not have the measurement. For example, if you want to use today's call volumes to forecast tomorrow's workload so that you can schedule support staff, you should have that information in time to prepare the schedule and notify your staff. If the data are late in coming, you cannot use today's data and may instead have to rely on the previous day's. Timely information can help you make more accurate decisions, which is important in the fast-changing environment of technical support.

Accessibility

Not only must the information you see be timely, it must be accessible. Information produced by the metrics system must be available to you and other decision makers who need it, and it must be available at the level at which the audience needs the information. For example, a first-level manager may want to see information for his department only, whereas a senior manager may want to see the same information rolled up for all departments that report to her. It would be unproductive for the senior manager to receive the same detailed reports meant for each of her first-level managers and perform the roll-up herself. A development manager, on the other hand, may want to see information for a particular product, and want the same level of detail that each first-level manager gets; again it would not be efficient for the development manager to have to crawl through detailed reports and extract only those data that are of interest to him. A good metrics system must ensure that it is possible to access the same information at multiple levels, and from different viewpoints.

Reliability

Your belief in the reliability of information produced by your metrics system will affect the credence you give that information in your decision making. If you are comfortable that the information is consistent and reliable then you will be more willing to base your decisions on that information; conversely, if you know the information has been unreliable in the past then it may play a smaller role in your decision, or not even be used at all. For example, a well-executed customer survey may provide information with a high degree of statistical confidence, and in the past you may have used the information to make some significant investment decisions. But even though the survey results had a high degree of statistical reliability the survey itself was not well designed, the information produced was misleading, and your investments did not pay off. You are likely to be wary of survey results in the future until you are sure the right questions are being asked, and that the information produced is a reliable indicator of customer opinions.

Relevance

By far the most important characteristic of any metrics system is its usefulness to decision makers. Presupposing a willingness on the part of the decision makers to use the information provided by it, a metrics system must produce information that is relevant to the decisions that need to be made by the decision maker. With today's technology it is possible to collect an incredible amount of data and produce volumes of reports. And many metrics systems do in fact produce volumes of reports; unfortunately nobody looks at them, and any time a decision has to be made staff personnel are sent scurrying off to collect and analyze data. As described earlier, measures should be linked in some way to the goals of your organization, because it is the goals that guide decision making; measures aligned to those goals will be more likely to be useful to you and your operating managers.

DESIGNING A METRICS SYSTEM

Designing a good metrics system is like any other system design project. You have to understand the purpose and scope of the metrics system, its target user community, and the specific requirements of the users.

Purpose and Scope

The first step is to define the purpose and scope of the project, usually by asking a lot of questions. What is the purpose of the metrics system that you are designing? What do you want to learn? What will you do with the metrics? What will change in the organization as a result of the metrics system? What are the benefits that the system's users will see? In a Technical Support Organization the purpose and scope are relatively easy to determine. The purpose of a metrics system is to assess and help manage the organization; the scope of the metrics system covers at least the key support processes, and usually all major activities in the organization. The benefits usually are that users have better visibility into current support operations, some ability to identify potential problems, and can make decisions based on shared facts.

Compile a list of organizational goals, and interview managers on how they translate these into departmental, process, and individual goals. Some managers may already have taken their goals and mapped them into specific actions they need to take to meet the goals; others may have an intuitive understanding of what they need to do and how they will measure their performance. One result of these interviews should be a hierarchical list of goals, actions, and measurements. In the earlier example of the organizational goal to improve contribution by 10 percent, at the organizational level you need to measure revenues and investments for the whole organization, against the standard of last year's revenues and costs. The sales department will be interested in the total revenue number relative to last year's revenue, because that department has a goal to increase revenues by 30 percent. The sales manager may in turn break down the revenue goal into revenue targets for specific support offerings; your metrics system would therefore need to be able to report revenues by support offering. The sales manager may also have broken down the total revenue amount into sales goals for individual sales representatives; each representative would need to know current sales performance against the individual goal.

Definition of Measures

The measures derived from an analysis of goals and actions are often supplemented by operating measures used by managers to run the business day to day. While these measures may not directly bear upon the goals of the organization, past experience has shown managers that it is important to track them as an indicator of future problems. These are still performance measures, because a standard is being applied to them and an assessment being made about the subject being measured; the difference between operating measures and other performance measures is that the standards are often internalized and may not be obviously linked to goals. Our 10-percent contribution margin goal earlier translated into a support delivery process goal to reduce the time to resolve customer issues by 20 percent. Clearly, a good performance measure would be the mean time to resolve customer issues; the goal dictates the measurement. The problem with this measurement is that by definition it gives information after the fact. But an experienced support manager may know that when the number of open support requests in process goes beyond a certain limit for a given staffing level, resolution times will go up. Another manager may have noticed that changes in the mix of support requests, such as more installation questions and problems than usual, also drive up resolution times. Reporting on the number of open support requests and trends in the mix of support request types can warn these managers of potential problems, and they can take actions (such as temporarily adding staff to the support delivery process) that can prevent those problems.

Timeliness Requirements

Another design consideration is the timeliness of the information that is produced by the metrics system. A very sophisticated system can produce reports and charts and detailed analyses, but they will be useless if the information is too old to take any meaningful action. Managers may have different requirements for the timeliness of information: Operating managers tend to want to work with *live* data, whereas executive managers can often wait a day or a week for most information, which they usually want in summary form anyway. We talked about this in the previous section.

Methodology

After collecting all this information from potential users of the metrics system, you have to agree upon the methodology that will be used in getting each measure. This is an extremely important step in the design of a metrics system for two main reasons. First, measures are usually reported widely within, and sometimes outside, the organization. Anyone who looks at a measure should either immediately or easily understand what is being measured, and how it is measured. Second, many measures reflect on individual performance, and people take a great interest not only in how they will be measured, but also how the measures are taken. The methodology for some measures is relatively easy to determine. For example, the methodology for most cost and revenue measures is set by corporate accounting standards. Similarly, raw counts of things, such as the number of support requests in a given time period, are commonly understood and not controversial. Other measures require more analysis and discussion. The methodology to use for some of these measures may be defined in process documentation, but many measures will still need some discussion and consensus before they are applied. What are the starting and ending points to use when calculating the *average time to resolve* support requests? Does a support request start when the customer initiates it, when it is accepted by the support center, or when all information is collected from the customer and analysis and research commences? Similarly, is an issue resolved when a resolution is found, when it is communicated to the customer, or when it is actually verified and accepted by the customer?

The next few sections of this book look at some of the areas of measurement. We will then discuss how to actually implement a metrics system.

MEASURING ORGANIZATIONS

Technical Support Organizations are systems with many inputs, outputs, components, and dependencies. They are made up of smaller organizations, people, and processes; and the interactions between all these components can become very complex. But a support organization exists for a reason: to deliver technical support to customers. To deliver support to its customers, the people in a support organization must perform many activities;

all of these activities need to be performed within the context of the specific goals of the support organization. Aggregate measures of the sum of all the activities and people in an organization provide us with organizational measures.

Measures of effectiveness at the organizational level should tie in directly to the goals of the Technical Support Organization. We gave the example earlier of a margin contribution goal, and how that goal was divided into goals at lower levels of the organizational hierarchy. We could then measure each lower-level organization against the goals assigned to it. At each level, then, we have laid the groundwork for measures of effectiveness. At the highest level the measure of effectiveness for this goal is whether the contribution margin was met, and not whether the lower-level organizations met their individual goals. If in fact all the lower-level organizations met their goals but the overall organization did not, then technical support management did not do a very good job dividing the high-level goal into lower-level goals.

Measures of operations at the organizational level are also tied into organizational goals. In our margin contribution example, the sales department was given a revenue target of a 30-percent increase. This could have been translated into quarterly or monthly revenue targets, so one measure of operation, at least for the sales department, would be support revenue. Similarly, the operations departments responsible for support delivery could track response times to ensure that the goal of a 20-percent reduction in response time is being met. Other common measures of organizational operations include the mix of support requests, intermediate cycle times during processing, escalation ratios by department, and so on.

Measures of finance at the organizational level are usually financial accounting measures such as organization costs and revenues. If, however, they are segmented along a dimension that is not part of the financial accounting system, you may be using managerial accounting measures. For example, your financial accounting measures may give you some idea of total revenues by support offering you provide, but you may be able to allocate these revenues across different departments in your sales organization to see how each department is performing (see Table 5.6).

TABLE 5.6 Example of Organizational Measures

	Asia	Europe	US-East	US-West
Support Requests Opened	13,556	12,452	18,977	16,738
Support Requests Closed	13,902	12,378	18,789	16,979
Mean Time to Close (Minutes)	20.12	21.89	19.87	22.72
Target (Minutes)	19.50	19.50	19.50	19.50
% Meeting Target	98%	95%	99%	91%
Revenues ($000s)	$789	$654	$893	$973
Target ($000s)	$800	$700	$850	$1,000
Expenses ($000s)	$558	$689	$750	$890
Target ($000s)	$600	$675	$745	$901

MEASURING PEOPLE

Measuring the performance of people is important, because incentive and compensation systems are often tied to the performance of individuals, and measurements provide an objective assessment of performance. Measurements of individuals can also help identify areas of potential improvement, and point to a need for additional training. In those rare Technical Support Organizations where all work is team based there is still a need to measure performance, albeit at a team level. Team members may, however, wish to track their own individual performance in meeting the team's goals.

When measuring people, the measures of effectiveness should be directly tied to the stated goals for each individual. We talked in Chapter 4 about goal setting for individuals, and how these goals must be quantifiable and measurable. Common measures of effectiveness of individuals include customer satisfaction with each individual's execution of tasks, the number and percentage of appropriate escalations, the quality of escalated work as perceived by the receiving individual, and so on.

Measures of operations at the individual level have to do with the production and efficiency of each individual. Common measures of operations at the individual level include the num-

TABLE 5.7 Example of People Measures

	Able	Baker	Chung	Dawoud
Support Requests Opened	34	47	23	67
% Escalated	12%	8%	1%	53%
Escalation Target	10%	10%	5%	50%
Quality of Escalation	4.5	4.2	5.0	3.9
Support Requests Closed	42	51	76	21
Mean Time to Close (Minutes)	20.12	21.89	19.87	22.72
Target (Minutes)	19.50	19.50	19.50	19.50
% Meeting Target	98%	95%	99%	91%
% Time on Support Requests	65%	61%	67%	43%

ber of support requests handled, the resolution rate, the time to resolve support requests, the total number of escalations, the number of hours spent on support requests, the number of accounts renewed for service, and so on.

Measures of finance at the individual level are usually related to the salaries and expenses associated with each individual, but could also include such measures as amounts billed to customers, amount of revenue recognized, and so on (see Table 5.7).

MEASURING PROCESSES

Processes in a support organization provide the infrastructure that enables individuals in the organization to perform the work necessary to meet the organization's goals. Process goals are therefore often derived from organizational goals, but they may also be derived from service-level commitments made to customers as part of a service level agreement. An example of a support delivery process goal is, Reduce the time taken to resolve customer issues by 20 percent. An example of an entitlement process goal is, Authenticate 95 percent of valid users within two seconds after a user has presented a PIN. A goal for a knowledge process may be, New issue reports must have an interim resolution with 24 hours of being created. A goal for the sales process could be, Achieve a 95-percent support contract renewal rate. Measurable process goals are absolutely essential in every Technical Support Organization, because the organization's goals have to be implemented by the processes in the organization, and so must be translated into process goals.

Process measures are useful to a support manager because they provide insight into the operations of the support organization. Good process metrics will show you not only where your resources are being applied, but also the quantities of resources used and the value of each process. Most importantly, process measures can identify potential problem areas. For example, if the average time to process a support request goes up beyond certain thresholds, then that measure can be an indicator that the process is not working as expected. At that time you can use other intersecting process measures, such as support request volumes and types, to identify any potential problems. Process measures are also useful in identifying areas for process improvement, even if there is no visible problem. For example, if you want to reduce the average time to process a support request by 10 percent, then you could use measures of the support delivery process, segmented over time, to see which process steps are the main contributors to the average time to process a support request. The segmented measures can tell you where to focus your process improvement efforts.

Measures of effectiveness of processes include customer and employee satisfaction with support processes, the number and impact of exceptions to routine processes, and the number of previously reported issues that are escalated beyond the support delivery process.

Measures of process operations include volumes of support requests; call hold times; average time to process a support request; cycle times; demographics of support requests by geography, sources, and support request type; and intermediate times between support processes such as the time between the transfer of ownership of a support request.

Measures of finance of processes include costs of each process, revenues collected by the sales department, costs to staff each process, and costs each time a process is invoked (see Table 5.8).

TABLE 5.8 Example of Process Measures

	Entitlement	Support Delivery	Knowledge	Engineering
# Transactions	61,723	59,401	9,823	893
% transactions passed on	96%	17%	9%	
Mean Cycle Time	0.14	9.23	53.76	253.44
Target	0.10	10.00	50.00	250.00
Satisfaction with process	4.9	4.1	3.8	2.9
Staffing Level	0	48	8	3
Costs ($000s)	$23	$1,862	$324	$127

MEASURING PRODUCTS

If your support center supports more than one product, you will benefit from measuring the products you support. Product goals are not often set in support centers, but when they are they usually take the form of quality goals. For example, the Research and Development organization of your company may have set a limit goal of the number of product defects it releases in a product. You may set a responsiveness goal for each product you support; the goal for mission-critical products may be different from the goal for products that do not normally affect the business operations of a user.

Product measures can be extremely useful to a support manager in many ways. Volume information on support requests, and average times to process those support requests, can be used for estimating staffing requirements. The number of support requests segmented by support request type gives information about product quality, and can point to the need for changes in the product. The relationship between the number of support requests reporting issues on that product, and the number of distinct issue reports arising from those support requests, can give you valuable information about the effects of product quality. For example, if you receive many installation questions on the same issue, it could mean that the installation process is not well explained in the product or its accompanying documentation. If, on the other hand, there are almost as many issue reports as support requests, the product may be of poor quality. If sufficient data are available, a support manager may be able to construct a product's support profit/loss statement by comparing what it costs to support a particular product to how much revenue is being generated by support fees. Most importantly, product measurements build up knowledge about how to design such products in the future, so they serve a valuable function in the product planning process.

As described previously, product measures of effectiveness generally report on product quality. Typical measures include the defect rate, documentation effectiveness, customer satisfaction with a product, and product compliance with specifications.

Measures of operations include the number of support requests on a product, and further segmentation by support request type, platform, release, and Technical Support Representative (TSR). Measures could also include the number of distinct issue reports, types of issue reports (e.g., documentation, interface, or defect), escalations to R&D, the number of resolutions available per issue report, and the time to develop the first resolution.

Measures of finance include segmentation of operating costs, revenues by product, and cost by support request type for a product (see Table 5.9).

TABLE 5.9 Example of Product Measures

	Alpha	*Beta*	*Gamma*	*Delta*
Support Requests Opened	26,055	21,783	9,625	4,260
Support Requests Closed	26,512	21,453	9,980	4,103
Mean Time to Close (Minutes)	14.10	16.23	20.63	91.35
Target (Minutes)	13.50	16.00	19.50	75.00
% Meeting Target	98%	95%	99%	83%
# New Issues	3,102	2,908	1,036	2,777
# Sent to Engineering	102	83	35	673
Cost to Support ($000s)	$902	$713	$402	$319

MEASURING CUSTOMERS

Customers of a Technical Support Center are the rationale for its existence, so it is vital to measure your customers. Customers give you feedback not only on product quality, but also on the quality of your performance in support delivery, feedback on your service offerings, and revenues in the form of support contracts. Customer measurement may be done with or without their knowledge. Some customer information is available in the Technical Support Organization, other information must be provided by the customer. Information that is available in the support center includes (after registration) demographic information on registered customers, demographic information on who actually requests support, products installed at a customer site, and the amount of support revenues associated with each customer. In many situations, knowing who's not calling can be as important as knowing who is calling. You can measure this by looking at the demographics of customers who do not request support from your TSO.

Information that must be provided by a customer is generally used in measures of effectiveness, such as customer satisfaction. There may be many measures of customer satisfaction, depending on your organizational goals. For example, one of your organizational goals may be to resolve all customer issues to their satisfaction within 24 hours of initial contact by the customer. Another of your goals may be to ensure that all new customers receive a welcoming call from a Technical Support Representative within five days of registering for support. You now have two measures of customer satisfaction.

Customer satisfaction measures, by their very definition, require the customer's assessment of the service. The most common way to gather assessment data from customers is through a survey, which may be conducted periodically, or after each support transaction. The design of interviews and surveys is beyond the scope of this book, but we should point out three areas of caution: question design, sampling methodology, and interpretation. Questions asked of customers must be carefully designed so that there is no ambiguity about the meaning and intent of the question, and questions should be asked only about things that you can and intend to change if the surveys results warrant. The sampling methodology must ensure that a representative sample of customers is surveyed. And the methodology for analysis and interpretation must be determined before the survey is conducted. If you conduct a survey of your customers, it is important for you to report the results of the survey back to all participants so that they feel they have not wasted their time.

Customer measures of operations include numbers of customers that actually use the support center in each time period, usage patterns, customer demographic information, and average time to resolve support requests, segmented by customer class.

Measures of finance relative to customers include revenues and costs by customer class, most expensive customers, customers that pay the most for support, and usage of support offerings (see Table 5.10).

MEASURING COMPETITORS

If your company's products face a lot of competition, you will want to measure the support performance of your competitors. As discussed in the Chapter 2, in highly competitive situations the perceived quality of technical support can often be a key differentiator in the mind of a customer. To stay competitive, you must

TABLE 5.10 Example of Customer Measures

	Gold	*Silver*	*Bronze*
# Registered Customers	3,488	18,947	76,990
Support Requests Opened	12,536	19,026	30,161
# Customers reporting issues	2,165	9,869	27,891
as % of class	62%	52%	36%
Support Requests Closed	12,603	19,089	30,356
Mean Time to Close (minutes)	7.35	14.86	30.50
Target (minutes)	7.50	15.00	30.00
% meeting target	99%	98%	96%
Satisfaction Rating	4.9	4.7	4.8

understand what kind of support programs your competitors offer, to whom they sell, what kinds of revenues they collect, and most importantly, how satisfied their customers are. Even if you are in a market that is not competitive, information on your competitors can give you new ideas for your own operations.

You can get this information by running what are called *competitive benchmarks*. In these benchmarks, you identify the competitors on whom you want the information, and the specific types and areas of information you want. Your competitors are then compared (benchmarked) to your organization in the areas of study. You can then use this information to change your operations if necessary.

You can run your own competitive benchmarks, but that could be difficult if your competitors do not want to reveal information to you. Another approach is to retain a market research company to perform a benchmark for you; however, this approach can become very expensive. A cost-effective approach is to participate in and use the competitive benchmarks conducted by a number of leading market research firms. You get to see how you perform relative to a pool of your competitors. A problem with market research reports is that they are anonymous (i.e., no companies other than your own are identified), and the areas of benchmarking may not be quite the areas you want to benchmark.

Measures of effectiveness when measuring competitors include customer satisfaction (with various things), product quality, and profitability.

Almost any of your measures of operations can be benchmarked against that of a competitor, to the extent the measure reports something the competitor is also doing in about the same way you do it.

Measures of finance can also be benchmarked. Sample measures include prices for service offerings, cost structure, salaries of TSRs, bonus plans, and sales commissions (see Table 5.11).

IMPLEMENTING A METRICS SYSTEM

All metrics systems must have the following key elements: data collection, analysis and synthesis, information representation,

TABLE 5.11 Example of Competitor Measures

	Our Company	Company A	Company B	Company C
# Registered Customers	99,425	106,246	75,023	362,145
% Customer Penetration	54%	68%	88%	41%
Mean Cycle Time	21.11	43.34	32.45	16.98
Overall Customer Satisfaction	4.2	3.4	3.8	4.5
Total Support Staff	95	86	61	275

and information dissemination. A representative system is shown in Figure 5.8.

Data Collection

Data are collected from a number of different sources. If your support center uses support automation tools, many of these tools provide data on their usage. Employees and customers are also sources of data, especially on customer satisfaction and product quality. Other sources of data could include external market research, competitive information, product quality information from the Research and Development group, and so on. Another data source is historical data, which is usually stored for this very purpose. The process and methodologies of data collection must be clearly mapped out, because the consistency and reliability of data are very important in a good metrics system. How the data are collected, from where, how frequently, and the meaning of the data elements are all things that are defined in the data collection methodologies.

Analysis and Synthesis

Standards are applied to the collected data during the data analysis and synthesis phase. These standards include goals, operations standards, financial budget numbers, and so on. But the standards also include rules on analysis and interpretation, and definitions for synthesis. This is where, for example, some-

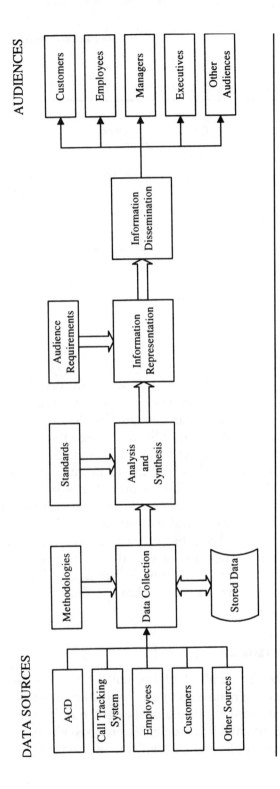

FIGURE 5.8 Overview of a metrics system.

164

thing like *time to resolve a support request* would be defined, and if it is developed from different data sources (like an ACD and a Call Tracking System) the rules for creating it would be defined. It is important because all users of metrics should have a common understanding of the definitions of all the metrics so that they can focus on the information in the numbers, and not on their meaning.

Information Representation

As stated earlier, different audiences have different needs for information and have different preferences for how that information is presented to them. This means two things: the level at which the information is accumulated or rolled up, and how it is presented. Operating managers may want to see information for their departments only, in both tables and charts; senior and executive managers may want to see only charts at a high level, with the option to look at greater levels of details. Customers will want to see feedback on the customer surveys in which they have participated. Employees will be interested in their performance measurements, perhaps in a great level of detail. In the information representation phase, audience requirements are applied to the analyzed and synthesized data to prepare the actual metrics reports.

Information Dissemination

In the last phase the packaged information is actually disseminated to all the audiences. The actual dissemination method (hard copy, e-mail, downloaded to a local workstation, push vs. pull, etc.), and the frequency of dissemination are all determined by user preferences.

Planning
and Budgeting

6

Contrary to popular belief, planning and budgeting for a Technical Support Organization is not mostly about accounting. It is about developing an operating plan for the organization to meet the company's strategic goals. Finances are certainly a key element of an operating plan; but so are organizational goals and objectives, programs that will be executed, and the assumptions made in developing the operating plan. The support organization's operating plan is in effect a contract with the company that details what the organization will achieve over the plan period, how it will realize those achievements, how much revenue it will collect, and the investments it will make. More time is usually spent on developing plans and programs than on translating the plans and programs into accounting measures.

Another myth is that planning and budgeting is a periodic exercise that can safely be ignored most of the time. In fact, changes in the technical support or company environment require constant adjustments to the operating plan throughout the plan period. Products may get delayed, sales may be higher than anticipated, and technology investments don't pay off as planned. All of these things change the assumptions made when developing the plan, and so can significantly affect the future actions that the organization must take. Planning and budgeting is therefore continuous throughout the company's fiscal year, though more time is spent on the exercise during the company-wide planning cycle. Many companies have annual budget cycles to meet the expectations of stockholders and regulatory agencies; however, the operating managers constantly review their budgets, and some companies even have *rolling* budgets that are updated every few months.

Developing a good operating plan is one of the most important tasks of any support manager. A good operating plan provides a road map of activities that need to be taken in the organization, and is the basis for performance standards to be used in the organization's metrics system. It is an excellent vehicle for communicating organizational goals, and gives a support manager the starting point for individual or departmental goals within the support organization.

This chapter talks about what happens during planning and budgeting, and how to prepare a good operating plan. We discuss how your workload is affected by external factors, and how you can forecast your future workload. Investments in staffing make up the major portion of all spending in a Technical Support Organization, so we show how to develop a staffing plan. We then discuss how staffing levels can affect service quality, and the importance of good scheduling. Finally, we talk about planning other budget items, as well as considerations for planning and budgeting revenues.

PLANNING AND BUDGETING OVERVIEW

Planning and budgeting are viewed in most support organizations as painful tasks done with great reluctance by support managers. Part of the pain is due to shortcomings in the company's planning and budgeting processes and personalities; the rest we believe is due to a lack of understanding on the part of support managers on why planning and budgeting are important, how to proceed, and what tools exist to make them useful and productive activities.

Importance of Planning and Budgeting

Planning and budgeting are necessary for the simple reason that they are necessary to get money to invest in your organization. Budgeting is conceptually very simple, and at a company level is not much different than budgeting at a personal level: You decide what you want or have to do, forecast your revenues, then adjust your investments to match what you can afford. The difficulty is deciding how much and where to invest. The planning part of the planning and budgeting process is where new programs are initiated, old programs discontinued or scaled back, interdependencies between the various programs identified, and trade-offs made by company executives on the programs that will be funded and the level of that funding. To prepare this corporate operating plan, company executives must have a good idea of the relationship between the value that will be derived from investing in a program, and the impact on the value of that and other programs of changes in the size of the investment. This is very similar to preparing a personal budget. For example, if you are purchasing a house you generally have a good idea of why you are making the purchase (the value of the program), the relationship between that value and the purchase price, and the impact of the purchase price on your lifestyle (other programs). You may be able to purchase a house that does not materially affect your current expenditures, or you may purchase a more expensive house if you can make adjustments in your lifestyle. As with a home purchase, even if the programs will not have a material effect on the company's operating plan, the planning exercise provides a framework for a review of new and existing programs.

Most of the planning and budgeting for Technical Support Organizations is usually done with the rest of the company, normally once a year. Company executives develop corporate goals and objectives for the coming year, and these are translated into operating goals and objectives for each organization in the company. Financial goals at the company level are similarly translated into preliminary goals and objectives for each organization. All goals, including financials, are negotiated at an organizational level during the budgeting process until some level of agreement is reached and goals are finalized. The financial goals at that time collectively make up the budget of the company. Budget negotiations are time-consuming and often contentious, but they serve a useful purpose in that they bring up cross-organizational issues that would not normally be raised at other times.

Planning and Budgeting Process

The corporate budget process may be top-down, when the targets are dictated from the top and implemented at the lower levels, or bottom-up, when estimates are created at lower levels and funneled up to corporate management; in practice the budget process is usually some combination of both top-down and bottom-up goal setting. Preliminary targets flow from the top down, estimates flow back up, targets are revised based on impacts on interdependent programs and flow back down, and so on, until agreement is reached or dictated (see Figure 6.1).

PLANNING AND BUDGETING IN TECHNICAL SUPPORT

The effectiveness of a support manager in the planning and budgeting process depends heavily on how well the manager has positioned the support organization within the company, how well other company managers understand the value of support to the company and its customers, and how well the support manager understands and explains the consequences of planning decisions.

Support Manager's Role

In a company of any size a support manager has to be able to articulate the value of the support organization to both customers and the company, make some estimates of how much revenue the support organization will achieve, estimate the investments required to implement programs in the organization, and then justify the estimates to other people in the company that control the purse strings. These people ask tough and pointed questions, and an unprepared support manager can come out of a budget-

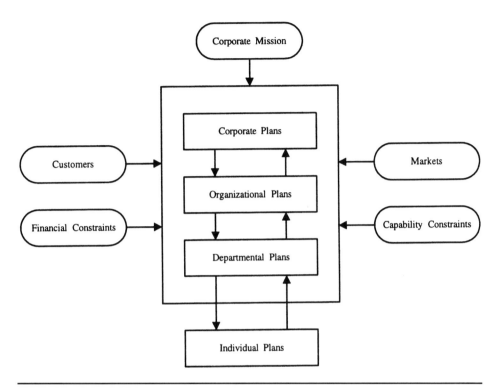

FIGURE 6.1   Overview of corporate planning and budgeting process.

ing process with not very charitable feelings toward the financial community in a company. Some of the questions come from ignorance, but most questions are asked because the corporate financial personnel have a fiduciary responsibility to the owners of the company to enhance profitability and leverage assets. Once you look at it that way, you see you have an opportunity to educate financial personnel and learn from the questions they ask.

To make the best use of the corporate budgeting process, support managers must prepare themselves by doing some groundwork. Nonfinancial organizational goals can be heavily influenced, if not set, by support management before or during the start of the planning cycle. As mentioned earlier, a support manager must continually publicize the value of support to both the company and its customers; it is this publicity that can ensure executive consent for the technical support organization's goals. Based on those goals, support management should make some preliminary estimates of revenues and costs, and use this information to prepare themselves for the budget negotiations.

Goals and Programs

The first step in this preparation is to understand the relationship between the goals of the company, the goals of the support organization, and the actual programs that must be implemented to achieve those goals (see Figure 6.2). Fortunately, in most existing support organizations those relationships are well defined: The key goal of most support organizations is to deliver support to customers, and most of that work is done in the key support processes. But there could be other goals and factors that also

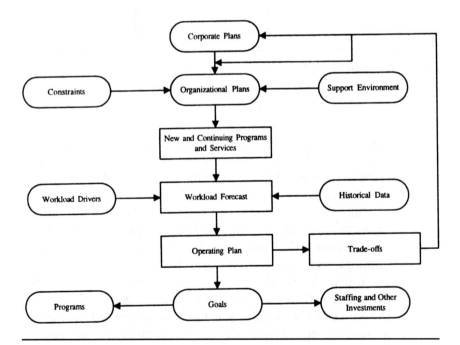

FIGURE 6.2 Technical support planning and budgeting.

create work. For example, your Technical Support Organization may be given the additional responsibility to generate revenues by selling new support offerings. This may mean that you now need to set up new sales and marketing programs in your organization. Similarly, your customers may be asking for new programs and services; these programs will not normally be specified at the corporate level, but as long as they fall under one of the goals of the support organization then they are candidates for the operating plan.

Estimating Workload

Once you have determined the programs that will need to be done to meet the organizational goals, you must estimate how much work will have to be done. Work will normally fall into one of two categories: changes to existing programs and services; and the introduction of new programs and services. The work performed in existing programs may increase or decrease, or even go away. For example, if you support all products of your company, there may be work arising from new products that will be launched in the coming year. Similarly, there may be reductions in the workload created by products that will cease to be sold in the coming year. To estimate how much the workload will change for your current programs and services, you must first understand what drives the workload, then make some assumptions about changes in the drivers. Using these assumptions you can then estimate the projected workload in the coming year, using some of the forecasting techniques described later in this chapter.

New programs and services will create incremental work that needs to be performed. It can sometimes be difficult to estimate the workload that is created by a new program or service. One solution is to make some estimates (guesses) and use those for initial planning; you can later take periodic assessments of actual workloads during the year and try to make adjustments to your estimates. Another option is to survey and benchmark similar programs, either within the company or in other companies of like size and market, and see if you can make some estimates from there. A third option is to hire someone who has had some experience with similar programs, and use that experience.

Staff Planning

The next step is to translate workload estimates into a high-level operating plan. The investments associated with people usually make up the highest percentage of investments in a support organization (sometimes as high as 90 percent), so the major focus in a high-level operating plan is on staff planning. As before, this is easy to do for some work, not so easy for other work. If you have metrics about current operations, you can usually estimate with some accuracy how many people you will need for the projected workload of similar operations. For new programs and services this is a more challenging exercise; you may have to make some educated guesses and use those until you can develop a more reliable forecast.

Technology Investments

Another vital part in the high-level operating plan is an evaluation of technology investments and planned process changes. As described in Chapter 7, there are numerous technologies in use in support organizations. Many of these technologies promise considerable improvements in productivity, and so can help reduce operating expenses (or the increase in operating expenses). Planned process changes can be similarly evaluated at this time; if you are planning to change some processes in your organization, you can estimate the effect of these changes on your productivity, and hence operating expenses. Evaluation of technologies and planned process changes can help you decide which ones to implement. If you plan to do so, then you must reestimate your staffing requirements taking into consideration the expected productivity increases.

Other Investments

Last, the high-level operating plan should contain some financial estimates of anticipated revenues and investments. These are generally based on assumptions made about the anticipated revenue base and new programs, and on a high-level conversion of staffing and program plans into operating expenses. For example, revenue estimates may be based on assumptions about changes in the size of the installed base, or on new programs to retain existing support customers. Approximate salaries and planned capital investments, together with gross estimates of infrastructure costs, and fixed and variables expenses (such as rent and telecommunications) can give you an idea of the extent of investment required to implement the programs in the operating plan.

It is absolutely essential to understand and document all the assumptions made in developing the high-level operating plan, because you will have to explain your reasoning to other people in the company, and show how you developed the high-level operating plan. The documented assumptions are also very important in evaluating trade-offs at the corporate level; if the plan is based on assumptions of dependencies on other programs in the company, then you can rapidly assess the impact of changes in those programs on your operating plan.

In most large and medium-sized companies other organizations, such as sales, marketing, research, and development, will be going through a similar exercise. The person responsible for the overall planning process (usually the corporate controller) will periodically bring together organizations in the company to resolve interorganizational issues. The resolution of these issues will often result in a need to modify the high-level operating plan, because the assumption set of the plan will have changed. In smaller companies planning and coordination may be done by the CEO, or by the company's executives as a group.

The high-level operating plan will eventually stabilize, as more interorganizational issues are resolved and assumptions validated by other people in the company. The stable high-level operating plan can now be translated into a firm operating plan for the support organization, and then used to finalize the operating plans for each department in the support organization. The final operating plans will include a financial budget, at a level of detail required by corporate financial staff.

WORKLOAD DRIVERS

Work in a Technical Support Organization does not exist in a vacuum. As discussed earlier, work manifests itself in programs determined by the goals and objectives of the company and the

Technical Support Organization, as well as customer expectations and other considerations such as product quality. Before attempting to forecast the amount of work your organization can expect, you must understand how and why your workload is the way it is, and what factors cause the workload to change. Factors that affect your workload are called workload drivers.

Understanding What Drives Your Workload

The work in each program in a Technical Support Organization is affected by different combinations of drivers; for example, the drivers of workload in the support delivery program may not be the same as the drivers of workload in the support sales program. The former may be driven more by the size of the total support customer base, whereas the latter may be driven more by the number of potential support customers. Even if the same set of drivers affect workload in different programs of technical support, the degree to which they affect the workload may not be the same. Poor product quality may result in more work in the support delivery program than in the knowledge creation program.

The best starting point for determining workload drivers is a thorough understanding of the current business programs and processes, and historical data about those programs and processes. From these you should be able to develop a model of the factors and their interaction with support workload, and perhaps even determine a predictable relationship between the factors and the workload. The most amount of work in a Technical Support Organization is done in the three key support processes discussed in an earlier chapter; this is also where the most amount of money is usually invested. For this reason, we recommend that support managers understand the factors that affect the workload in these three processes, and the extent to which the workload is affected by those factors.

Table 6.1 gives some examples of workload drivers that are common in support organizations.

Relationship between Drivers and Workload

In some cases it is relatively easy to determine that a causal relationship exists between workload and one or more factors.

TABLE 6.1 Common Workload Drivers

Category	*Subcategory*
Customer	Number of customers
	Number of sites
	Number of units installed
	Customer expertise with product
	Customer usage of products
	Point in customer's application lifecycle
Product	Product quality
	Product complexity
	Stability of product technology
	Quality of product documentation
	Availability of third-party support
Connectivity	Number of platforms on which product runs
	Network complexity of typical installation

Managers can make use of data produced by the metrics system, supplement that with external data, and examine the historical relationship between different factors and the workload being affected. For example, in most organizations there is some relationship between product sales volumes and support request volumes. The relationship is usually direct, and can be estimated by examining historical data. An example of this relationship is shown in Figure 6.3.

In other situations, it may be possible to identify the drivers of workload but not the exact relationship that exists between the drivers and the workload. This could happen when there are many drivers of the workload, or if there are no data available that can be used to quantify the relationship. For example, you may want to estimate the workload that will be generated by a particular class of customer. You know from past experience that many factors will affect the amount of work that will be generated, including each customer's expertise with your products, the quality of the products, the *mission-criticality* of the customer's usage of the products, each customer's internal policies

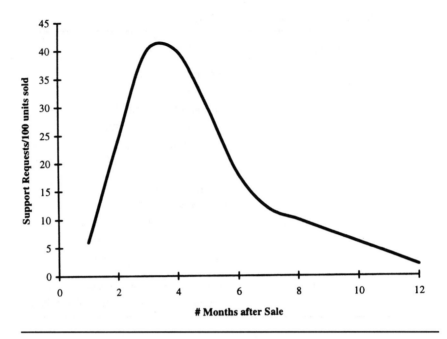

FIGURE 6.3   Relationship between unit sales and support request volumes.

and procedures, and so on. But you have no way of estimating how much each of these factors consistently contributes to the overall workload. In these situations you may not be able to develop accurate forecasts using only quantitative techniques, and may have to rely on a Delphi forecasting method (discussed later in this chapter).

Finally, you may not even be able to reasonably establish any factors that affect your workload in a particular situation, let alone establish a relationship between those factors and the workload. Admittedly this is rare, but this may happen, for example, if your company introduces very new product technology, or if you implement a new technology to deliver support. If there is no organizational experience with the technologies, it may be impossible to even come up with a reasonable set of workload drivers. In these situations you may have to rely exclusively on experience, both yours and that of others who have worked in similar situations.

FORECASTING TECHNIQUES

About Forecasting

Once you have established what drives your workload, you must forecast how much work you will get in the coming year. Forecasting is an inexact science or an art, depending on how you look at it. It is certainly possible to create sophisticated forecasting models using advanced mathematical techniques, but no forecasting model or technique can guarantee you an accurate prediction of the future. This is because forecasting techniques are based on your assumptions, and the quality of the forecast is influenced by the quality of the assumptions you make. You can improve the quality of the forecast by rigorously validating the assumptions you make, but in any but the most trivial models there is no guarantee that the assumptions you make are perfect, or even that the set of assumptions you make are the only things that affect the forecast. A forecast can give you an idea of the future workload with some degree of uncertainty; the better the forecast, the smaller the degree of uncertainty.

You should therefore never make business decisions solely on the basis of numbers from a forecasting model; all forecasts should be tempered by your experience and subjected to *tests of reasonability*. If your experience as a support professional tells you that the results of a forecast do not feel right, then you owe it to yourself to validate that forecast.

Having said that, forecasting models can be a valuable tool for support managers. The purpose of forecasting techniques is to minimize the degree of uncertainty in your forecast; in other words, forecasting techniques take your assumptions and produce a fairly reliable forecast based on the assumptions. This section describes the main forecasting techniques that are in common use; treatment of the mathematics of forecasting is beyond the scope of this book but may be found in most books on statistics or decision science. To help you we have *italicized* the terms you could look up in an index of such a book.

Delphi Method

The simplest way to forecast future workload would be to poll a number of people familiar with what is being forecast, and the drivers of that workload. You could then gather the polling data and derive a reasonable forecast that incorporates the views of all the people you polled. This is actually a fairly good technique; a formal methodology, called the *Delphi Method*, is a way of interviewing subject matter experts individually, collecting their forecasts, and sending them back for successive revisions until a consensus has been reached (see Figure 6.4). This technique is particularly effective in small or new organizations, and for new programs, where there is not a lot of history to work with and the subject matter experts have first-hand knowledge of business conditions and workload drivers. It is somewhat sub-

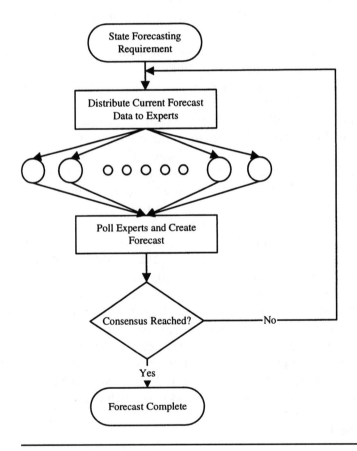

FIGURE 6.4 Delphi method.

jective but it can be a quick way of consolidating the experience of all the participants.

Causal Methods

Another class of forecasting techniques is called *causal methods*. As their name would suggest, these techniques work on the assumption that there is a consistent cause and effect relationship between what is being forecast (the *dependent variable*) and one or more *independent variables*, using a technique called *regression analysis*. In these methods the independent variables are the workload drivers you identified for the workload you are forecasting. For example, after examining historical data you may identify a consistent relationship between the independent variables of unit sales and the size of the installed customer base (the workload drivers), and the dependent variable of support request volumes; and base your volume projections on the number of sales and size of the installed base in the previous few months.

Causal methods are very powerful because you can examine the causal effect of many workload drivers on a single dependent variable, and select for your model only those that make sense and have a strong effect. The potential weakness of causal methods is that you need to know the future values of your independent variables; after all, even if you identify the relationship between the drivers and the workload, you still need to know the behavior of the drivers in the future. For example, if your projections are based on unit sales in previous periods for which you know actual numbers, you can reliably forecast future volumes (see Figure 6.5). But if you need to forecast based on unit sales in future periods, the accuracy of your forecast is very dependent on the accuracy of the unit sales forecast. Another issue with causal methods with more than one independent variable (or driver) is the possibility that the drivers are not independent of one another. The more interdependence there is among your workload drivers, the less reliable your forecast will be. We gave the example earlier of support requests being driven by unit sales and the size of the installed customer base. If you are in a market where one customer typically buys only one unit, then the size of the installed customer base will grow by the amount of the

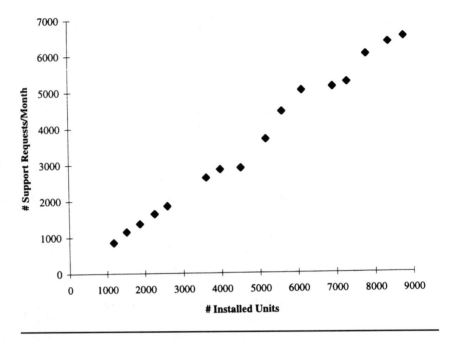

FIGURE 6.5 Example of a causal relationship.

unit sales; in other words, the unit sales and the size of the installed base are not independent of one another.

Growth Rates

In those situations where it is difficult to establish a consistent and reliable relationship between the workload drivers and the workload, you may be able to use time as a surrogate for the combination of all the workload drivers. A class of forecasting techniques, called *time series methods*, are based on the assumption that the contribution of the combination of independent variables in the past is a good predictor of their contribution in the future, so you can use time as the single independent variable. Time series methods examine historical data for workload patterns over time, and project that pattern to forecast future workloads. For example, one way you could forecast your future support request volume would be to look at the *historical growth*

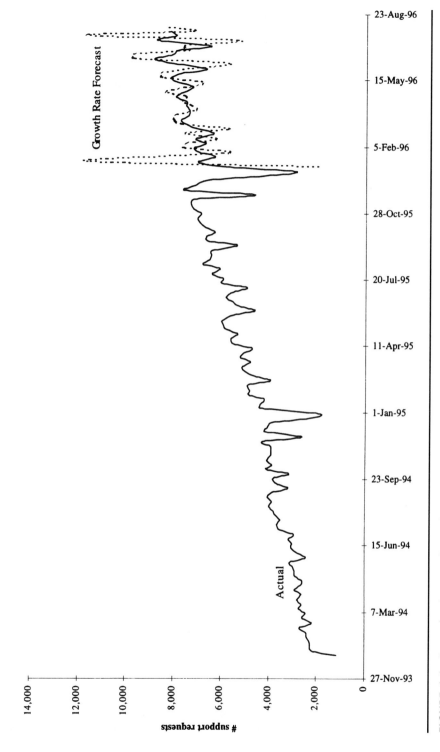

FIGURE 6.6 Example of a growth rate forecast.

rate of your support requests, and just apply the growth rate to the support request volume in the current period to derive the expected volume in the next period (see Figure 6.6). The major problem with this approach is that if the support request volume in the current period is an aberration, then your estimate for the next period will not be very accurate.

Moving Averages

A way to work around the distortions caused by aberrations and smooth out the irregular periods is to take the *moving average* of the past few periods and use that as a predictor of the next period. For example, you may decide that the support request volume in the next month will be the average of the support request volumes over the last three months. This may give you a reasonable approximation, but the big problem with this approach is that if your recent volumes changed suddenly (for example, you start supporting another product), it will be a while before your projections catch up with reality. This is because the older months (which had lower volumes) will drag down the projection.

To reduce the influence of the older periods you can use *weighted averages*, which give more weight to the recent periods. For example, you may decide that the support request volume next month is best estimated by 50 percent of the support request volume last month, 34 percent of the volume two months ago, and 16 percent of the volume three months ago (see Figure 6.7). This technique is more responsive to trends, but deciding the weights to use requires a lot of experience and trial and error. Slightly more sophisticated techniques called *exponential smoothing* can help make better forecasts, but they too require some guesswork and don't pick up trends in data too well.

Trend Projections

Probably the most popular time series technique is *trend projection*, which fits a line to a series of historical data points, and then projects the line into the future (see Figure 6.8). This technique is quite easy when it is possible to fit a straight line to the historical data point, and gets a little more complicated when the

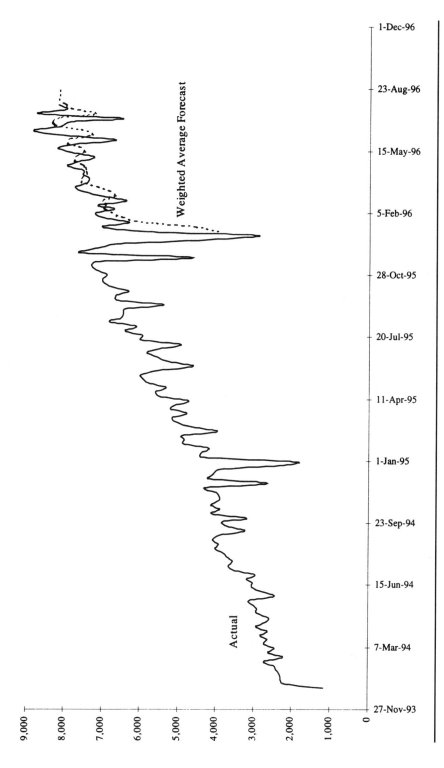

FIGURE 6.7 Example of averaging techniques.

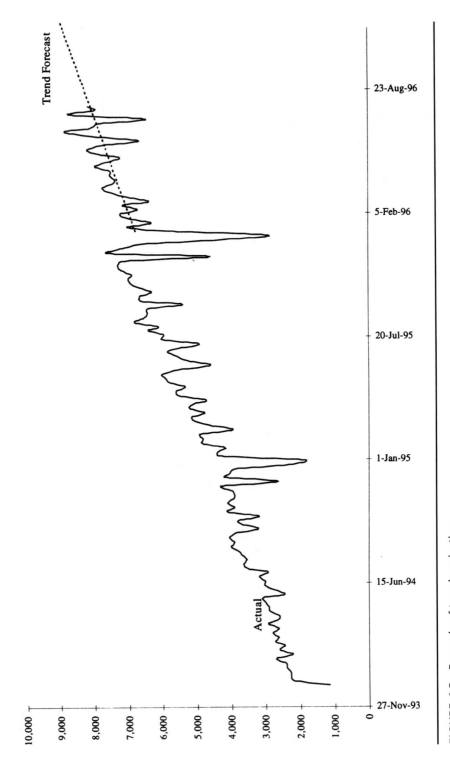

FIGURE 6.8 Example of trend projection.

trend line is not straight. Even so, sophisticated trend models can develop a line that matches all the historical data points, and this line can be used to make a forecast of the future trend.

The problem with trend projection, indeed with all time series methods, is the basic assumption that the historical data provide a good indication of the future. This may be true in relatively stable environments, but few support organizations experience such consistency of behavior. In reality, changes in the support environment occur all the time and the rapid pace of change means that the past is at best a guide to the future, but not a predictor.

One area where the past is usually a good indicator of the future, assuming no changes in the product and market mix, is in the *seasonality* of workload. Most support organizations experience dips and surges in the workload at specific times of the year. For example, many support organizations show a change in workload (or in the rate of growth of workload) around national holidays, such as Christmas or the New Year. In the United States, there is almost always a dip in support workload around Thanksgiving. Such seasonal variations in workload can be estimated, and *seasonality adjustments* made to forecasts to give a better representation of the forecast workload. An example of a forecast workload with seasonality adjustments is shown in Figure 6.9.

SEGMENTED FORECASTS

In organizations with few programs, or organizations that support only a few similar products, it may suffice to use forecasting techniques to directly develop an overall organizational forecast, without developing a forecast for each product or program. In larger organizations that support many different products through many support offerings, possibly from multiple support centers, it may be necessary to create a forecast for each of a number of segments, and then develop a budget for each segment before adding up all the budget forecasts to arrive at the organizational forecast.

Why Segment?

The reasons for this are best explained with a simple example. Consider a large support organization that provides technical

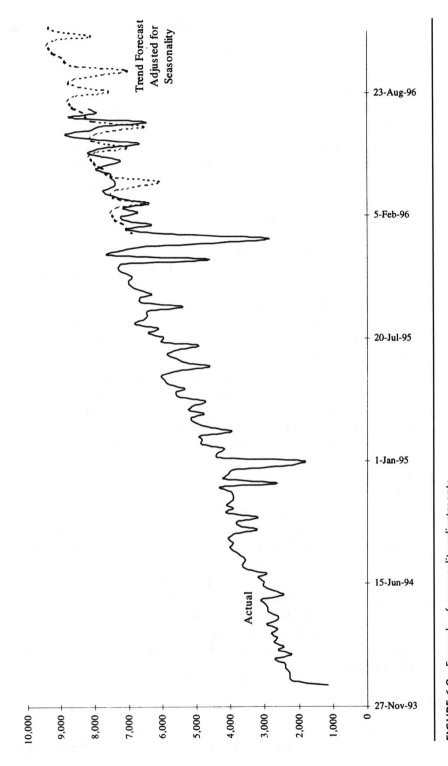

FIGURE 6.9 Example of seasonality adjustments.

support on two product families. Each family has its own support center, and each center provides three types of support: via e-mail, via telephone into a telephone bank, and a premium personalized service. Last, the product families are targeted at different markets: One family is sold primarily to large business organizations, the other to individual end users. We now need to forecast the total workload required for the key support processes in this environment.

One approach would be to apply some of the forecasting techniques previously described to historical data on the total workload, and make an estimate. But even if the total workload forecast is reliable, we are still faced with the problem of dividing up the total budget into budgets for each support center. Should it be based on the proportion of work that was done by each center in the past? Perhaps. But what if the mix of workload is changing; for example, if the end-user product family is being phased out of the company's product offering (see Figure 6.10). How will this impact the mix of work? A better approach instead may be to develop a forecast for each support center, then add up the forecasts to develop an overall workload forecast. In a similar manner you may want to further segment the forecast for each center into forecasts by the type of support offering. If you intend to use workload forecasts to develop staffing projections, and if the time required for different types of support requests is significantly different for each type, then it may even make sense to develop a forecast by support center by support offering by support request type, and develop staffing requirements on that basis. A word of caution: Too much segmentation may result in budgets that overstate the actual requirements, because the potential for sharing resources across segments is often neglected.

You may have realized by now that we are developing our forecasts along a number of different dimensions of segmentation, described in Chapter 5. In general, you should forecast down to the lowest meaningful dimension of segmentation that can significantly impact the mix of what it is that you're trying to forecast. In our preceding example, we could have further segmented our forecast by the severity associated with support requests in each support request type. That may have been an interesting exercise, but if the mix of severity levels does not sig-

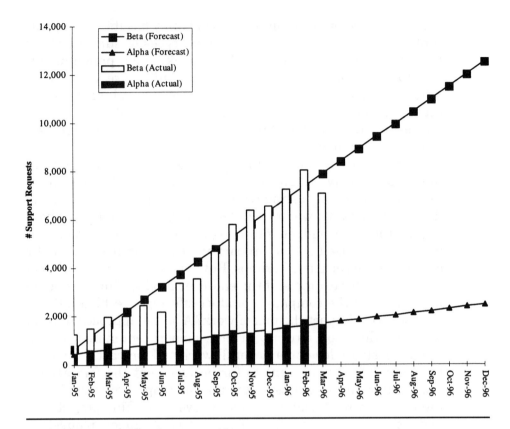

FIGURE 6.10 Example of segmented forecast.

nificantly impact our staffing calculations, then it would not make sense to carry the segmentation that far.

Note that the further you carry the segmentation, the more data you need to be able to make reliable forecasts. Obviously you will not be able to carry out any segmentation if you do not have a quantifiable basis for the segmentation and the forecast.

Segmenting over Time

One type of segmentation we highly recommend is time based. Even if you are preparing an annual budget we recommend that you segment your forecast to give you estimates of workload over shorter time periods, such as quarters, months, or even weeks. This is useful in environments where there is a high growth rate in the workload, or if the mix or workload can change considerably during the course of the year. These changes can have a significant impact on your resource requirements from period to period, and you can develop a more accurate budget if you take the changes into account. A typical example of this is the seasonality variations discussed earlier.

Tests of Reasonability

If you use quantitative forecasting methods, such as causal or time series methods, you should examine your forecasts and see that they appear reasonable. Such tests of reasonability vary from company to company, but you can do some spot checks. Are both product sales and product support workload headed in the same direction? If not, you may want to verify your assumptions and analysis. Is the change in the forecast workload substantially different in the changes in the individual drivers? There are many other questions you could ask along those lines. We recommend you bring together some of your colleagues to validate your assumptions and forecasts before you actually use them to prepare budgets. Remember, a forecast is an estimate of the future, and the purpose of forecasting techniques is to reduce the uncertainty of the estimate. Forecasting techniques cannot replace experience and intuition that managers develop over the course of their careers.

ESTIMATING GROSS STAFFING REQUIREMENTS

Now that you have estimated your workload, you need to estimate your staffing plan. For some of the workload you may have no simple way to translate the workload into a staffing requirement. For example, your organization is going to introduce a new customer retention program and will need to develop a marketing campaign. Without actually designing the program in some detail, it may be very difficult to determine exactly how much and what type of marketing labor will be required for the program.

The best you can do in these situations is use a variation of the Delphi forecasting technique described earlier to estimate how much marketing labor you will need, and then translate that into a staffing plan.

In other situations you may be able to develop some rules of thumb to help you estimate the staffing requirement. For example, many companies put a cap on the number of people that may directly report to one manager, as well as a minimum number. Using this range you can estimate the number of managers that you need in your organization.

For most of your support programs, however, you will have forecast some numbers of support requests coming into each of one or more support centers, possibly segmented by product family and/or support offering, and perhaps even by support request type. For budgeting purposes a gross estimate of staffing will suffice, because what you are interested in is your staffing requirement for the whole period. At this time you are not so interested in the actual staffing levels and scheduling.

Estimating Staffing Levels Using Processing Rates

We present two techniques in the following section that you can use to estimate staffing requirements. The first technique calculates the staffing requirement based on the current rate of processing support requests. Consider an example in which you have to estimate your staffing requirement for a forecast workload of 3,000 support requests in a month. An examination of historical data shows you that for a particular segment of support requests, an average TSR processes nine support requests per day. You can get this number by dividing the number of closed support requests in that segment every month by the total number of TSRs you had in place, who were supposed to process those requests. Exclude new hirees who were not yet ready to handle support requests, but do not exclude TSRs who were out in training, on vacation, or out sick, because they are part of your staff and you need to factor in absences that will occur in the normal course of things. We will account for the new hirees later.

We first calculate the number of days your support center is open. Assuming that you have ten holidays a year, and assuming your support center is closed on weekends, then:

$$\text{Number of working days} = 52 \text{ weeks} \times 5 \text{ days} - 10 \text{ holidays}$$
$$= 250 \text{ days}$$
$$\text{Working days/month} = 250 \div 12$$
$$= 20.83 \text{ (which we may round up to 21 for illustrative purposes)}$$

Calculation of the number of TSRs required is then easy:

$$\text{Number of TSRs required} = \text{Number of support requests} / (\text{daily rate} \times \text{days in month})$$
$$= 3{,}000 / (9 \times 21)$$
$$= 15.87$$

Since we cannot have fractional TSRs, we can round this number up to 16 TSRs needed for a month in which we expect 3,000 support requests.

You can do this for each month, and develop a staff requirement for the whole year. But remember, these are fully trained TSRs. Compare this to your current staffing levels and attrition rates to determine how many new fully trained TSRs you will need in each month during the year. For each new hiree TSR, you have to plan for some training time before that TSR can be put to work on support requests. If this period is two months, you must hire new TSRs two months before you need them; in other words, you have to pay two months' salaries. This directly affects your budget! An example of the hiring schedule is shown in Table 6.2.

Estimating Staffing Levels Using Labor Time

The second technique uses a slightly different approach, and may be easier to use when you do not have a historical rate of support requests per TSR. To use this technique you must know the average time required to process a support request, and make some assumptions about the availability of an average TSR. You must first calculate the total labor time required. Let's say that it takes 27 minutes on average to process each support request. Thus in a month in which we expect 3,000 support requests:

TABLE 6.2 Hiring Schedule and Staffing Levels

	Jan	Feb	Mar	Apr	May	Jun	Jul	Aug	Sep	Oct	Nov	Dec
Trained TSRs Required	15	15	15	16	16	16	17	17	18	19	20	20
Expected TSR Attrition	0	0	0	1	0	1	0	1	0	0	1	0
New TSRs Required	0	0	0	2	0	1	1	1	1	1	2	0
New Hiree Schedule	0	2	0	1	1	1	1	1	2			
Total TSRs in Budget	15	17	17	17	18	18	19	19	21	21	20	20

$$\text{Total labor requirement} = \text{Time to process 1 request} \times$$
$$\text{Number of expected requests}$$
$$= 27 \text{ minutes} \times 3{,}000 \text{ requests}$$
$$= 81{,}000 \text{ minutes}$$
$$= 1{,}350 \text{ hours}$$

The next step is to calculate the average availability per TSR. We have already assumed 250 working days in a year. If we assume that in a year a TSR will further be absent for 20 vacation and sick days, and 10 days of training, the TSR is available for a total of:

$$\text{TSR Availability} = \text{Working days} - \text{Days absent}$$
$$= 250 \text{ working days} - 20 \text{ vacation days} -$$
$$10 \text{ training days}$$
$$= 220 \text{ days}$$

$$\text{Availability as \%} = 220 \; / \; 250$$
$$= 88\%$$

Next we estimate the number of hours each day that we actually expect a TSR to work directly on support requests. In most support environments, TSRs are expected to do other things in addition to processing support requests. In the course of a day a TSR may be expected to spend time in a laboratory, on research activities, on documentation and other special projects, and may also be required by law to take some breaks. In our example let's assume that a TSR can spend five hours a day processing support requests. We now calculate the number of hours a TSR is available each month to work on support requests:

$$\text{TSR Hours Available} = \text{Number of hours per day} \times \text{number of days} \times \text{availability}$$
$$= 5 \text{ hours} \times 21 \text{ days} \times 88\% \text{ availability}$$
$$= 92.4 \text{ hours}$$

The last step is to calculate the number of TSRs needed:

$$\text{Number of TSRs required} = \text{Labor hours needed} \div \text{TSR monthly hours}$$
$$= 1{,}350 \div 92.4$$
$$= 14.6$$

Since we cannot have fractional TSRs, round the number up to 15 TSRs needed in a month in which we expect 3,000 support requests.

A big assumption made in the second technique was that the TSR moves from support request to support request, with no time in between. This may happen in a high-volume support center, but even in those situations there is a small but measurable time between calls. Our average of 27 minutes per support request may actually result in 29 minutes between support requests handled by a TSR; it is not practical or reasonable to expect a TSR to perform work in the extra two minutes, so the additional time must be absorbed as a labor overhead. If we use this higher number, the total labor requirement goes up from 1,350 hours to 1,450 hours, and the staffing requirement to 15.7, or 16 TSRs. If you can estimate the average time between support requests handled by a TSR, you should add that to the time to process support requests.

EVALUATING SUPPORT AUTOMATION TECHNOLOGY INVESTMENTS

As a part of the planning and budgeting process, you may have to justify the purchase of some support automation technology, such as a problem resolution system or a search engine. Evaluation of automation technologies on their strategic value and technical merits is discussed in Chapter 7. This section discusses the financial assessment of any technology investment that is made with the expectation of a financial return on investment, usually realized through increases in productivity. Remember that not all investments are made with a financial return in mind. For instance, a Technical Support Organization may invest in a sophisticated fax-back system just to provide an additional service to customers, and not with the expectation of reduced costs by redirecting reduced incoming support requests from telephones to a fax machine.

Return on Investment

Many investments in technical support automation technologies are, however, made with the expectation that there will be a reduction in costs of delivering support to customers. In reality, as the absolute number of support requests continues to climb, the effect of automation is usually to slow down the rate of increase of costs. This typically manifests itself in increased productivity of TSRs, and this increased productivity means that fewer additional TSRs may be needed to handle projected increases in workload. Many technologies do in fact increase productivity considerably if they are successfully installed and properly used.

Benefits of Investments

To analyze what kind of financial return you may expect, you need to carefully evaluate the benefits of the technology as they apply to your particular support operations. A basic analysis of return on investment weighs the amount of the investment against the anticipated economic benefit over some period of time. We demonstrate an analysis by considering an investment in a problem resolution system, which promises two types of productivity gain. The first productivity gain is realized by increasing the success rate in quickly and accurately identifying previously reported issues. The second productivity gain is a reduction in time to search through previously reported issues, something that is done for all support requests.

Consider an example given earlier of the support center whose average time to process a support request is 27 minutes. Historical data show that 80 percent of all support requests are on previously reported issues, and 20 percent are on new issues. However, the success rate of quickly identifying support requests on previously known issues is 60 percent; the remaining 40 percent are not quickly identified and so require additional research. Although the mean time to process support requests on known issues is 15 minutes, it actually takes on average only nine minutes to process those requests that can quickly be identified as known issues, and 24 minutes to process those that take a little longer to identify as known issues. Support requests on new issues take an average of 75 minutes to process. This is summarized in Table 6.3a.

Implementation of the problem resolution system will result in better organization and accessibility of known issues, and is expected to increase the quick search category of support requests on known issues to 80 percent from 60 percent. All other

TABLE 6.3a Example of Support Automation Analysis

				Mean Time to Process
All Support Requests			100%	27 Minutes
	Known Issues	80%		15 Minutes
		Quick Search (60% of Known Issues)	48%	9 Minutes
		Longer Search (40% of Known Issues)	32%	24 Minutes
	New Issues		20%	75 Minutes

TABLE 6.3b   Example of Support Automation Analysis (Continued)

				Mean Time to Process
All Support Requests			100%	25 Minutes
	Known Issues	80%		12 Minutes
		Quick Search (80% of Known Issues)	64%	9 Minutes
		Longer Search (20% of Known Issues)	16%	24 Minutes
	New Issues		20%	75 Minutes

things being equal, the effect of this shift will be to reduce the mean time to process a support request from 27 minutes to 24.6 (rounded up to 25) minutes, as shown in Table 6.3b.

As mentioned earlier, once information has been collected about an issue, a TSR will search through a knowledgebase of known issues. The second type of productivity gain from a problem resolution system arises from a reduction in the time required to perform the search. To estimate the impact of this type of productivity gain, we continue with our earlier example. Let us assume that a problem resolution system can reduce the search time for the three categories of support request as found in Table 6.3c.

TABLE 6.3c   Example of Support Automation Analysis (Continued)

Type	*Before Automation*			*After Automation*		
	Search Time	*Other Time*	*Total Time*	*Search Time*	*Other Time*	*Total Time*
Quick Search	5 Minutes	4 Minutes	9 Minutes	1 Minute	4 Minutes	5 Minutes
Longer Search	15 Minutes	9 Minutes	24 Minutes	10 Minutes	9 Minutes	19 Minutes
New Issues	30 Minutes	45 Minutes	75 Minutes	15 Minutes	45 Minutes	60 Minutes

Using these new processing times, you can now calculate the effect on overall mean processing time. This is shown in Table 6.3d.

In this situation, the automation technology has reduced the overall average time required to process a support request from 27 minutes to 18 minutes, an improvement of 33 percent. The productivity improvement is highest in the Quick Search subcategory (from nine minutes down to five minutes, or 44 percent) and lowest in the New Issues category of support request (from 75 minutes down to 60 minutes, or 20 percent). This is as one would expect, because the problem resolution system is meant to reduce only the search time, and the search time is a smaller percentage of the total time spent on new issues than it is on known issues.

A productivity improvement of 33 percent does not automatically result in a 33-percent savings in costs or staffing. If we use an average of 18 minutes per support request, and two minutes between support requests (as described in the example in the previous section), then the staffing requirement for a month in which we expect 3,000 support requests would drop from 16 TSRs to 11 TSRs, or 31 percent. In practice, the reduction in the staffing requirement would be reflected in improved responsiveness (see the later section on queuing) or more time for the TSRs to perform other work. Cost savings would be realized only to the extent that the value of the other activities performed by TSRs is equivalent to or greater than the value of processing support re-

TABLE 6.3d Example of Support Automation Analysis (Continued)

				Mean Time to Process
All Support Requests			100%	18 Minutes
	Known Issues	80%		7 Minutes
		Quick Search (80% of Known Issues)	64%	5 Minutes
		Longer Search (20% of Known Issues)	16%	19 Minutes
	New Issues		20%	60 Minutes

quests. Eventually as the workload grows, the 16 TSRs can be reapplied to processing support requests; with an average time between support requests of 20 minutes, the 16 TSRs should be able to process over 4,400 support requests in a month.

Costs of Investment

So far we have considered only the expected benefits of the automation; we have not considered the extent of the investment required to realize that benefit. Without getting into great detail about the finances, we can assume that an investment such as a problem resolution system will require an initial capital outlay to purchase (or build) and install the system, and then some ongoing maintenance of the system. Furthermore, there is a period of time while TSRs adapt to the new technology, before they are able to realize its full potential. Assuming that the benefits described earlier are greater than the cost of ongoing maintenance of the system, at some point the initial investment will be recouped. From a strictly financial perspective, it is only after this point that the support center realizes the value of its investment.

An example of a simple return on investment analysis is shown in Table 6.4.

In this example, we show the expected workload and the number of TSRs we estimate will be needed to handle the workload. With automation, the number of TSRs needed will decrease, but since we are unlikely to terminate trained staff already in place we end up with more TSRs than needed for about one year. These TSRs can be applied to other tasks in the support center, or you can realize the benefit of extra staff by improving your service levels (see the section on queuing models). The actual savings from implementing the automation system start accruing approximately one year after the automation effort is started, and take another year to recoup the initial investment and ongoing maintenance costs.

QUEUING MODELS

Many support organizations provide an *immediate support* model, usually available for support delivered over the telephone. Customers requesting support call into a central telephone num-

TABLE 6.4 Simple Return on Investment Analysis

	Q4-94	Q1-95	Q2-95	Q3-95	Q4-95	Q1-96	Q2-96	Q3-96	Q4-96
Projected Support Requests		9,000	9,450	9,923	10,419	10,940	11,487	12,061	12,664
TSRs Needed without Automation		15	15	16	17	18	19	20	21
Associated Costs ($000s)		$375	$375	$400	$425	$450	$475	$500	$525
TSRs Needed with Automation		12	13	13	14	15	15	16	17
TSRs in Place		15	15	15	15	15	15	16	17
TSR Savings		0	0	1	2	3	4	4	4
Actual Savings ($000s)		$0	$0	$25	$50	$75	$100	$100	$100
Automation Costs ($000s)	$150	$50	$25	$25	$25	$25	$25	$25	$25
Net Benefit in Quarter ($000s)	($150)	($50)	($25)	$0	$25	$50	$75	$75	$75
Cumulative Benefit ($000s)	($150)	($200)	($225)	($225)	($200)	($150)	($75)	$0	$75

ber at a support center and wait in a telephone queue until a TSR takes the call off the queue. Many surveys of customers have shown that they generally do not like being put on hold for extended periods of time. It behooves support organizations, therefore, to design their operations to minimize the wait time that customers experience on hold. Support managers often establish *service levels* for their support centers that define the performance goals for that organization. These service levels usually describe the *mean wait time* (or some variation thereof) that callers may experience when they call. For example, a service level may be, "Callers will experience a mean wait time of 30 seconds, or, Ninety percent of calls will be answered in 45 seconds or less." In this section, we will go over some basic characteristics of queues, and the planning and operational implications of these characteristics.

To design a queuing system we must make some assumptions about the characteristics of call arrival patterns, about the types of calls, and about the support organization's performance in handling the calls. The rate at which calls arrive is generally stated as the average number of calls per unit of time. For example, at a peak period we may expect ten calls/minute. Due to the random nature of when calls may come in, this does not necessarily mean that a call arrives every six seconds. It means that during the peak period, some calls will come in exactly six seconds apart, others come in, say, two seconds apart, yet others come in ten seconds apart, and so on. The net effect over a large number of calls is that on average there are ten calls/minute. The call arrival rate is said to be described by the *Poisson probability function*, whereas the time between calls is described by the *exponential probability distribution*. Figure 6.11 shows the probability distribution of calls/minute in the example of an average of ten calls/minute.

This distribution shows that in a given minute the probability is highest that there will be either nine or ten calls, but there is also a probability that there may be less than or more than ten calls in that minute. Over time, the number of calls will average out to ten calls/minute.

One assumption that is commonly made about the types of calls is that all calls in this queue are essentially similar in nature, and can be serviced by any of the TSRs handling calls. Given that calls are essentially similar, we further assume that calls take an average amount of time to service (mean service time), and the actual service time follows an exponential probability distribution around this mean. For example, if the mean service time is 10 seconds, then a certain percentage of calls will actually be serviced in fewer than ten seconds, and a certain percentage in more that ten seconds.

Using all these assumptions, we can model a queuing system that is in a *steady state*; that is, calls are arriving at the rate we assumed and are being serviced at the rate we assumed. From this model we can derive certain performance characteristics of the queue as we vary elements of the model. The two performance characteristics that are of greatest interest are the *mean wait time* experienced by callers (i.e., how long do they have to

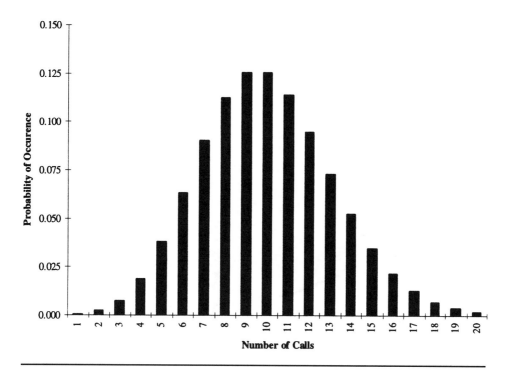

FIGURE 6.11   Probability distribution of calls.

wait on average to get service), and the number of callers in the system at any given time.

In a simple queuing system such as this, there are only three elements that can change: the number of calls coming in, the number of TSRs handling those calls, and the average time it takes to service each call. Each of these things affects the average time callers have to wait on hold. Some of the relationships between these three things and the wait time are intuitively obvious: The more TSRs you have serving callers, the less time callers will have to wait to get service; if you have more callers coming into the queue than are being serviced, then the latecomers are going to have to wait a very long time indeed; the lower the time it takes to service each caller, the less callers will have to wait in the queue.

What's not so intuitive is how much the mean wait time changes when you change the call arrival rate, the staffing level,

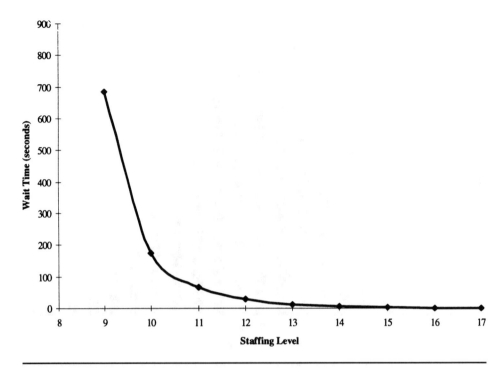

FIGURE 6.12 Wait time variation with staffing changes.

or the mean service time. Take a look at the chart in Figure 6.12, which shows how the wait time experienced by callers changes as you vary only the staffing level of TSRs. The shape of the curve shown in the chart remains essentially the same for different combinations of staffing levels, service times, and call arrival rates, which means that the conclusions apply to most support-center situations.

As expected the wait time decreases as the staffing level increases, but the relationship is not linear. In this example, the wait time decreases more when you go from a staffing level of nine people to ten people than it does when you go from 14 people to 15 people. The practical implications of this behavior are quite significant. Depending on where your support center is on this curve, putting one more TSR on the phones may have a very dramatic effect on wait times, or virtually no effect at all. You may be able to use this chart to identify a need for additional staff at certain periods during the day, or you may realize that adding more staff isn't going to do very much to improve wait times. Another implication is that if you are operating on the edge, say, with ten people in this example, and one of them takes a short break; then for the duration of the break you will be operating with nine people, and your wait times will very quickly escalate to high levels. For this reason scheduling phone time *and* breaks is very important if you want to provide a consistent service level to your customers.

Yet another implication of this chart is that the wait time increases as the pool of people available to take calls decreases. In other words, it is better to have as few queues as possible and to maximize the number of people that can service the calls coming into one queue. Table 6.5 shows what happens when a queue gets split into many smaller queues. In this example, we take a queue that gets 120 calls/hour and is staffed by 24 TSRs, with an average service time of ten minutes/call. The mean wait time is then 45 seconds per call. If we split it up into two queues of 12 people each, and each queue gets 60 calls/hour, then the wait time per call will go up to 135 seconds. In the extreme, if we split up the queue into 12 queues of two people and ten calls/hour each, our wait time goes up to 1,364, or almost 23 minutes per call. What this means for support center organization is that you can improve your service levels by training your TSRs to handle as many calls as possible, by reducing the number of telephone queues coming into the center, and by maximizing the pool of TSRs available for each queue.

Another element that can vary in a queuing model is the service time. Figure 6.13 shows the relationship between wait time and the service time for a given call arrival rate and staffing level.

TABLE 6.5 Effect of Splitting Queues

# Queues	1	2	3	4	6	8	12
Staff/Queue	24	12	8	6	4	3	2
Calls/Hour/Queue	120	60	40	30	20	15	10
Wait Time (seconds)	45	135	240	353	592	843	1364

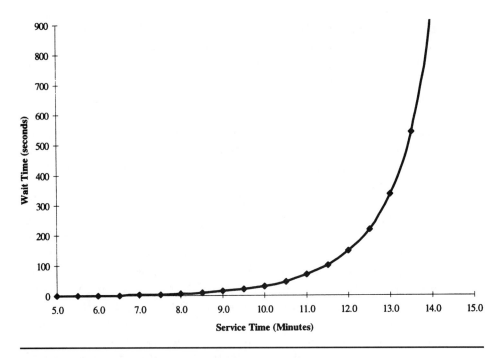

FIGURE 6.13 Wait time variations with service time changes.

As might be expected, the wait time goes up as the service time increases. As the service time goes higher, the rate of increase of the wait time also goes up. This is a fairly common situation when new features are added to the products you support. The added complexity may result in longer conversations between your TSRs and callers, and significantly increase the wait time for callers in the queue. This model also gives a basis for evaluating the impact of reengineering your support process, or introducing new support technology into your support center. For example, if you install a search system that you expect will reduce the service time from 12 minutes to ten minutes, then in the preceding example (40 calls/hour, staffing level of ten) your wait time should go down from about 150 seconds to 30 seconds without any additional staff. However, if you want to introduce the technology yet maintain the average wait time at three minutes, you will be able to reduce your staffing level from one to nine people, or increase the number of calls your ten people can handle from 40 calls/hour to 50 calls/hour.

The key concept to remember about queues is this: The relationship between the wait time and the call arrival rate, the staffing level, and the service time is not linear. By examining the effect of the call arrival rate, the staffing level, and the service time on wait times experienced by callers, support managers can make operational decisions that result in predictable service levels, and minimize costs at the same time.

SCHEDULING

Queuing models are valuable in determining how many TSRs to schedule at different times of the day. In many support centers the call arrival rate changes over the course of the day. For example, if you support products sold primarily to businesses, call volume may be quite low early in the morning, peak in the midmorning, dip at lunchtime, and pick up again in the midafternoon before tapering off in the evening. If you have the same number of staff scheduled through the day, then there will be periods when you have more staff than you need, and other periods when your staff is working at full capacity.

Figure 6.14 shows the daily call volume variations for a support center located in the Western United States, which supports customers all over North America.

Figure 6.15 shows the relationship between wait time and the call arrival rate, for a given staffing level of ten and a service time of ten minutes.

In this example, if your acceptable wait time is three minutes (180 seconds) or less, then ten TSRs can comfortably handle 50 calls/hour. But if your call volume falls below that number to, say, 40 calls/hour, then the mean wait time will drop to 30 seconds. Similarly, if you have only ten people scheduled and your call volume surges to 55 calls/hour, then you need more people or your wait times will increase dramatically. The practical implication of this is that you should examine how your call volume varies during different periods of the day, and schedule the appropriate number of staff to handle the expected call volume during each

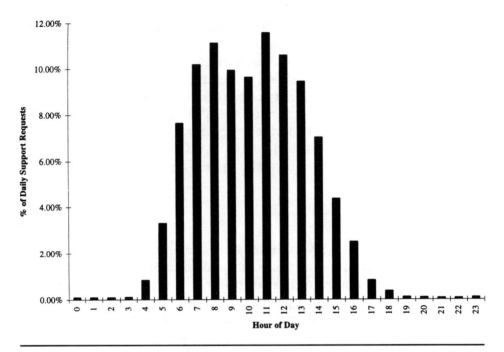

FIGURE 6.14 Workload variation during a day.

period. This will maximize the utilization of your staff, as well as give you some insight into when you can schedule time for research, meetings, training, and other off-line activities without materially affecting your service levels.

A frequent complaint of many customers of support organizations is that they have to wait an unacceptably long time to be put in touch with support personnel competent to handle the support request. This is partly because of inefficiencies in the distribution of support requests, and may also be due to lack of qualified support personnel. However, a major reason for long delays experienced by customers is poor scheduling of available resources.

What is scheduling? For the purpose of this chapter we will define good scheduling as ensuring that the right resources are available to meet responsiveness and quality goals. This is not an easy goal to achieve, because it requires a good understanding of workload patterns, cycle time distributions, and staff skill sets

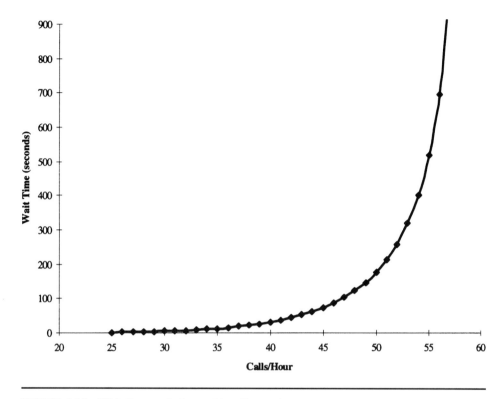

FIGURE 6.15   Wait time variations with call rate changes.

and availability; and the ability to optimize the schedule within the constraints imposed by the factors mentioned.

Responsiveness and quality goals are those goals that you set for your organization to further your mission of customer satisfaction. The responsiveness goals relate to measures of time (e.g., 95 percent of all support calls are acknowledged by a support person within two minutes; average wait time for callers will not exceed one minute etc.), and must be established by you. Quality goals are related to the value-added steps in your process, and measure how closely your personnel adhere to standards. The importance of both sets of goals is, of course, that they both significantly affect customer satisfaction.

As may be expected, workload arriving at your support center usually follows a pattern of some sort. The pattern depends on the time frame you are examining, the type of products you support, and the characteristics of your customers. For example, if you support business software, you may notice daily peak loads in the morning and afternoon, but a drop in incoming workload at lunchtime. You may have very little workload before and after regular office hours. Similarly, you may notice that most support requests come in on Monday and Tuesday, but few on Friday. Over a longer time frame, you will notice a dip in workload around most holidays, followed by a spike shortly thereafter. If, however, you support consumer software, you may notice that your peak loads come in the evenings and on weekends, and increase during and after holidays. In both cases, you may observe a peak of demand shortly after a new product is introduced into the marketplace.

It is also useful to understand the distribution of the time it takes for your personnel to process support requests. In quality parlance, this is called *cycle time*. If you track such things, you will find that a lot of support requests are processed in a relatively short time frame, but a few take a long time. This distribution is quite common, and is the basis of many mathematical models used to estimate waiting times experienced by callers. If your cycle time distribution does not follow the standard pattern, you may have to do some more sophisticated modeling.

By using the arrival rates and patterns, and the distribution of cycle times, you can estimate how many staff you need to handle the workload you expect, given your responsiveness and quality goals. A typical method is to calculate expected workload by the half-hour time period for a week in advance, and therefore determine how many staff are needed during each half-hour period. Depending on your support request volumes, you may be able to segment your arriving workload by product group, or staff specialty, and so determine your staffing needs by product group or specialty.

In order to do good scheduling, you must also know the skill sets of your staff, and the availability of each staff at any time. Depending on your organization's policies, your staff are available anywhere from 50 percent to 80 percent of the time, on average over a long time period. Staff may be gone on vacation or for training, be scheduled for other activities, or have personal scheduling preferences.

And now for the most difficult part: matching staff availability to resource requirements while minimizing loss due to overstaffing, and keeping in mind legal and other requirements regarding scheduling people. For example, you may not be able to schedule anyone for more than 50 hours/week (or less than two hours/day), or for 20 hour shifts, and so on. You must provide for a lunch break as well in an eight-hour shift. Fortunately, there are some scheduling programs in the marketplace that are quite efficient and can do a good job with this task.

OTHER INVESTMENT ITEMS

There are many investment line items that go into a detailed budget; from a management perspective, however, they fall into five broad categories: people investments; technology investments; infrastructure investments; sales and marketing investments; and partnering investments.

We have spent some time talking about investments in people and technology. Developing an accurate workload forecast can lead to a good staffing plan, and that in turn determines the major part of the technical support organization's total investment budget. Staffing plans must take into account both direct staff, such as Technical Support Representatives and consultants, and indirect staff, such as management, marketing, finance, and so on. Investments in training, costs associated with recruiting and hiring, bonuses and rewards, and travel and entertainment must also be considered in arriving at the overall staffing budget in the operating plan.

Technology investments are those investments you make to improve the effectiveness and efficiency of your personnel. Your plans must show not only the investments that must be made, but also the expected benefits of those investments. This way you can be prepared to demonstrate the effect of not making, or reducing, the scope of technology investments.

Infrastructure investments are those investments you need to make in physical infrastructure to make your organization functional. These include resources for your employees, such as workstations and laboratories; and also physical facilities, such as offices, telephones, meeting rooms, and so on.

Sales and marketing investments are those investments you make in the packaging and selling of your support offerings. This is covered in Chapter 8.

Partnering investments are the investments required to maintain your relationship with your partners. Examples of this are: the costs associated with outsourcing (or insourcing) part of your support operations, costs associated with training and managing distributors, and costs associated with support alliances with other companies.

Table 6.6 lists some common budget line items.

TABLE 6.6 Sample Budget Line Items

Category	Line Item
Direct Staff	TSR salaries and associated expenses
	Support Delivery management salaries and associated expenses
	Consulting/contracting expenses
	Training
	Travel and entertainment
	Recruiting and hiring
Indirect Functions	Marketing expenses
	Human resources expenses
	Sales expenses
	Finance expenses
Technology	Client hardware and software
	Server hardware and software
	Maintenance and support fees
	Depreciation
Infrastructure	Facilities costs
	Furniture
	Telecommunications
General and Administrative	Supplies
	Postage and so on
	Partnering
	Legal fees

PLANNING REVENUE

Planning for support revenues is no different from planning for any other kind of revenue. Most support organizations have a captive audience: the customers of the products that the company makes. Customer leads are generated by the sales organization, either through direct sales or sales through any one of a number of channels. Identifying customer leads for sales made through channels can be difficult in those situations where there are multiple levels of channels, and sales to the end user are not reported back to the company. In those situations it is common to wait for customers to register for support, and concentrate the sales effort at that time. You may, however, be able to establish a causal relationship between units shipped by your company and, after a suitable delay, the number of new customers contacting you for support.

Once a customer has purchased support from your Technical Support Organization, you have a considerable effect on the customer's support repurchase decision. Of course, the customer may switch products for reasons you cannot control, but to the extent that the customer continues to use your products, the quality of service you provide and the value the customer perceives affects the *support renewal rate*, that is, the percentage of existing customers that repurchase support from your organization.

The techniques used to forecast revenues are no different from those used to forecast workloads, described earlier in this chapter. In this case, you develop your revenue drivers, determine the relationships between those drivers and revenues, and use one or more forecasting techniques to develop a revenue forecast. Revenue forecasting is generally segmented by support offering, and is heavily influenced by product sales and support renewal rates.

Products and Tools

Most businesses have one objective in common: to grow the company. And there are at least four primary methods of achieving that objective. The first is to find and obtain new customers. This is often the most costly method of growing a company, but essential for a company to increase its market share. Another is to simply keep current customers. Keeping them with your company means they do not become new customers of another company. A third way of achieving the objective is to sell more products to current customers. And a fourth is to increase efficiency and effectiveness, thereby reducing costs.

The Technical Support Organization plays a critical role in each of these methods. Technical support is often a key component in a buyer's purchase criteria. In addition to product functionality, business stability, and other important factors, prospective buyers are often concerned about how well they will be taken care of after they've handed over their hard earned money. Even though your organization has invested significant dollars to identify, build, QA, market, and sell the product to get to this point, customers are just beginning their experience with you as a company and therefore the support component is very important.

The support organization plays an extremely important role in keeping customers as well. This is done primarily by keeping customers satisfied, thereby increasing their loyalty and willingness to purchase additional products from your company. Just getting a customer is no longer enough. Especially in a maturing industry where the market is becoming more and more saturated, customers are becoming more knowledgeable, and getting customers from your competitors may be just as appealing as enticing potential customers who have not yet experienced your market space.

The practice of selling more products to your customers, after the initial purchase, is not new. Businesses have been doing it with new products, updates, upgrades, accessories and the like for years. What is gaining new momentum, however, is the concept of asking the Technical Support Organization to become more active in the sales process. Not only in special circumstances when the sales organization needs specific product expertise, but day to day in almost every conversation a Technical Support Representative (TSR) has with a customer. There is a trifurcated reason for this. First, customers are desiring one-stop shopping more and more, and offering to sell products, upgrades, add ons, and so on is another step toward delighting customers. The second is that support people, based on their experience with what customers like, don't like, and are doing with the company's products, make wonderful resources for customers who are looking for information on how to do things better or differently with the products they've bought. Third, because the customer is usually the one to initiate contact with the company when technical support is the primary objective, the support person has a fabulous opportunity to solve a problem, thereby building credibility with the customer. The customer thinks of the TSR as just that, a support person who's provided them a solution, rather than a sales person, who is often stereotyped as aggressive, pushy, and not always motivated to act in the best interest of the customer.

For example, when a customer on a support plan calls numerous times about the same topic, it becomes clear to the TSR that the customer is not comfortable with the specific topic in the product. Today we typically ask our support personnel to cheerfully help the customer through the problem, maybe explain why it occurred, and maybe provide information and suggestions on how it may be prevented in the future. In a few instances the TSR may suggest the customer consider a class on the topic, and if the customer is lucky, the TSR might even be able to tell her where and when classes are held, what they will cost, and whom to contact to sign up or just to obtain more information. Truly proactive organizations have gone even further by giving the TSR a quick way to fax the information to the customer and sign her up on the spot, or initiate a request to someone in the training organization to call the customer before the day is out. If the customer knows she wants training, allowing her to sign up on the spot is most convenient. It provides additional revenue to the company from the training class, assures customers don't go away and then forget about it, and will likely decrease the after-sale costs of servicing customers going forward, since they'll be more knowledgeable and therefore more able to solve their own product questions.

Another example would be people who are trying to install a new product on their PCs. They get an error message and call the company for assistance. The support person cheerfully solves the problem by telling customers they need more memory. If the support call is concluded at that time, one might argue that the objective of providing customer satisfaction was not met, primarily since the customer still had additional steps to take to solve the problem. To further meet the customer's needs, a more complete solution would be for the Technical Support Representative to be able to sell the additional memory and place the order on the spot, if the customer so desired. Customer satisfaction could go even higher if the Technical Support Representative could reassure the customer that simple written instructions on how to install the memory on the customer's specific computer would be included in the same package as the memory itself. This example could be used for printer drivers, patches for operating system software, sound cards, and more. In summary, asking support personnel to take on some of the tasks of selling can often be done under the objective of providing exceptional customer service and increase customer satisfaction as a result. We'll discuss this in more detail in Chapter 8.

Finally, decreasing after-sale costs of providing technical support to customers by increasing efficiency and effectiveness is a method that can be undertaken regardless of your specific technical support strategy. By decreasing the costs of providing technical support, more of the company's funds can be allocated toward activities which more directly drive the potential to increase market penetration and market share through research and development, marketing and sales. This method will be discussed in length in this chapter.

PRODUCTS TO SUPPORT

An important aspect of a technical support strategy is the decision of what to support. A Technical Support Organization often, but not always, supports all products produced by the company; however, most service organizations start out with the luxury of supporting products developed, QA'd, marketed, and sold by your company. However, it doesn't usually take long before you need to begin supporting products not developed within your company. These products may not be fully quality assured or QA'd within your company. When being sold, customers may not know which pieces of the development and sales effort your company does. And in reality, customers don't care.

Customers do not know, nor should they be expected to know, the inner workings of our companies. When we bring a product to market, the customer should be able to expect a consistent level of support across brands, if not by product name. Many companies are just learning this customer expectation. As a leader in your company's Technical Support Organization it is important that you bring this to the attention of the development, QA, and marketing individuals leading the project early on.

There is no proven best method for selecting the products your organization will support. Instead, it is prudent for you, as the primary customer advocate in your company, to create awareness with the organizations involved in bringing the product to market. This may mean developing a strawman set of guidelines, then calling the appropriate people together to discuss, refine, and consistently adopt the strategy for supporting products. This should be done for all products to be supported, regardless of whether they were completely developed, marketed and/or sold within the company or not. It is also important to note that it is possible, and sometimes necessary, to have different support strategies for different products. The objective is to provide a consistent level of support delivery, based on respective expectations set, across all strategies.

A strawman should include a purpose statement so all members know what it is you are trying to achieve, while also indicating what is outside of the objective of this task. It would also be beneficial for various categories to be broken out, with explanations as to why they are being broken out. Outlining the needs of each scenario, with suggested response times, quality measures, and agreed upon checkpoints is also a fundamental piece of the strategy. The basis of these explanations should always be from the customer's point of view. This strawman document can then be used as a discussion tool for helping all parties to come to a better understanding of the implications of the decisions and agreements reached with other companies whose products you will support.

Often these opportunities are identified and sponsored into the company by someone in Business Development; or by the VP of Marketing, VP of Engineering, or even the president. When working out your strategy on what to support, it is important to include three types of people. The people listed who might be thought of as the company deal makers, the people in charge of making the technology work or the marketing and sales processes happen in support of the deal, and the support personnel responsible for supporting the product in the end. This is an effective methodology for all support managers, including those who work for a support outsourcing company. The aspect which will vary is the identification of the people involved, as they will likely be different for managers in outsourcing firms based on the products and markets to be supported.

Once a strategy has been developed, all affected parties need to demonstrate commitment to the strategy. However, someone will still need to own the strategy to ensure that it is being followed and supported as needed. This does not mean that decisions about the strategy are done in an autocratic manner. Rather, it means that it is important for a single person to take responsibility for being the focal point to bring issues to, and for bringing the appropriate people together as needed to address those issues.

Typically that person is a senior TSR or a person specifically asked to manage all escalated support issues that arise.

Even when your organization is supporting products developed and sold entirely within your company, you will still need to define and communicate your strategy on what you will support. For example, although your company makes a fabulous piece of entertainment software, the fact that your company does not make or distribute the operating system, the CPU, or the video cards that are critical for the game to function properly, you will get calls from your customers on those topics. One strategy is to handle some of the more basic calls, providing customers with phone numbers to access the manufacturer's service entity and provide them with pertinent information for the customer to provide the manufacturer's support representatives. Another strategy would be to draw a fairly firm line by not answering any, even the simplest, inquiries on products not offered by your company. This strategy doesn't win very much. It may be adopted in an effort to minimize the after-sale cost of supporting your product. However, this backfires more often than it works, since customers do not appreciate or value the strategy, and will spend your representatives' time trying to get them to solve the problem anyway, which is hard on your representatives. A third strategy is to try to handle all calls, even those on products not developed at your company. This is most often done by mature organizations that have already amassed a large amount of knowledge and information on the subject, that have strong networks with key manufacturers through some type of technical support alliance, and often are already, or are thinking of, generating some revenue by becoming outsourcers for other manufacturers.

In the end, each strategy has its pros and cons, and must be considered in light of your organization's knowledge level, capability, and mission.

SUPPORT'S ROLE IN THE DESIGN AND RELEASE PROCESS

Regardless of which strategy is adopted for supporting customers, it is imperative that technical support personnel play a role throughout the entire development cycle of a product. Once a product has been identified, the product strategy set, and the designing begins, support personnel should be involved. During the design process, they can provide valuable input on what causes customers to have questions, and what customers actually do with functionality compared with what we originally think they'll do with it; and they can begin thinking about the training that will be necessary for the Technical Support Organization to effectively support the product. When the product goes into the development phase, the support personnel can play an active role in the product quality assurance, documentation, and beta efforts of the product; can contribute to the creation and editing of marketing materials; and can help develop the training for the Technical Support Organization. During the product release process they can also be key conduits between the release team and the support organization, keeping the organization aware of and prepared for any possible issues that may result from the release of the product. Upon release of the product, the individual will be invaluable as an expert to whom others in the support organization can go before escalating an issue outside of the organization.

The benefits of involving the Technical Support Organization in the product design and release process are more than sufficient to warrant allowing the time for the involvement. In one company, all members of the release team had to actually sign a release document that indicated that they knew of all known outstanding issues with the product, and were willing to take responsibility for the product's release in that stage. At any time any person on the release team could prevent release by withholding their signature. This included the support person on the team. The benefits of this process were numerous and included all members of the team having a better understanding of the big picture of the company by understanding the trade-offs of shipping a product with known problems to hit an important date for getting a product on the shelf in time for the holidays, or holding a product with known problems and missing the important retail deadline.

All team members had a better understanding of the implications of their decisions, and the support organization had a much better idea of what to expect and therefore what to prepare for in order to meet the support needs of the customers of this product.

TOOLS—HIGH TECH AND HIGH TOUCH

The service industry is continually evolving. As products become increasingly fully featured, novice users are adopting at faster and faster rates, and there is tremendous pressure on a business's ability to grow and succeed (see Figure 7.1).

In addition, the concept of technical support is emerging from a point where only the Technical Support Organization is responsible for customer satisfaction, to a point where the entire company is responsible for customer satisfaction (see Figure 7.2).

The new paradigm is holding the entire organization responsible for productivity efficiency, customer satisfaction, data collection, data accessibility, and responsible implementation of technology (see Figure 7.3). And it is being asked to do so by utilizing sophisticated technology while still developing loyal, highly satisfied customers. This winning combination of high-tech and high-touch is a critical component of a world class Technical Support Organization.

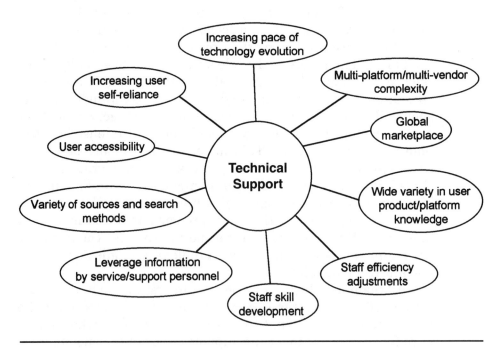

FIGURE 7.1 Technical support pressure points.

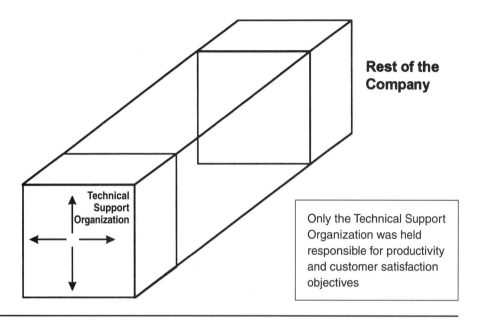

Rest of the Company

Technical Support Organization

Only the Technical Support Organization was held responsible for productivity and customer satisfaction objectives

FIGURE 7.2 Past paradigm: artificial boundaries.

In addition, companies in virtually every market segment are deploying new technology and development tools to design and implement their own applications. Some, such as budgeting, event tracking, analysis, and reporting programs, are used internally to increase efficiency. Others, such as design-it-yourself greeting cards or automated airline ticketing machines, aim to make products and services more convenient and customers more self-reliant.

All of these advances, however, have one characteristic in common: They require technical support. There are more users, many of whom have little or no experience with computer- and network-based systems, and there are more sophisticated equipment, networks, and applications at millions of remote locations that need to be able to run 24 hours a day, seven days a week. The result is a growing workload on the Technical Support Organizations. Compounding the problem is that often these Technical Support Organizations are being asked to do more with less.

Until recently, the traditional approach to provide technical support assumed the need for a conversation between the user

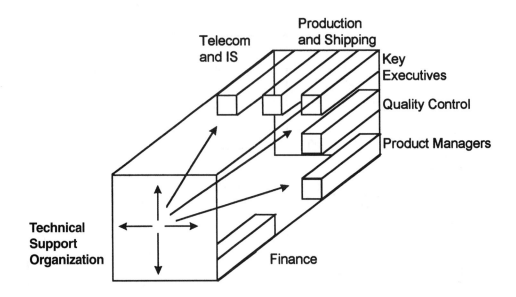

The entire enterprise is being held responsible for:
- •Maximum productivity efficiency
- •Customer satisfaction
- •Data collection
- •Data accessibility
- •Technology implementation

FIGURE 7.3 Emerging paradigm: outside the box.

and the Technical Support Representative. This seemed to work quite well, and tools became available that support access to and processing of technical support information. The tools focused on efficient call handling, management and tracking; and metrics for recording, reporting, and capture of customer incidents.

However, three primary influences are driving this significant shift in the model of providing technical support and achieving high customer satisfaction. They are a focus on customers as the long-term, central component to a company's success; technology as an innovation and an agent of change; and an increasing requirement of companies to help customers become more self-reliant. Many technologies are converging today to allow this to happen: data processing, distributed computing, voice and data networking, and telecommunications. Together these are converging into an area referred to as CTI, or *Computer Tele-phony Integration,* which is essentially the blending of computing power with the strength of telephony. The business values of these converging solutions are many and include improved service quality, reduced operating costs, increased staff productivity, increased revenue opportunities, and increasingly valuable customer and management information.

There are many tools that help translate these opportunities into business benefits, and many tools often can play more than one role. However, for discussion purposes we will consider them in three main categories: access tools, process tools, and enabling tools, including the Internet (see Figure 7.4).

We are in no way attempting to cover all the tool options available or under development today, but rather will discuss those that seem to have made the greatest impact within the realm of delivering world-class technical support.

Access Tools	**Process Tools**	**Enabling Tools**
• Tools designed to improve customer accessibility to the person who can best help them solve problems.	• Tools designed for the purpose of improving the delivery ability of the Technical Support Organization.	• Tools that allow and encourage customers to become more self-reliant and independent in using various products. The Internet is taking a leading role in this tool category, along with modifications to products that provide users with the means to become more independent in their ability to use products and troubleshoot problems.

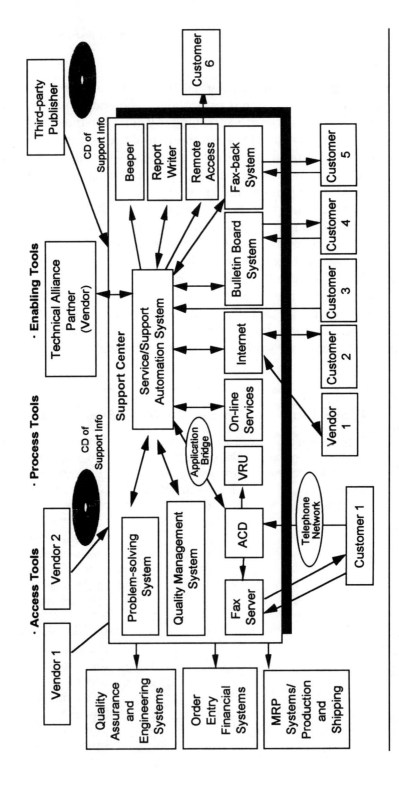

FIGURE 7.4 Complete technical support solution includes many components.

ACCESS TOOLS

In the early days of technical support delivery we had some essential components, including people and their minds, some sort of tracking mechanism—often pink message sheets stacked on a spindle on someone's desk—and a telephone. Within the last decade there's already been a significant impact to date with tools designed primarily for improved access and process ability. These tools are focused on efficient call handling and distribution, effective call management and tracking, management information and statistics, and capturing of customer incidents.

Access tools were among the first tools in the service evolution. They were tools designed for improved customer accessibility, or to get customers most quickly to the person who could best help. The most prevalent tools in this category are ACDs, or Automated Call Distributors; ANI, or Automated Number Identification; single line voice and data sharing; fax; e-mail; and the Internet. As previously mentioned, many tools can be helpful in more than one of the categories used in this book. For discussion purposes we will talk about ACDs, ANI and single line voice and data in this section on Access Tools. The others will be discussed in the section on Process Tools.

The function of the ACD is call answering, call routing and transfer, and call time reporting. Applications are often larger call volumes (anything over 50 calls per day makes this technology worth investigating), caller-directed routing, and preview calling (a type of caller identification). Benefits of an ACD include the ability to efficiently link callers to the appropriate Technical Support Representative without requiring human intervention. For example, upon calling a support center the caller may be asked, via the ACD system, to press 1 if they own the product they are calling about or 2 if they do not yet own the product they are calling about. This then allows those callers selecting 2 to be sent to a group of service personnel trained to handle presale questions. Before actually sending the call to an individual, the ACD may ask a second question like, "Press 1 if you are calling about product A, or press 2 if you are calling about product B." Once a customer makes a selection, the call will further be processed to send the caller to someone in the presale group who's had training on product B. All of this happens in seconds and without much impact on the customer. The keys to allowing the ACD to work well for you include providing six or fewer options at a time, always allowing the customer the option to press a certain key to speak with a person, and phrasing the options in a way that customers understand rather than in a way that only you or your employees understand. For example, too many companies make the mistake of asking customers to "Press 1 for customer service or press 2 for technical support." Since many new customers don't know the difference between customer service and technical support, and since no two companies define the functions of customer service and technical support in the same way, using those terms doesn't work well. Instead, phrasing the option with examples of what a customer will be thinking about will result in a higher adoption and success rate. And always be sure that your message begins with "Thank you for calling . . . ." It's such a simple but effective touch in helping the technology to take on a high-touch feel.

ACDs also provide valuable call productivity metrics, providing metrics on volumes of calls for a particular reason or group, management information for guiding employee performance, and tracking efficiencies of scheduling scenarios. Not all ACDs have the same functionality or reporting capabilities, so as with anything, determine your system requirements before you make your purchase decision. Following are suggestions to ask your ACD vendor. These can also be used to help determine your ACD system requirements.

1. How many product support groups can a Technical Support Representative be assigned to?
2. Can each Technical Support Representative identify a level of skill (first line support, second line support, and so on) for each product support group he or she logs in to?
3. How many total product support groups can the system support?

4. How does a Technical Support Representative log into multiple product support groups?

5. Who (Technical Support Representative or Support Manager) controls the set of product support groups and priorities for each Technical Support Representative?

6. Can a call be queued against multiple product support groups concurrently, and if so, how many?

7. What conditional variables are available for the way in which calls are distributed (also known as the routing pattern)?

8. How will the real time and historical reports account for:

   • Technical Support Representative time utilization

   • Positions staffed for a product support group

9. What features of your current system would need to be modified by this implementation?

10. How would this technology be implemented in a multi-site environment?

ANI, or Automatic Number Identification, is also becoming more prevalent, although it is not consistently available throughout the country and is available on a very limited basis internationally. ANI simply receives the calling party's number and presents it to you when the call is coming it. In conjunction with some of the other service offerings, you can identify numbers you do not want to receive calls from, and block them; or they can be sent to a database to see if the caller has called before, is on a service plan, or is a registered customer before being forwarded to a designated individual a group based on instructions you've created and held in the ACD system. This works well when the customer is almost always calling from the same telephone number.

Single-line voice and data sharing is one of the most recent access tools to hit the market in an affordable manner. Single-line voice and data sharing allows the customer to use the same telephone line to both talk with a Technical Support Representative (TSR) and allow the support person to *see* and take control of the customer's keyboard. Alone it provides greater flexibility in offering training without incurring the expense of gong on-site, and more simply it allows the TSR to *show* the customer something in addition to being able to explain it over the phone. As this technology becomes more accessible, sophisticated, and cost effective, the opportunities are tremendous for it as a tool in the technical support industry.

PROCESS TOOLS

Another significant step in the evolution of the support organization has been the addition of information processing. Process tools have the purpose of improving the delivery ability of the support organization. Customer information systems linked to knowledge bases, remote access, and problem-solving help have been key investment strategies for many businesses dedicated to improving their overall service strategy and customer satisfaction levels. Voice-response systems, fax-server/fax-back systems, and online tools (e.g., the Internet) are changing the way service is provided.

One of the most fundamental of all the process tools is the customer information management system, also referred to as *Problem Management Systems*. Commercially available customer information management systems began hitting the market in the early 1990s, with the initial purpose of providing a central repository of customer and product information, support request/issue logging and tracking capability, and with the capability of capturing customer profiles and history. Applications most apt to use such technologies include sites whose customers repeatedly utilize the Technical Support Organization for technical support assistance, and organizations wanting to maximize investments in the technical support strategies.

The customer information/problem systems on the market today have been designed to support a variety of different strategies. In its simplest form they can be thought of in four categories described below. The support strategy chosen for your Technical Support Organization should drive which tool is right for your company.

Four Categories of Customer Information (Problem) Management Systems

Enterprise-Wide	*Process Driven*
Services the entire company.	Supports cross-company processes.
Includes a comprehensive database, workflow, and measurement tracking and reporting.	
Utilizes client server technology.	

Department Focused	*Proprietary*
Supports Technical Support Organizations utilizing LANs.	Customized using commercially available development tools and relational databases.

Today customer information management systems are quite prevalent in all types and sizes of support centers. They are linked to other technologies, such as the ACD previously discussed, allowing for a caller's information to be shown on a Technical Support Representative's computer screen seconds before the telephone rings. Although TSRs in most support centers combining these two technologies might be tempted to answer the phone with a personalized greeting, such as "Hello, Mr. Smith, how may I assist you today?" most support professionals have realized that a personalized greeting at that point in the call may be a bit too presumptive. This is because first, it may not actually be Mr. Smith calling, but a secretary, technician, or Mr. Smith's younger brother. And, although customers appreciate personalized service, greeting a person by name even before they've said a word may be a little invasive for some folks.

So although utilizing a customer information/problem management system with ACD to provide for these *screen pops* may not be a great tool for greeting a customer by name before they've had a chance to say hello, it is an effective tool for providing the service representative with a little information about callers before they need to plunge into the call. The few seconds between the screen pop and the customer's voice coming across the phone line help reduce the stress of the TSR's job by giving them an idea of who is on the other end of the phone line, an idea of what the call might be about, and a brief chance to glance at the caller's profile and call history.

Other common technologies being integrated with the customer information management system today are knowledge bases and problem-solving help systems (also known as problem resolution systems) that will be discussed in more detail later in this chapter.

The benefits of a customer information management system can be tremendous. They provide for the ability to have increased knowledge of your customers: who they are, their product purchase patterns, their call patterns, records of detailed call histories, and more. For those organizations that have discovered the value of their customer base to the company, a customer information system helps a company market to that customer base in a more sophisticated and efficient manner. For example, you might decide to target a sales campaign of your newest version of Reptile Rock educational software for children to customers who have already purchased your Dancing Dinosaur package. Or using the call history information tracked in the customer information management system, you may be more successful in selling an upgraded service plan to customers who have called your organization eight or more times during the past year, while suggesting your lower value plan to customers who have called fewer than four times in the past year.

Customer information management systems that are configured and used to track customer profiles, some marketing information, and call and product purchase histories are valuable tools for segmenting your customers for sales opportunities, for sending announcements, and for simply providing more specialized service. For example, let's say your company develops and sells financial software, including a General Ledger, an Accounts Receivable package, an Accounts Payable package, an Inventory package, and a Payroll package, and customers can purchase any combination of the five. Then let's say that your company identifies and fixes a problem in the Payroll package, which is significant enough to warrant contacting your customers who own your Payroll product in hopes of preventing them from encountering the problem. Without a well-used and populated customer information management system, you'd probably be thinking you need to contact all customers; since you're not sure which ones have Payroll and might be affected, and which ones don't. Not only does this create the additional expense of communicating with all customers, but you're also in the position of unnecessarily informing customers who do not have that particular product and therefore have no possible chance of experiencing the problem. Even if the additional expense is not a concern, alerting customers who do not currently have the Payroll product but who may have been contemplating purchasing it, may cause them to reconsider their purchase intention because of the problems they now know others are having with the product. With a comprehensive, well-populated customer information management system, you will have the opportunity to segment your customers to send messages only to those for whom the message was intended. It allows you to provide more tailored communication to different groups of customers, motivating and tracking their response separately from other customer types.

Customer information management systems also increase the productivity of your support personnel by providing them with historical call information and product information about each customer. This provides the TSR with important information from which to draw in servicing the customer, while increasing customer satisfaction by not having customers repeat information they know they've given someone in the company previously. Both the TSR and the customer save time, the customer feels important to the company, the representative can tailor and personalize the support provided each customer, and the customer has a more positive experience overall.

One more benefit of a customer information system is the intracompany communication it provides. When customer profiles, product purchases, buying patterns, and call histories are captured and accessible by nearly anyone within the company, the ability to provide the customer with an exceptionally positive experience, regardless of whom they contact in the company, is substantially enhanced. Commonly this is called *cradle to grave* customer service, since it can capture the first contact a caller has with the company as a potential caller, then follow the caller through the product purchase cycle and throughout their life as a customer of your company.

The value of a customer information system may start within a company as a solution for a specific function or department. However, once the power of such a tool is experienced within a company, it often gains momentum in becoming an enterprise-wide tool for use by the entire company. Other technologies, in addition to the ACD, frequently integrated with a customer-information management system are bug tracking systems, technical knowledge bases, fax servers, and problem-solving help.

Potential detriments of this tool are the costs of installation and ongoing maintenance and the possibility of reduced Technical Support Representative efficiency until they adjust to using the system during the course of servicing a support request. However, the growing majority of companies today have concluded that the return such a tool can provide is worth the investment.

A second process tool type is the remote access tools. These tools provide for the ability to render on-site service without being on-site. They are often used by organizations needing to provide on-site service for nonhardware related issues and to increase product knowledge and use through real-time training, without the trainer or the customer incurring travel time or expense. The benefits of the remote access tools include the ability to increase responsiveness, improve the ability of the Technical Support Representative to respond to a support request, increase the knowledge shared with customers, and reduce service costs by decreasing the time to resolution. The potential drawback to this tool is the requirement that both the customer and TSR have the appropriate communication software and data connectivity.

Problem-solving help, or problem resolution, is a third process tool designed primarily to capture, increase, and leverage the collective knowledge of your organization. Support organizations are very vulnerable to loss of data without the investment in a knowledge base with problem-solving help. We invest heavily in the staffing and training of our teams, then watch them leave work every evening, taking a great portion of all the knowledge they've accumulated with them. Without an investment in a knowledge base to capture this information, our employees' brains become the primary repository of the tremendously valuable information we have about our products and customers. In addition, even when all your employees, with all this knowledge, are present and accounted for, the sharing of that information without the assistance of a problem-solving help tool is haphazard at best.

Content for these knowledge bases can come from many sources. Three primary sources include the organization itself, vendor-distributed stand-alone CDs of information, and third-party multisource knowledge bases.

It's not uncommon for a Technical Support Representative who received, investigated, and resolved a new support request one day, to be out at lunch or on vacation two days later when another TSR receives the same support request. The result is, the second representative reinvesting time already spent by the first representative to investigate the reported problem—a complete duplication of effort. Another outcome is the second customer having a much longer time for resolution than necessary. Even if the first representative was in the office that day, sitting six seats away from the second representative, there is still a good chance that this inefficiency would occur. And imagine if either of the representatives had to try numerous possible solutions as they narrowed down the options for resolving the issue! The waste of time as well as the customer's potential for dissatisfaction both increase unnecessarily. Then to top it off, what if a third and a fourth TSR were to encounter the same issue before word of the solution finally was communicated within the organization? The result would likely include repeated, unnecessary inefficiency, which could be resolved with a knowledge base and problem-solving tool that could be used to capture all customer issues and solutions to those issues. In addition, many of these tools have the ability to track the most frequently used solution and offer solutions to the representative based on the frequency with which it has been previously used, in order to maximize the effectiveness of the representative's time.

The benefits of a self-generated knowledge base do require an investment. The decision to deploy a well-designed and populated knowledge base requires both financial and resource investments. This is an important factor to include when considering a knowledge-base tool. For the tool to be most effective, someone must invest the time and energy to gathering, organizing, and editing the content so that it is comprehensive, applicable, and quickly demonstrates value to those individuals who are being asked to use it. If that investment is not made, your team members will quickly find it lacking in quality content or organization, and stop seeing it as a valuable resource; leaving you with a sizable investment in a piece of under utilized technology.

If your Technical Support Organization supports products that require the use of or interaction with other products, vendor-distributed and third-party multivendor knowledge bases may also be a good source of information to strengthen the content of your knowledge base. Vendor distributed knowledge bases are frequently stand-alone knowledge bases that primarily cover topics and issues for the products offered by their company, with little coverage on issues that include the products from more than one company. Vendor-distributed knowledge bases offer a strong solution for organizations that have standardized on one company's products. They typically provide comprehensive, accurate, and current information on that company's products, since often the content comes directly from that company's support organization.

Third-party, multisource knowledge bases are also good content providers. They are usually developed by someone other than the product provider, and cover a broad number of topics. The degree of comprehensiveness depends upon the method by which the content is obtained. One multisource content provider method is to secure contractual agreements with the product providers to obtain information directly from them. The multisource provider then manipulates, abstracts, and indexes the content received directly from a product provider together with all the other product provider information. Another method of obtaining content is by providing outsourcing for various product providers, then editing, abstracting, and indexing the information to make it available to other support organizations. The benefit of the first method is that the information is obtained directly from the product provider. The drawback is that the data are not tested by the knowledge base publisher. The benefit of the second method is that the solutions are tested for accuracy, since they are not necessarily just taken from the product provider, but have been used by the knowledge base creator's service staff to resolve support requests. The drawback for this method is that it may not be as comprehensive as the first method, since the support organization may not have encountered everything the product provider already has documented.

Both methods are offered on CD, and distributed either monthly or quarterly. Each also allows you to easily find solutions to an issue involving products from various vendors. For example, a single vendor knowledge base from Novell can provide great support information on Novell products. However, if a support request involves a Novell network, Microsoft operating system, Borland application, Compaq computer, and Hewlett-Packard printer, a third-party multivendor knowledge base that includes content from all products, would be a better source for resolutions to the support request. Both also provide for a more content-rich knowledge base, especially when combined with your own knowledge base content generated by your own organization and offered with a strong search mechanism.

Knowledge bases with problem-solving help can be tremendous assets in capturing, organizing, and making knowledge more generally available throughout the support organization and then with customers, either directly or indirectly. Your Technical Support Organization retains the cumulative knowledge even when people leave, making the entire organization more knowledgeable and less vulnerable. In addition many companies go even further in sharing knowledge by allowing their customers direct access to some or all of this information. Access can be given to customers based on service plan purchased or customer type, and the information accessible can be limited based on your guidelines.

Tips for Making the Most of Your Knowledge Base Technology Decision

1. Select a knowledge-base technology that easily integrates with your other technologies, especially your customer information management system and chosen online or World Wide Web access method.

2. Select a technology that has a powerful, sophisticated, yet easy to use search and retrieval mechanism.

3. Invest in populating the database with quality information before deployment from the product vendors themselves and third-party vendors, as well as that generated within your own organization..

4. Create a process that allows for Technical Support Representatives to easily use and contribute to the ongoing building and *cleansing* of the content.

5. Invest in appropriate resources to compile and edit solution content for accuracy, grammar, and viability (this is especially important if plans include allowing customers direct access to this information) before being made accessible to other team members or customers.

6. Train and encourage employees, and customers if they will be given access, on how to use and contribute to the content.

7. Consider additional ways to use the content (newsletters, voice response systems, top 20 questions and answers as part of what customers hear while they're on hold waiting to speak to a service representative, etc.) to leverage the investment.

Voice processing is another step in the evolution of the call center. It is an effective tool for functions that include repetitive calls, such as order taking, literature requests, product pricing requests, and order information. The technology is also very effective for providing simple answers, solutions to the most frequently asked questions, and product usage tips.

It is often used in applications dealing with repetitive inquiries and high call volumes of calls of short duration. Utilizing the technology in situations where a quantity of calls are for lower value information, such as the company address or fax number, directions to a training center, and hours of availability, are also good applications. Voice processing is also often used as a front end for high value calls. For example, a call to a local Macy's department store begins with a pleasant greeting, then follows with options for store information as well as with the opportunity to access an operator or the department desired. Selecting the option for store information gives you the store's hours, address, directions to the location, a directory of departments, sale dates, and more.

Voice process systems provide a number of benefits to support organizations as well as customers. One of those is increasing customer accessibility by giving customers the ability to gain needed information without having to depend on a person to provide the information. When tied to a well-populated knowledge base, it can actually extend service hours by helping the customer obtain information or place product orders beyond the staffed hours of the support center. An example here is the Genie Newstand, an online service, which allows customers to order products 24 hours a day without interacting with a human being. The service asks for your name, address, phone, fax, payment method, and product or information required. In this example, because the toll number was part of an advertisement, the Voice Response system also asked for the name of the magazine where you saw the advertisement. If a fax number was provided, confirmation of the order was sent via fax within 24 hours; if not, a confirmation call was made to the phone number provided. Many companies also use this as a tool to which receptionists forward calls. For example, a caller to a software company asking for information on training classes may be forwarded to a voice response system that gives the caller the opportunity to hear information on various classes, receive the desired information via fax, or sign up for a class; or forwards the call to a person if the caller needs additional information.

The benefits of a voice processing system include cost savings for support-related activities, as well as increased productivity of your support staff. By allowing the system to provide basic information on repetitive calls, an organization's costs go down by not incurring the cost of an actual person to handle each call. Each call is typically shorter, since the call is more focused and to the point. An added benefit is increased productivity of the staff by spending time on tasks and calls that are not of a repetitive nature and need the special attention only individualized service can provide. This not only creates greater efficiencies in servicing customers, but it also allows your staff to spend time on calls and issues that are challenging. Allowing your staff to spend time on more difficult, less mundane tasks will increase their motivation and enthusiasm for the job, which translates into higher customer satisfaction.

However, voice response systems can also have their drawbacks if the implementation and purpose is not well thought through from the customer's perspective as well as from the company's perspective. Having customers interact with a voice response system does not address the emotional element of the caller, which at times may be a detriment. For example, if callers are calling for product information, there is no immediate interaction to help build their decision to actually make the purchase. However, this can be addressed by following up on all product inquiries as your organization would any other lead. Another example is if the customer is dissatisfied with something regarding the company, an interaction with a voice response system will not identify it during a conversation the way a person might. This too can be addressed by designing the system to easily allow the caller to reach a person or leave a message for a call to be returned at any time while the customer is interacting with the voice response system. Designing the system to ask customers a few customer-satisfaction questions at the end of their utilization of the system, and then inviting, but not requiring customers to do so, also helps to address this drawback of utilizing this valuable piece of technology.

The last process tool of the evolving service center that we'll talk about in this book is the capability of fax processing. The function of fax processing is to most easily provide documented information to customers. The three most popular applications of fax processes today are fax broadcasting, fax servers, and fax on demand.

Fax broadcasting allows information to be communicated in writing to all customers whose fax numbers you've recorded. Three very frequent uses of fax broadcasting include lead generation, surveys, and notification. Lead generation is simply faxing instead of phoning or mailing current or potential customers with a new product or service offering you want them to consider purchasing. Instead of investing in a four-color photo, an envelope, stuffing, and postage costs, sending a well-designed fax in the middle of the night is a much less expensive alternative.

Faxing a request to all or a segment of your customers, for survey information during the early morning hours, is also an effective use of this valuable technology. An added benefit is that the average return rate for a faxed survey, which can be returned by fax, is 15 percent higher than responses received from a mailing. It seems that recipients are more likely to respond to a short, well-designed fax survey on which they can quickly mark their responses and then return than they are a more formal looking document that needs to be mailed back.

A third popular use of fax broadcasting is to use it as a communication device on urgent topics. If you've identified on December 28 that a bug in your software will delete all files on your hard disk when your system date sets itself to January 1, you could be in for a big phone or Federal Express bill. Or, if you've got fax broadcasting and you've captured your customers' fax numbers along with other pertinent profile information, you might send a well-worded fax explaining the problem and the solution to those customers you anticipate will be affected by the problem. It could save you significant dollars as well as serious embarrassment.

Fax servers are effective tools for disseminating information. They allow the faxing of documents from service representatives' desktop PCs without incurring the inefficiency of having them leave their desk to fax a document. Fax servers can also be set up to access master documents, such as a letter explaining a detailed procedure to solve a complicated product issue, giving the TSR the ability to customize the document with a personalized greeting, modify the body of the text if needed, and close with a signature stamp before faxing it off to the customer. Moreover, if the fax server is linked to a customer information management system, it would be able to pull the customer's fax number from the customer's profile information and record the date and type of fax sent in the customer's call history. Some customer information management systems even provide the ability to keep a copy of the actual fax attached to the customer's record.

Fax on demand is an other very popular use of fax processing. It is used primarily for providing document retrieval capability directly to customers. By calling a dedicated number, customers receive the option to tell the system which fax document they desire by pressing the keys associated to the desired document on the telephone keypad. If callers don't know which item they are looking for, they can select the option for a fax on demand catalog, which is usually the first item. The system then asks the caller for the fax number, and faxes the selected document, individual item, or catalog, within minutes of the call. The system runs 24 hours per day without human intervention other than to keep the documents up to date. Customers love it because they can obtain information anytime at their leisure, and in a written rather than verbal format. Like fax servers, this technology benefits the company by increased leveraging of information by documenting something once and sharing it many times. It also benefits both the company and employees by reducing the work load of the customer service representatives and operators by reducing activities involving repetitive tasks. The company saves on printing, collating, labor, and postage costs. Finally, it also ensures consistency of message, since whether it's a marketing message or steps to address a product issue, it's the same every time.

Regardless of the type or reason for your fax, spend some time on the wording of the content and the format of the document. Just like anything else provided to customers or potential customers, a fax document should be professional in content and format.

COMBINING ACCESS AND PROCESS TOOLS FOR IMPROVED CUSTOMER SATISFACTION

Technical Support Organizations are making significant strides in investing and integrating access and process tools to service their customers to even greater degrees. For example, when we as customers stop to do a commonplace task, such as buying fuel for our cars, do we think about who services the registers and systems that allow us to conveniently pay, in seconds, by credit or debit card so that we can be on our way as quickly as possible? Probably not. But the Technical Support Organizations at these oil and gas giants think about it all the time. In 1992 one of these companies was under criticism from its stockholders for not achieving the desired results. In response, a concerted effort was launched to identify and implement ways to run the business more effectively across all operations.

Until this time the retail technical support center that serviced the systems utilized by the gas stations to process transactions approached improving service primarily by increasing staff and all the associated elements, including such things as space, equipment, management staff, and so on. Under the new directive the approach changed. Instead of automatically throwing people at the problem in an effort to solve it, the option of increasing staff was weighed against the cost of deploying new technology. In addition, this assessment had to be done within the context of meeting customer expectations.

The first technology to pass the criteria was a customer information and problem management system. The system stores data about customers, in this case gas stations, such as profiles and system configurations. Previously the support organization had been using a mainframe-based system that provided only limited reporting capabilities and was not particularly user friendly. Windows and Novell were identified as substitutes. Selection criteria for the customer information management system was based on three elements: user friendliness, ability to easily modify the system by the company's technical support personnel, and ease of maintenance of the application and database. The selected system included key-word search capability. It also tracked customer profiles, system configurations, software purchases, service contracts, support incidents, and problem resolutions.

The second investment was to integrate ANI (Automatic Number Identification) functionality into the telephone system. The chosen solution allows a call to come into the center's PBX or telephone system, and initiates a query to a marketing database on the calling number based on the ANI looking for a match. When it finds the match it pops the customer profile on the Technical Support Representative's desktop in the customer information management system seconds before the call comes through.

ANI lends itself well to this application, since the company's support sites, the gas stations, permit easy identification of the location initiating the call and therefore the system requiring assistance. The support center reported a reduction in call time of 20 to 30 seconds per call, which on an average volume of 40,000 calls per month was the equivalent of four full-time personnel.

The third tool implemented was a voice response unit (VRU) able to absorb 4,000 calls per month that otherwise would have gone directly to a Technical Support Representative. The calls included requests from station cashiers for the keystrokes that are required to generate an *end-of-shift* report, or for keystroke instructions on how to cancel or reverse a sale transaction. Among other frequently asked questions, the VRU provided instructions on the procedure for reloading paper into the slip printer, and how to clean the paper sensors in the printer. Questions once answered by support center personnel were leveraged by providing the solution via the VRU.

Together, these investments in technology helped the organization increase efficiency, as well as paved the way for a transition from a mainframe environment to the PC world, another company-directed initiative. They have also allowed staffing of the support center to reduce itself, over time, by over 50 percent since the time the directive was given, while the systems handle over 200,000 customer activity records. And since technology deployment is often a step-by-step process, the center's next step is to implement a fax-back system to provide written step-by-step information to callers.

Another example of utilizing combined access and process technology tools is from a leading banking institution. In 1987 the service organization within this institution was created to provide a single point of contact to its internal business partners, bank units, for first-line support of all technical problems; and to coordinate problem resolution. By the fall of 1994 the organization was supporting 100,000 employees and nearly 200 different applications on various hardware configurations. One of their primary problems was that the business partners needed faster information regarding system outages. The service organization was often notified of an outage by a business partner before or at the same time the bank's operational units began experiencing the problem. The Technical Support Organization wanted to adopt a more proactive approach.

A team was formed to launch an automation strategy with the goal of increasing first contact call resolution from the current 75 percent to 90 percent. The following objectives were established: Provide a single, uniform operating environment for outage reporting, tracking, and resolution; provide any-to-any access to tools or knowledge bases from any PC in any location; implement automated fault management; use knowledge-base tools for problem isolation and resolution; and provide business partners with access to tools, including the customer information management system and a voice response system, or VRU.

The deliverable was a trouble-tracking and ticketing system that intercepts alerts from the network management system, and automatically notifies the appropriate business partners of the problem before they experience it. The alerts are also sent to the customer information management system, which automatically creates a trouble ticket and posts key information on an LED wall display board. The information on the display board furnishes management with the current status of all major applications. Previously this was done by a person writing the status on a white board along with all of the other outages. As the status of the outage changes, the display board is updated and the notification of the events are forwarded to a system that calls the business partner and delivers a prerecorded message about the status of the outage via digitized voice. The system also requests receipt notification of the message. This all now happens within a minute after the alarm is originally generated.

Customers, employees, and management have judged the effort successful and have given the go-ahead to augment these access and process tools with more enabling tools. The objective of the next phase is to enable the business partners to increase their ability to resolve issues themselves, minimizing their dependency on the Technical Support Organization. The Technical Support Organization intends to accomplish this objective by putting enhanced diagnostic tools in the hands of the business partners, and expand the partners' access to information within the customer information management system. They are looking toward the Internet and other tools to provide online documentation and access to information to increase the partners' abilities to self-diagnose and resolve problems.

The third example of successfully deploying a service strategy which utilized the power of access and process tools is of a popular worldwide fast-food chain based in southern California. This technical support team supports more than 4,000 restaurants and 120,000 people throughout the world. The team's mission is to promote technology and self-sufficiency, and to effectively manage problems.

The restaurants use PCs linked to cash registers, and the technical support team wanted to be more proactive in accurately recording, analyzing, and reporting information relating to the technical support team's service needs. The team was experiencing trouble getting call statistics in a reasonable period, primarily because the information was being collected manually. To rectify the situation an ACD was selected and integrated with the corporation's existing PBX or telephony system. In addition, a customer information and problem management system that records customer profiles, tracks calls and the resulting issues and resolutions, provides up-to-date status on outstanding issues, and tracks product bugs was chosen and implemented. It was linked to the ACD and to a knowledge-base system. The original content for the knowledge base came from information previously gathered by the Technical Support Organization, and technical support information obtained from subscriptions to vendor-distributed and third-party multisource knowledge bases.

These tools, deployed in a well-integrated manner, have increased the Technical Support Representatives' confidence and efficiency in servicing their customers, while providing technical support management with better information to lead the organization. The next technologies to be adopted include an integrated VRU, fax processing tools, and another level of sophistication in call management that provides callers with information on the length of the queue, anticipated time before they'll receive assistance, and helpful product hints.

Although each situation facing these companies is unique, there are some common themes. All of the companies recognized a problem, clearly identified their goals, and created a process for addressing the problem. While the solutions varied, the most successful approaches were driven by business needs, and gave strong consideration to the impact the systems would have on customers and employees. The use of access and process tools is becoming fairly common in today's world of providing technical support to customers. However, as in each example here, the future direction is clearly to include enabling tools that are more complex and often build on access and process tools already in place. It's one of the principal ways that Technical Support Organizations are responding to new reality led by the growing demands placed on them with increasing volume, scope, and complexity.

Responding to the Reality of Today's Technical Support Organization

1. Understand the business need
2. State and communicate a vision
3. Define the goals
4. Establish the objectives
5. Identify a process
6. Identify criteria for solution selection
7. Develop a deployment plan
8. Deploy
9. Monitor impact and result
10. Modify as needed

ENABLING TOOLS

One 1993 study, completed by the Help Desk Institute (an organization gathering, compiling, and sharing information pertinent to service support professionals), showed that corporations have spent 1.4 trillion dollars on information technology in the ten previous years. The majority of that investment went into networks, desktop machines, and telephony. Significant portions were dedicated toward access and process tools in an effort to increase the efficiencies of call handling and distribution, improve the effectiveness of call management and tracking; providing enhanced management information and service statistics, and expanded ability to capture customer incidents.

While access and process tools are in fairly widespread use, and continue to be adopted at higher and higher rates, another service approach is fast emerging that centers on providing service when, where, how, and sometimes just before customers realize they need it. These are called *enabling tools.*

Enabling tools allow and encourage customers to become more self-reliant and independent in using various products. They can be used to improve customer satisfaction and communication of information, and to more effectively leverage a technical support staff. Enabling tools achieve these results through improved access to knowledge; they also leverage knowledge by focusing on knowledge capture and reuse, assist in call avoidance strategies by distributing knowledge to customers, and support the service strategy of being a revenue or profit center by allowing for new and expanded service offerings.

Organizations are being very creative in their uses of enabling tools and the services offered as a result. Although enabling tools are almost always designed and offered as a way to increase customer satisfaction, they are not necessarily designed or offered specifically from within the Technical Support Organization. Frequently, the original concept for the enabling service comes from information gathered within the support organization on the way customers actually use products compared to the way product designers originally anticipated customers would use products. It also comes from information observed by the support and marketing organizations in an effort to determine the root cause of the reasons customers need to call the technical support staff for assistance.

In many ways enabling tools need to build upon well-integrated process and access tools already in place. Enabling tools are often driven by the characteristic of increasing customers' ability to service themselves. A simple example of this that we've become very accustomed to is the ability to place an international call with the touch of a few keys on a telephone key pad. The result is that the function of the operator is to assist us with more challenging telephone tasks, while we have complete control over repetitive transactions. With some telephone systems even the ability to arrange conference calls takes little more than coordinating the people to be included in the conference call, knowing the phone number of their location, and keying in the appropriate numbers. More than half the people holding ATM (automatic teller machine) cards deposit and withdraw money from their account on a regular basis without ever interacting with a bank employee. And we do this with relative convenience from nearly anywhere in the world.

Today we can design our own personalized greeting cards in many card shops, Walmarts, K-marts, and Targets throughout the country thanks to American Greetings. We can order our week's groceries via computer at any time of the day or night, specifying the exact brands and sizes of what we need, paying by computer, and designating the delivery date thanks to a new offering from Safeway stores, called Peapod. And we order a meal from McDonald's at some gas stations at the same time we're filling our car's gas tank, pay for it within the same transaction, and pick up the meal as we leave the station. These are a few examples of the way enabling tools are affecting our lives today.

Ticketless travel is now a commonly used option provided by most airlines so that customers don't have to bother with keeping track of their tickets. However, the customer is not the only beneficiary. The companies benefit by not incurring the costs of printing, processing, and mailing tickets—repeatedly if travel arrangements are changed—or dealing with customers who have lost their tickets, and the associated labor expense. Even the airline employees win by removing a frequent issue for customer dissatisfaction. To enable customers even more, airlines are now equipping curbside baggage handlers with an enabling technology that allows ticketless passengers to check their bags at curbside even without a boarding pass in hand, without compromising the security of the flight.

At first glance, you may question what enabling tools have to do with Technical Support Organizations. However, when we consider that on average, 60 percent or more of the support requests received by Technical Support Organizations are how-to related questions, identifying and providing enabling tools which encourage customers to become more self-reliant becomes an important component of a company's overall support strategy. And often, when the support strategy is a well integrated element of the company strategy, enabling tools are both a technical support tool created with the desire to achieve greater customer satisfaction, and another step in the evolving design of the product.

As computers become more predominant in homes and small businesses, so is the potential for skyrocketing demands on technical support. And so is the increasing demand for mobile computing. A survey of 500 frequent business travelers by Dell Computer Corporation, Austin, Texas, found some interesting facts and customer needs and expectations about the use of portable personal computers. What Dell learned included: 58 percent have taken them on a trip, specifically 49 percent have used them on airplanes, 41 percent use them for faxing, and 54 percent use them to transmit documents by modem.

Recognizing this extension of computers into the home and small office, and on the road, some of the computer hardware and software manufacturers are building enabling tools into their products to reduce the need for technical support assistance, especially the assistance requiring direct contact with a Technical Support Representative today. Hardware manufacturers are building enabling technology right into the machine by including the capability for a person to conduct an entire desktop inventory and to run sophisticated machine diagnostics at the touch of a button. In addition to designing more stable computer systems, computer hardware manufacturers are working to link computers to customer information management systems and knowledge bases, both as a reactive mechanism and as a proactive mechanism, in an effort to increase customers' ability to troubleshoot and do maintenance on their systems. Some of the impetus behind this direction has come from studying the evolution of other industries' products. For example, when Henry Ford first introduced the automobile it was nowhere near as reliable or sophisticated as today's cars. Through the evolution of the automobile, not only did the car and its components improve in capability and quality, but so did our understanding of how important it was and what it took to proactively service and maintain such an item. As a result today's car owners know to get oil changes every 3,000 miles, and more comprehensive tune-ups every 15,000 miles. In addition, owners still have service centers to go to when the unexpected occurs in between scheduled checkups. This is where some of the big players in the computer hardware industry are headed; the next generations of computers will include more functionality to provide better proactive maintenance service, improved *just in time* service and instruction, and reactive service that gives the user even more control.

Enabling tools don't necessarily reduce the stress that we feel doing some tasks, such as preparing our tax returns. However, some of those tools can make it much simpler, such as MacInTax from Intuit. MacInTax can walk you through your tax preparation process, asking questions as a tax preparer might, offering suggestions and definitions, and pointing out inconsistencies and missing information. The purpose is not to take the place of the user's accountant or tax preparer, but rather to speed and ease the process of doing what many think of as an undesirable task. The product didn't start out as helpful or enabling, but is continuing to evolve into a tool that gives users more control and confidence in their ability to complete the task at hand. It even allows users to take information from a financial transaction reporting product called Quicken and, depending on how the user has categorized the transactions, integrating the two products can even speed tax preparation. And not to be forgotten is the ability for users of the Quicken product to pay bills by integrating with another product called CheckFree.

Another example of enabling tools being used in computer software endeavors is Microsoft's use of wizards. The wizard functionality within the software itself uses intelligent agents and profilers to follow how a product is being used and then anticipates when the user will need help.

Even the healthcare industry is catching on to the importance of utilizing enabling technology. As an example, a medical center's more than 50 home health care nurses now carry notebook computers equipped with a modem and a medical software package installed. Carrying the notebooks allows the nurses to log patient charts without having to go to the center. This use of technology to enable these service providers resulted in nurses being able to increase their number of patient visits by ten percent.

Deploying a well-designed customer information and problem management system integrated with an e-mail package, comprehensively populated knowledge base with problem solving help, order management system, and fax server becomes a powerful tool for allowing customers to help themselves. Allowing customers to access the customer information management system, linked with these other repositories of information and processing tools is a significant step toward helping customers help themselves. With some creative thinking, sophisticated integration, and possibly an additional application, access and process tools can become very powerful enabling tools—tools that achieve the purpose of making customers more self-reliant and successful in product use by allowing them to log in to submit a request, check the status of a request, search the knowledge base for solution, or update their own profile information.

THE INTERNET

The Internet is one of the hottest technical support enabling tools being utilized today. It's been described as an institution that resists institutionalization, something that belongs to everyone and to no one. It began as a research project within the U.S. Defense Department during the Cold War, with the purpose of investigating techniques and technologies for connecting computer networks of various kinds. The goal was to produce communication protocols that would enable different computers to communicate across linked networks even in the case of nuclear attack.

Scientists soon discovered the advantages of connecting their computers together. An example of such a network, Bitnet, was developed by research scientists to help promote collaborative research efforts between their different universities. The network existed independently of the original network, but the advantages of joining the two were too large to resist. Eventually more and more scientists began to use this network as well.

In 1986, the U.S. National Science Foundation (NSF) started

the NSFnet, which is one of the main backbone communication services connecting many of these smaller networks, like Bitnet, together. This network of network systems was called the Internet because it was the interlink between many networks.

Basic Internet History

- 1960s—ARPANET established
- 1970s—TCP/IP becomes the standard
- 1980s—Creation of NSFnet to cater to universities
- 1990s—Introduction to commercial traffic

As the Internet grew, a new community of users grew as well. However, these users formed a community unique to the *electronic environment* in which it existed. This community has been described as a *virtual community,* where people communicate, conduct business, meet new friends, and discuss a wide range of topics—all electronically, never really in person. This new type of community provided a freedom and flexibility unlike that of other communities by not being tied to time or space. In addition, the ability for communication to be with a single person or a multitude has created opportunities for business and personal growth. As with many opportunities that sound too good to be true, there are downsides to this community. One of the most challenging being that because it is completely an electronic environment, there is no way of knowing if the people you are communicating with are truly who they say they are.

To address the problems inherent in an electronic environment, the new virtual community began to establish some rules to help govern themselves. These rules are known as *Net Etiquette*. They include being honest about your communication, remaining legal in your activities, and being polite when dealing with others. However, our societies are only beginning to define and understand the ramifications of what is legal or illegal.

For example, this *cyberspace* has spawned a brand new commercial industry. Companies such as CompuServe, Prodigy, America Online, and others are providing commercial networking services and creating a new outlet for commercial ventures. No one organization (department, company, or country) owns the Internet. There are organizations and companies that help manage different parts of the networks that tie everything together, but no single governing body controls what happens on the Internet. This has been compared to the English language, which as an institution is public property. Taught, used, and modified by many; owned by all and by none. In addition, the networks within the Internet are located in many different countries and are funded and managed according to local policies.

Congress is currently looking at how this expanding medium should best be regulated or controlled within the United States, but basic laws are yet to be written. However, the potential for this new environment is so compelling that businesses are making huge strides in leveraging its potential. Businesses, especially Technical Support Organizations, are exploiting the potential of this new institution through four primary uses: Internet mail, discussion groups, long-distance computing, and file transfers.

Internet mail is similar to e-mail, with the added benefit of being global in scope. Discussion groups, or *newsgroups*, are forums where information dissemination, discussion, and even debate can be carried out. Long-distance computing is just that, the ability to design, model, prototype, and develop concepts into products around the world. And file transfers allow Internet users to access remote machines and retrieve programs or text. All are ideal mechanisms for a Technical Support Organization looking to leverage its knowledge and resources while making customers more self-reliant.

Providing basic information to customers via Internet access is fairly straightforward. As the provider you'll need a server, which could be as simple as your own workstation or as complicated as a dedicated server, on which to store your content. You'll also need a Web page creation tool, an account with an Internet service provider, a modem, some content, and a firewall for security purposes. Your customers will need a PC with a modem, a browser such as Navigator from Netscape, and an account with an online provider such as America Online or CompuServe.

Requirements for Technical Support to Offer Internet Services

- Server
- Account with an Internet provider (e.g., BBN Planet)
- Web page creation tool (e.g., Adobe Systems, Inc.)
- Data content
- Firewall
- Modem (28.8 Kbps or higher speed is recommended)

Requirements for Customers to Take Advantage of Internet Services

- Personal computer or workstation
- Internet connection
- Web browser (e.g., Netscape Navigator)
- Modem (28.8 Kbps or higher speed is recommended for electronic software downloads, and 14.4 Kbps or higher for other services)

Technical Support Organizations are becoming very inventive and entrepreneurial in their uses of the Internet to service customers in a manner that results in high customer satisfaction. Some of the most common uses are providing customers with access to the Technical Support Organization's basic information, such as hours of operation, services offerings, training offerings and schedules, frequently asked questions and answers, release notes, product and company information, and even employment opportunities. More experienced Technical Support Organizations are providing their customers with direct access to the product support knowledge base, allowing customers to register themselves, and permitting access to the company's customer information management system. Each of these options gives customers the ability to keep information about themselves and their systems current for the company's records, lets them answer some of their questions themselves, gives the company more current customer information, and provides customers with expanded service hours. Both objectives of increasing and leveraging the technical support knowledge and resources, and providing enhanced levels of customer service are achieved.

Those technical support teams that are even more sophisticated are working to provide one-to-one and one-to-many training via the Internet. They are handling sales transactions for various products, with delivery and payment handled via the Internet. And they are hosting real-time discussion forums, where customers are able to interact directly with developers.

A technical support team from Silicon Graphics created a studio Web site that is used to offer some of their Premier Services. The site provides for real-time conferencing, weekly live forums (with customers communicating directly with SGI engineers), a product bulletin board, threaded discussions, access to the technical support knowledge base, and white papers. The weekly forums with the engineers are scheduled and moderated by a Technical Support Representative who moderates the questions asked of the engineer, and communicates them to the entire audience. The content of the knowledge base and the white papers are marked with topic indicators so that they are easily grouped and sorted. The same documents are also marked for various customer types, providing customers with information on products they have without overwhelming them with information on products they do not yet own. This studio Web site also offers sophisticated computer-based training linked to code snippets, the tech support knowledge base, and product documentation. The training is designed to be completed on one's own or interactively with an instructor in a one-on-one or classroom session. Tests have been developed as a part of the training program as well.

In addition to knowledge-base access and the ability to request replacement software and technical information, the technical support team at Sybase, Inc., offers additional Internet-based services. These services are available around the clock, so Sybase customers can manage their technical support cases in real time, gain immediate access to software fixes, and access technical information as soon as it becomes available. The Internet-based services are provided at no additional charge to all Sybase support customers as a part of their purchased support plan. Features offered include electronic case management whereby customers can manage their technical support at their convenience by logging new cases with the ability to attach pertinent backup files, update open case information, view a list of customers' open cases, and close cases. The cases are logged directly into the Sybase technical support database, and are automatically queued for processing according to the priority level set by the customer and the response time associated with the customer's support plan. And customers receive an e-mail notification whenever an update for each case has occurred, keeping them well informed. A reporting option even lets customers quickly and easily create reports on all their cases or only on their open cases.

Another offering is electronic software distribution, which allows customers to obtain software fixes at any time with the ability to quickly locate information about defects that have been corrected. This is possible because the system displays software fixes available only for that customer's licensed products and platforms. The objective of these efforts is to provide a way for customers to increase their productivity in working with the company's products, and to help customers become more self-sufficient by offering a variety of technical support services electronically.

High-technology companies are not the only ones leveraging the power of the Internet. Federal Express, the delivery company, is providing its larger customers with the ability to do online tracking of packages via the Internet. In the past, a customer would have to contact Federal Express to track a package that had not shown up at the designated location on time. The Federal Express service representative would find the status of the shipment and communicate it back to the customer. Today, some customers simply connect to the Federal Express Web site via the Internet to check the status of shipments themselves, in minutes. Similarly the travel and entertainment industries are utilizing the Internet to become more customer friendly by giving customers the ability to research a business or vacation destination;

investigate travel options (method, carrier, and fees); and make travel, lodging, and even dinner (eat there, pick up, or order delivery), concert, and theme-park reservations via the Internet.

The obstacles faced by Technical Support Organizations today in being able to utilize the Internet for the objective of providing technical support are fairly few, yet somewhat challenging. Security of systems and data integrity is one of the largest. However, with the assistance of the corporate Information Systems division, and by using some of the Internet service and data security providers, this is becoming a more manageable topic. A second is the effort to design a process to make Web-site content current and comprehensive. It is better to wait to launch your Web page until you have solid content and a process to keep it updated, than to launch it with sparse or incorrect content just to have an Internet presence. First impressions are just as important on the Internet as they are in other aspects of business. As a result, customers' first impressions need to be positive, or they many not give you another chance. The third challenge is to get customers to change their habits and use the Web site instead of calling the technical support center as a first action for problem resolution. Some customers will do this without much encouragement; the novelty will intrigue them enough. Other customers will need encouragement. Some technical support centers have given discounts on products and service-plan enrollments as incentives. Others are offering t-shirts, sweatshirts, mugs, and other items with the corporate logo. Regardless of what strategy is chosen, it should include a well-thought-through communication plan, similar to that done to announce and sell any other new service or product. The communication is best received when it is simply written, explains the benefits and reasons for utilizing the service, explains what is needed (special software or hardware), includes specific directions on how to utilize the service, and answers anticipated questions about the service usage, escalation procedures, and so on. And finally, an Internet support strategy should not be expected to replace other technical support access and delivery mechanisms completely, at least not right away. One of the best sources for getting ideas on how to use the Internet for your technical support purposes is to log on and surf the net yourself. Check out companies known for their ingenuity, customer service, and graphics design capability, (Disney, L.L.Bean, and Silicon Graphics, among others) and build from what they've done. In addition, check out the conferences and technology shows that highlight the Internet as a main topic, and be creative in your implementation.

CONSIDER THE PURPOSE

Technology is a valuable mechanism for supporting growth through customer satisfaction; when done well, its value becomes more apparent within your business over time (see Figure 7.5).

There are tremendous needs and significant benefits for the Technical Support Organization to use access, process, and enabling tools. In the process of selecting these tools for deployment, it is important to remember to keep the customer, the technical support employees, and the company in mind to ensure

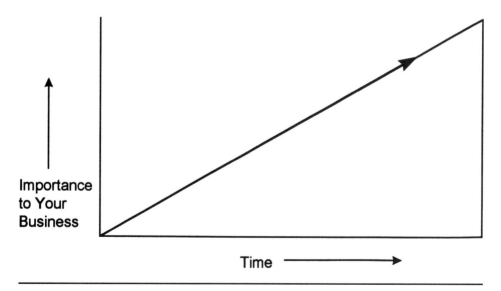

Importance to Your Business

Time

FIGURE 7.5 Leveraging technology will support growth and result in greater customer satisfaction.

a good solution. Technology systems are best viewed as ways to enhance and leverage, not replace, the efforts of the Technical Support Organization. Select the options and combinations most appropriate for your customer type, knowledge level, aptitude and interest. In addition, customers will adapt to different technologies at different rates. Recognizing this and factoring it into deployment plans will increase the chances of a successful outcome. By selecting meaningful tools, integrating them effectively, and investing in communicating the benefits of the tools and how to use them to customers and employees, customer satisfaction can increase while effectiveness and efficiencies drive costs down and create a more interesting and rewarding job for technical service personnel.

Positioning
and Marketing

According to *Webster's New World Dictionary, Second College Edition,* positioning is the manner in which something is set in place, situated, and arranged in an effort to influence others attitude towards, or opinion on, it. Marketing encompasses the business activities engaged in to move goods or services from the producer to the consumer and can include selling, advertising, packaging and other activities.

Just like anything else, service is a product and the positioning and marketing of services is just as important for service product as for non-service products. You may choose to deliver services internally, externally, or both. You may provide all or some services at no additional cost, considering it a cost of your company's business. Or you may charge modest or substantial fees. Regardless of your chosen strategy, it is important to invest in identifying and communicating messages that help you position and market your organization and its products both inside and outside the company because if you don't, someone else will. And letting someone else define and communicate to your customers, partners and employees, who you are and what you're about, is a risky alternative.

An effective way for many Technical Support Organizations to position and market themselves is through achieving high levels of customer satisfaction, which positively influence the company's bottom line. At the highest level this can be summarized into two parts:

- Setting expectations
- Meeting and/or exceeding expectations

Setting expectations is essentially making sure you, your customers, your employees, and your company all have the same understanding of what will be delivered when, where, how, and to what degree. Customers will require their expectations to be met or exceeded on a regular basis before considering themselves highly satisfied or delighted.

SELECTING A STRATEGY

A strategy is the planning, directing, and maneuvering of resources into the most advantageous position to achieve a desired result. Basic questions you'll want to answer before selecting a technical support strategy include: Is part of the strategy to generate revenue from the support offerings? If so, is the objective to off-set costs by a certain percent? Attain a cost/revenue breakeven? Become a profit center? Who are your customers (meaning: What is the definition we will be working from)? Are customers only those people who buy your product? Must they have purchased the product directly from you? What if they purchased from an authorized third party? What if they obtained it from an unauthorized source?

If they are using your product, regardless of how they obtained it, are they considered customers? If they purchase your product from one source rather than another, do you think of them differently? Will you treat them differently? Are people within your company customers? In all cases? Will you be the first line of service delivery? Second? Third? And is this an absolute or a preference?

These are the types of questions that will help define your support strategy. In many companies customers are often narrowly defined—for example, as someone who buys product from us—in which case a couple of immediate questions should be asked, such as What does *product* mean? Does it mean tangible goods only? Or does it include nontangible goods such as training, consulting, telephone support, and so on?

Another question is what does "buys . . . from us" mean? Does that mean they must have purchased product directly from your company? An authorized source? And if not, how does that affect the service they receive?

These questions may be challenging and may require your company to reconsider its current definitions of some basic business elements. However, this exercise is necessary for the development of a solid, comprehensive technical support strategy and underlying offerings.

Service offerings are products which should be integrated into the company's overall product line, be included in the broader marketing and positioning of the company's entire product offering, and need to be understood and adopted by marketing, sales, finance and operations. If the strategy is for services to generate revenue (to apply against costs, or as a profit center), it needs to be considered as a significant contributor to the company's revenue stream.

DOING THE ANALYSIS

Some people learn by reading, others by watching, others by doing, and yet others by some combination of styles. At the same time different people value different things. Some people value time over money. Others money over time. Some people value knowledge above everything. Others are willing to endure less knowledge as long as they still get the correct solution in a timely and friendly manner. In summary, what people value varies by individual, circumstance, and perceived cost for value received. The more this is understood and built into the design of the support offerings, the greater the success (adoption, enrollment and re-enrollment rates).

Example: Great Plains Software, an accounting software firm, was providing technical support to all customers with same-day response, while their competitors were often taking up to a week to respond to a call for technical support assistance. Yet some of Great Plains' customers were still dissatisfied with the company's responsiveness. Upon further investigation Great Plains learned:

1. Although Great Plains was a leader in responsiveness among its competitors, its end-user customers did not necessarily know or value this, since the only accounting software they had was Great Plains, which gave them no occasion to call and thereby compare Great Plains' technical support to Great Plains' competitors. Therefore, one of Great Plains' measurements, benchmarking against its competitors, was not important to this customer type. However, it was still quite valid and important to a different customer type.

2. Although Great Plains customers were generally pleased with the company's average response time of three hours, for a few customers (especially those having questions when running payroll checks off the Great Plains system at 5 p.m. on the last day of the month) the three hour response wasn't good enough. Even though those same customers raved about the wonderful response time only a few days before when calling about a general question regarding a different aspect of the system.

As a result Great Plains determined three things around which it then built its service offerings:

- Customers need options on elements they deem important (time, cost, access method, comprehensiveness of offering)
- The offerings needed to be flexible. For example an option was needed so a customer could receive a response within three hours for most items, with the opportunity to get immediate response on the exceptional high priority call.
- Customers and Great Plains needed to be working from the same definition of the service offerings, commitments and deliverables.

Through this exercise Great Plains was identifying trends and segmenting customers. Identifying trends and segmenting customers supports the ability to develop offerings in which customers will perceive value for themselves as unique entities. Not segmenting customers will result in a one-size-fits-all program that will meet some customers' needs, but which will also completely miss meeting the needs of others.

Some of the trends to watch and segment from are:

- *Product and service patterns.* When do people purchase? How long after purchase do they begin to install? When are the most popular times of installation (evening, day, weekend)? How long from beginning to end of install?
- *Service usage patterns.* Where do customers turn first for assistance if they have a question during the install process? Where do they first turn for postinstallation questions? Do they tend to call on the same product area more frequently than others?
- *Service requirements.* When customers call at different times and for different needs, are their requirements different? If so, how are they different?
- *Demand/frequency.* Is there a time during which a customer calls more often—possibly in the first 30 days after product purchase or product installation. Or maybe customers call more often when they are working with a specific area of the product.
- *Communication methods.* Some customers prefer to have a person walk them through the solution during a phone call. Some prefer to receive specific written directions they can follow at their leisure. Others prefer interactive written communication so that they can control the pace.

Identifying these trends will provide information for segmenting customers into a variety of categories, allowing programs to be built that are deliverable by the Technical Support Organization while meeting specific customer needs.

Talk with customers to obtain this information. User Groups, phone calls, and surveys (paper, fax, online) are all good ways to obtain the needed information. When talking with customers, ask not only what they need, but also how important each item is to them and how often they anticipate using it. Ask what level of content, response time, and communication method is preferred; and at what fee would the cost outweigh the desire to use the specific service.

In addition, invest in understanding what customers perceive to be their alternatives. Research competitor's offerings to ensure that your offerings are competitive in a direct comparison.

Look outside your industry. Research offerings of companies who are not direct competitors but to whom customers might be comparing you. This is especially important for organizations responsible for providing support to home consumers. Although technology is being adopted at incredible rates, many people are purchasing and using computers for the first time, and are not sure what they should expect servicewise. As a result your customers may compare the technical support you are providing to that they recently received from an airline, a mail-order house, or the place where they bought their TV or washer and dryer.

Visit other companies, those in your industry type and those in other industries to which your customers may be comparing you. Making the time in a busy schedule to arrange and do these visits is sometimes intimidating. And very rarely will an exact match of business styles, marketplace, strategy, and so on be identical from one company. However, it is an effective way to broaden thinking and creativity.

In summary, think outside the box of what you know, your company has done, and your competitors are doing, to identify what customers will value in service offerings for your specific product lines.

DEVELOPING YOUR SERVICE OFFERINGS

Recognizing that customers are different and have different needs requires the development of a variety of service offerings. Most often the resulting offerings are developed around a combination of the following six elements:

1. Service type, such as problem resolution, training, consulting, and so on.

2. Proactive and reactive. Historically, technical support was most often a reactive function, responding to customer needs on demand. This is changing. Today more and more Technical Support Organizations are adopting a strong preventative strategy, in the belief that preventing customers from encountering problems is the best customer satisfaction there is.

3. Length of service agreement. Fitting into budgets, recognizing product use styles, and acknowledging customers' ever growing knowledge level is an important aspect of service offerings. Some people will look at a support contracts as a way to being more independent once they've gained some confidence. Other customers will see a support contract as insurance, giving them the security that assistance is easily available whenever needed.

4. Flexible payment methods can encourage or discourage using the service. Prepaid contracts, prepaid packages of contacts (by number of contacts, time spent), credit cards, 900-number billing, and special service credit cards for blocks of time or contacts are all payment methods in use today.

5. How customers can access the service organization is also important. Telephone, fax, e-mail, Internet, pulling information from a fax-on-demand or integrated voice response system, and logging in to the service center's customer information management system are some of the possibilities.

6. Features, or what is provided within an offering, can be a combination of elements. As simple or extensive as desired, some organizations have gone so far as to price all features separately, allowing customers the ability to choose their service plan the way some companies allow employees to choose their benefits from a cafeteria-style plan.

The features of an offering are what will determine its value. The content that is provided is one of the most compelling features of an offering. The content is the information that is provided or accessible as a part of a particular offering. It may be in a support person's head, a manual, or a knowledge base. It may require the intervention of another person. In addition to content, value is also associated with how easily and thoroughly the content can be searched to find specific items by individuals who are not familiar with the structure of the data. Great data is worthless if it cannot be easily culled by the person requiring the information.

Accessibility, response, and resolution time are other important features in determining the value of an offering. (For purposes of this discussion, accessibility refers to a customer's ability to reach a Technical Support Representative immediately. Response time means the time it takes a Technical Support Representative to return a customer's support request if the customer was not able to reach a Technical Support Representative upon calling in. Resolution time refers to the time it takes the Technical Support Representative to provide a complete solution to the customer.) Customers would like answers, education, and assistance when, where, and how they need it. Available access methods, response times and resolution times are fundamental to meeting this need. However, not all needs require the same access, response, or resolution time. Developing different options, such as offering immediate access, response within ten minutes, response within four hours, and response within two days, will help meet this need. It is also best if customers can choose the level they need at the time they identify their technical support need. However, although being flexible for customers is a tremendous asset, it needs to be offered in such a way that the Technical Support Organization is virtually certain it will be able to meet and exceed the expectations of the customer, including this expectation. This can be done by offering a few basic service accessibility or response-time options for various fees, while allowing customers the ability to easily upgrade the response time for selected situations.

Using the previous Great Plains example, a service plan providing an average two-hour response was one of the options offered. However, for customers who chose this option, paying for a six- or 12-month service agreement in advance could easily upgrade a specific service call by paying an additional $30 for immediate response. This allowed customers to choose a less expensive plan (two-hour response instead of immediate access) as their basic plan, while knowing they had the option to upgrade to immediate access for a single call by paying a little extra money. Of course, customers could also have upgraded the entire plan from two-hour response to immediate access by simply paying the difference between the two plans, prorated for the remainder of the contract. This plan also worked well for the service organization, since they knew to plan for a guaranteed response of two hours for a certain group of customers, and could have a little extra staffing flexibility to cover those upgraded calls, since there was revenue to cover such flexibility.

Specifying two or three service people to a customer account is also an option valued by some customers. Similar to a sales organization assigning a salesperson or system engineer to a specific customer account, this ensures that customers will have someone at the service organization who knows their situation, people, and needs. This offering is not for everyone, and should therefore be appropriately priced. However, because there are almost always customers who value such a relationship, this feature should be part one of the options of a comprehensive offering.

Customer communication preferences can differ with regard to medium. Some people work best talking with a person over the phone; others are more direct and prefer to submit a question and get a response on-line. Some customers prefer to be stepped through a solution in a manner that allows them to ask questions along the way. Others just want the information so that they can go forward at their own pace. And yet others desire access to the exact information the service organization uses so that they can solve their questions and learn at their own pace.

Basic marketing tells us that we don't want to make customers decide too often if they want to purchase (or reenroll in) something, since every time the question is posed a second question almost immediately enters the customer's mind: What are my options? And when this question is asked, there is always a chance the customer will decide not to purchase (or reenroll) our product or offering of the same or greater value. Therefore, every time we put the customer in the situation of having to ask that question, we risk losing some revenue from them. To minimize that risk, most service offerings have a contract length of 12 months. However, for those customers who, for whatever reason, do not believe they will need a full 12 months of service (this may be the case with customers who have had a product for awhile), a contract spanning a shorter time frame may be desirable. Per-incident call paks, where a customer pre-pays for a group of calls, the number of which is reduced by one for every new support request incident the customer contacts the Technical Support Organization about, is also a popular offering.

Nearly all customers desire to understand not only the solution or answer to their questions, but also what they did that caused the question or problem in the first place, and what they can do in the future to prevent it. A good service call always addresses all of these components; however, there may be times when the information is too lengthy to cover in a phone call intended for quick problem resolution. As an option, training opportunities may be offered as parts of the service offering features. The training could take the form of classroom training, could be as simple as a video, or could be an interactive one-on-one session, with neither party having to physically move. This could be accomplished by scheduling a training appointment and, if taking control of the customer's keyboard is important, providing the customer with the software needed to allow a data, as well as voice, tutoring session. With the advent of single voice/data lines, and the adoption of video conferencing, this will become a more cost-effective and efficient way of providing customers with helpful information.

Publications, such as newsletters and question-and-answer updates, are all good value additions to any service offerings. Again, the content communicated and the method of communication (paper, Internet, bulletin board, fax) are all dependent on the makeup of your customers.

Designing a program of offerings that meets customers' varied needs while still appearing simple can be a difficult task. We suggest developing three offerings as a first step, then adding additional offerings or variations of the three offerings as a second step. To cover the greatest number of customers, the three categories may be thought of as no-brainer, moderate, and ultimate.

The *no-brainer* offering is one that customers barely have to think about before realizing that it is a good, no-frills value. It should be priced low enough that cost is rarely an objection, and should have meaningful components in which nearly all customers will find something of value. In software, this may be the guarantee of notification of any problems identified within the software (and directions on how to correct the situation or obtain the corrected software) within 24 hours of identification. The big win for both the customer and the company would be the proactive nature of the offering. The customer would be able to correct the problem before experiencing it, therefore saving time, frustration and money. At the same time the Technical Support Organization would be able to cost-effectively (possibly via fax or e-mail via the Internet) prevent serious drops in customer satisfaction while avoiding significant after-sale costs from disgruntled customers.

The *moderate* offering provides basic, getting-comfortable-with-the-product values. It would include the same or better elements of the no-brainer offering, and likely include the option for direct contact with a service person via the customer's preferred medium as an additional value.

The *ultimate* offering is packed full of information, access methods, discounts, and special services. This offering is too expensive and has too many features for most customers. It is there for those who have a need for and are willing to pay for significantly enhanced service. This may take the form of a guarantee to speak to one of two designated Technical Support Representatives every time. This offering may be an absolute guarantee that the customer will never have to wait for assistance. It may provide customers direct access into their accounts on the company's customer-information system so that they can directly log requests, check status of outstanding calls, see the escalation of the call, and more. Or it may be a completely custom-designed offering for each customer that purchases this level of support offering.

Following is a sample service offering for a software product sold to small to medium-size businesses, with an average sale price of $3,000 to $5,000.

No-Brainer Example: Maintenance

- Telephone assistance via an 800 number for a per-call fee with same day response
- Software updates every six months
- 15-percent discount on product upgrades
- Online access to product, service, and company information (includes software patches, drivers, etc.)
- Fee options: $125/12 months; $65/6 months

Moderate Example: Standard

- Four incident call pak (telephone access via an 800 number) included in fee, additional per incident call paks could be purchased for an additional fee
- Guaranteed response of four hours or less
- Software updates every six months
- 25-percent discount on product upgrades
- Online access to product, service, and company information (includes software patches, drivers, etc.)
- Fee options: $295/12 months; $225/6 months

Moderate-Plus Example: Standard Plus

- Four incident call pak (telephone access via an 800 number) included in fee, additional per incident call paks could be purchased for an additional fee
- Guaranteed response of one hour or less
- Software updates every six months
- 25-percent discount on product upgrades
- Online access to product, service, and company information (includes software patches, drivers, etc.)
- Fee options:$495/12 months

Select Example: Premium

- Unlimited incidents (telephone via an 800 number) for no fee
- Guaranteed response of four hours or less
- Software updates every six months
- 30-percent discount on product upgrades
- Online access to product, service, and company information (includes software patches, drivers, etc.)
- Fee options: $795/12 months; $525/6 months

Select Example: Premium Plus

- Unlimited incidents (telephone via an 800 number) for no fee
- Guaranteed response of one hour or less
- Software updates every six months
- 30-percent discount on product upgrades
- Online access to product, service, and company information (includes software patches, drivers, etc.)
- Fee options: $1,095/12 months; $ 725/6 months

Ultimate Example: Comprehensive

- Unlimited incidents (telephone via an 800 number) for no fee
- Assigned technical representatives
- Guaranteed response of one hour or less
- Software updates every six months
- 35-percent discount on product upgrades
- Online access to product, service, and company information (includes software patches, drivers, etc.)
- Direct access to customer account in customer information system
- Fee options: $3595/12 months

Example: Matrix provided for customers for ease of selection

Offering	Guarantee	Price
Comprehensive	1 Hour	$3,595
Premium (12 mos.)	1 Hour	$1,095
	4 Hour	$ 795
Premium (6 mos.)	1 Hour	$ 725
	4 Hour	$ 525
Standard (12 mos.)	1 Hour	$ 495
	4 Hour	$ 295
Standard (6 mos.)	4 Hour	$ 225
Maintenance (12 mos.)	Same Day	$ 125
Maintenance (6 mos.)	Same Day	$ 65

Regardless of how support offerings are designed, they will be more effective if the Technical Support Representatives know and understand what the offerings are before announcing them to customers and/or partners; systems are in place to make meeting the commitments of the offerings simple and easy; and the terms of the offerings are consistently enforced by all members of the Technical Support Organization.

PRICING YOUR SERVICE OFFERINGS

There are two basic elements to pricing service offerings. One is the relationship between value, importance, and willingness to pay for individual features from the customer's perspective. Second is the cost to create, deliver, maintain, and collect on the offerings.

The relationship between value, importance, and willingness to pay for individual features from the customer's perspective is an important but imperfect element. This information can be obtained from focus groups, customer user group discussions, and surveying customers. Very few organizations actually do this perfectly, since customers don't always act in real decision-making scenarios as they think they will when completing such comparative survey information. However, it is valuable information from which to begin developing, pricing, and costing service offerings. Keep in mind, however, that service offerings, like many other products, require ongoing analysis and modification to keep up with customers' ever-changing needs and desires.

Once the analysis has been completed to determine the services customers want and what they would be willing to pay for those services, financial models need to be built. The models should include costs and revenues, and often take the form of a balance sheet and profit-and-loss statement.

To be helpful the models need to be built on complete and accurate data whenever possible. To make it easy to modify, assumptions should be clearly identified and built into the spreadsheet model in such a way that a change in estimated percent enrollment, fees, and so on can easily roll over into the calculations.

Enlist the assistance of the finance organization to ensure that the model is comprehensive, well designed, and believable. This assistance will give validity to the model when it undergoes scrutiny by others in the organization.

There may be unknown elements in the model, such as percent of units shipped generating a call, percent of calls that will generate additional revenue opportunities, or the average revenue from a revenue call. Check within your own company to obtain any experience or knowledge for a baseline of what might be expected. Investigate published studies and surveys that have been done with other companies that are already offering revenue-generating services.

Be sure to consider all direct and indirect costs, including the costs to create, communicate, and deliver the offerings. Also include any costs to inventory any physical goods that may be covered in the offerings. And don't forget to include the costs of other departments that will be involved in the creation, announcement, and delivery of the offerings. This ensures that all internally provided technical support services are accounted for. It also makes it simpler to credit costs and/or revenues to a particular product line if desired.

The model can then be used for a variety of purposes including communicating and building understanding with people outside of the Technical Support Organization on the workings, successes, challenges, and opportunities of the proposed support offerings. Use it to validate the proposed offerings, gather feedback for further refinements, and gain increased awareness of the contributions the Technical Support Organization is, and can make in the future, to the company's bottom line.

MARKETING AND PROMOTION

For a successful support program two types of marketing and promotion should take place: internal and external. Internal marketing and promotion of any organization is essential for the organization to represent its functions well within the company. Specifically a service organization must market and promote itself to ensure that the voice of the customer is heard and that the service organization has the resources needed to do the job the company expects of it.

Good internal communication includes creating and sharing detailed plans that indicate payback and time frame on new projects. Once the project is approved, regular progress reports to the rest of the company keep everyone informed and aware of the progress being made. This is especially critical when the project is in response to a need identified by another part of the company, or when the project directly affects another group.

Internal marketing can and should take many forms, including promoting successes and leveraging failures. Promoting successes is the more natural approach and can be done as simply as publicly sharing compliments and appreciation from customers at company or division meetings, publishing graphs that easily show consistent delivery against stated goals, communicating projects and the associated hours and returns for the efforts the Technical Support Organization invested to help another area of the company, or simply translating the costs of finding and correcting a product problem before it left engineering.

For example, in its early days Intuit, Inc., had a company meeting once a week, which everyone was encouraged to attend. At the meeting, product and shipping issues were shared, marketing plans were discussed, sales rates were communicated, and service rates and issues were provided. In addition, a customer story or two, or three, were the first items on the agenda.

At Great Plains Software—a company recognized as one of the best places to work in America in the book *The 100 Best Companies to Work for in America* by Robert Levering and Milton Moskowitz, and in *Making It in America* by Jerry Jaskinowski and Robert Hamrin, for exceeding customer expectations—the Technical Support organization did a number of things to market itself within the company. This included starting company and department meetings with a customer story—each of the senior staff meetings began with the executives sharing a customer story. The Technical Support Organization created a Wall of Fame that displayed the hundreds of cards, letters, and lists of gifts received from appreciative customers. Among the gifts were boxes of Washington apples, cases of champagne, styrofoam coolers of steamed Maryland crab, flowers, candy, and other small gifts. One of the more extravagant was the customer who flew a support representative and her husband to Chicago, picked them up in a limousine, treated them to dinner, put them up at one of Chicago's nicest hotels, and gave them tickets to a Chicago Bears football game—all for a little extra effort the support representative provided to help the customer in a difficult situation. In addition, the Wall of Fame also stated, in beautiful hardwood numbers, the number of support calls the team had taken without missing a single guarantee. In the company's main meeting room, customer products and/or t-shirts, caps, and so on were displayed in a Customer Wall to remind everyone that the customers who used Great Plains products were people just like the people at Great Plains who were trying to get a job done.

On the other hand, using failures, or projects that just did not go as well as planned, can also be used to promote the Technical Support Organization. Done properly a negative situation can be turned into a learning situation for the company, and leveraged to make the right investments so that similar failures do not occur in the future. Some of the most successful leveraging has resulted in the approval for much needed equipment in the support organization, the blessing to invest in helpful technology, the agreement to have service personnel participate in the product release process with the same right to *stop product shipment* as anyone else in the company; and the agreement that anything going to customers, resellers, or partners will be presented to the Technical Support Organization first so that the Technical Support Representatives are knowledgeable and prepared when customers call about new programs, products, or processes.

Above all, leaders of Technical Support Organizations must see it as their job to be the primary voice of the customer within the company. Doing this effectively requires the respect of the rest of the company. This respect can be built by continuous, proactive, fact-based marketing and promotion of the support organization's mission, goals, and accomplishments. Blended with being the customer's constant advocate while keeping the company' s best interest in mind, and looking for a solution that works for the customer, the company and the support employees will achieve tremendous results and influence.

External marketing is equally if not more important, and all marketing and promotional activities must consider the needs of the customer, partners or resellers, and industry influencers, as well as the company and the employees who will be responsible for delivering the service.

When marketing to customers, make it simple. Programs can be simple or complex. Either way the message to the customer needs to be simple, clear and straightforward. One good test is to ask people outside your company to read the communication and ask them a few questions to determine what they understood and what steps they believe need to be taken as a result. If the response is what you were hoping for, chances are that you have a good message. If not, work it again. One company asked employees, at random, to take finalized messages home for their spouses and significant others to read and to identify any confusing messages. The participation was outstanding and the feedback resulted in changes that prevented many customers from calling with questions, therefore providing significant cost savings. This was especially true on order forms (directions on how to fill something out or how to calculate the cost of an order) and directions on how a new process works.

Second, remember that customers do not know, nor do they care, how your company is organized. The best example seen in many service organizations today is when a customer calls a company for assistance and is given such options as "Press 1 for sales, press 2 for technical support, press 3 for customer service." Most companies know to give the caller the choice of also pressing 0 for operator assistance, which is definitely the right thing to do. However, customers calling with what they think is a defective product may not know which of the three options is the right one to most expeditiously get them to the organization that can best help them. A better solution is to more completely describe the type of services for which an option should be selected rather than simply listing organizational departments.

Third, whenever possible give customers all the information they need to make a decision, and even give them a recommendation of what is suggested based on what you know about them. This makes customers feel like they are known entities to your company, beyond just a sales number, and makes their decision process easier. An example of this is a notice that a support plan is about to lapse. You could simply send a letter telling the customer that their service is about to lapse on a particular date, and refer them to an attached marketing piece that talks about your service offerings. Or, you could, in addition to telling customers that their service is about to lapse and when, provide information on what plan they're currently enrolled in, the activity (number of contacts, duration of each call, products called about), and a recommended plan going forward based on the customer's historical usage pattern. In addition, the letter could actually be an invoice that requires a check mark on the service plan desired, customer signature, credit card, or purchase order number. This latter idea is not new; it has been used by magazine publishers for years as a way to make decision making and reenrollment as easy as possible. And it works. One company did this and experienced a 28-percent increase in response to the notice without even requiring a follow-up call.

If a price increase or program change is what the communication is about, be sure to provide it early enough so customers can readjust their budgets to accommodate the new programs. A new program is also a way to show appreciation to current or longtime customers by grandfathering them into the new program under the old prices (assuming they're lower than the new prices). And if you're going from a free to a fee service program, it may be worth considering a mailing that requires signatures of customers showing they've received the information.

Marketing and promoting service programs to partners are also important ingredients in a successful service offering. If the intent is to involve partners or resellers in the communication or sales effort of the offering, be sure they understand the program well. The reasons and methods of testing the marketing and promotional messages are similar here to what were described earlier for marketing and promoting for customers. In addition, be sure to provide partners and resellers with the reason for the change. If it's a business need, explain the change in those terms. Most of your partners and resellers are competent business people who will understand your reasoning and appreciate the business-to-business tone of the communication. Also provide your partners and resellers with anticipated objections and responses for overcoming objections, simple tools to involve them in the sales of the new service offerings, and a financial reason for supporting the change. This last point is the part of the offering that will gain new offerings the greatest support, especially if the intent is to leverage partners and resellers in selling the offerings.

Incentives can be as simple as a percent of the sold service offering; earning a certain number of points for trips, gifts, and so on; or as complex as building sales of the service offerings into their business plans just as they do for other of your company's products. If commissions, points, or similar incentive programs are offered, it is important to determine who receives the incentive at the start—whether it be the corporate office, the local store or outlet, or the individual sales person.

Two other sources for introducing and gaining customer acceptance of new or modified service offerings are the corporation's sales force and a telesales staff specially tasked with selling into the installed base of customers. Both should be leveraged in communicating and selling the service products offered by the company, and the incentive compensation plans of both sales organizations should be revised to reflect and reward the sale of service products. In some cases a quota may also be appropriate. The details on how the sales organizations will play a role in the sales of services will need to be determined with the leader of the sales organization. If your company does not have a telesales organization focused on selling services and products into the installed base, suggest it. It can be tested by simply bringing on a few quality, part-time sales people for a test period. Invest the time to train both sales organizations on the service products, responses to anticipated objections, the benefits to the customer and the company, and the benefits to the sales people themselves. Provide scripts, especially for the telesales team, to help ensure communication of the salient points of the service, and to help them close the sale. If a customer information management system (discussed in Chapter 7) is effectively used by the Technical Support Organization, make it available to the telesales staff as well, so they can use customer-specific information to provide the basis for selling a particular service to a customer. For example, before telesales people call on customers, they could check the customer information system to determine what service plan a customer is currently on or was last on, how long since the enrollment expired or how long until expiration, previous usage patterns, and more. The more the sales people know about the customer and can tell them about the customer service history, the more credible they will be when recommending another service product.

Whenever possible, also use your investments in technology to keep customers from lapsing from their service plans. This can be done quite easily by creating a process that mails, faxes, or e-mails notices to customers that their service agreements are about to expire. The first notice should be timed to arrive at the customer site ten to twelve weeks before the service plan expiration date. A second notice could then be sent to customers not replying to the first notice approximately six to eight weeks before the plan's scheduled expiration. Two to four weeks prior to plan expiration, the telesales team could contact those customers who have not yet responded. Reenrollment rates with a plan like this are often 75 percent and higher. They should be, since it's based on the magazine publishing industry model for magazine subscription renewals. However, support organizations have an added benefit. With the use of the customer information management system, the renewal notice letters can easily be tailored to individual customers by giving them their current plan information, plan expiration date, recommended service plan to renew into, and specifics on customers' own call histories. This history might include items such as number of service calls made to the service organization, average response time, topic of each call, and possibly the name of the person who called from the customer's location. This information reinforces the fact that the customer is known to the company. A simple calculation can also be done to help determine which plan should be recommended (plan A if more than ten calls in the last six months, plan B if four to ten calls during that time frame, or plan C if fewer than four calls were received). This coupled with a professionally formatted letter, a respond-by date as a call to the customer to take action, information on all available services and fees (not just the one recommended), and payment terms and methods, helps draw in a significant number of renewals without requiring human intervention. Once more the customer and company benefit. Utilize a fax broadcast system to fax these professional, customer-specific notices at two in the morning, and the company benefits even more by reducing the costs of the reenrollment processes by eliminating printing, processing, and mailing costs.

Along with communicating the service programs and offerings to your employees, customers, and partners is the endeavor of positioning your service offerings with industry influencers. Specifically people who are involved in reporting on the technical support, customer service, and help-desk industry. The people and companies who are influential within your company's industry area will also be valuable contacts to make and develop relationships.

There is significant value in creating and cultivating these relationships. These people in turn influence others through their writings and talks. Influencers can help tell your story, reaching audiences you or your company may not be reaching in a way or as frequently as desired. These industry luminaries are often well connected and can create opportunities for your company to be better known and respected by the influencer's identifying your offerings as something noteworthy. Creating these relationships helps to leverage others to tell your story, or at a minimum helps you attain opportunities that you might not otherwise have to tell your story. By talking positively about your efforts, the influencer is basically telling audiences that your programs are worth taking a look at. This can have significant, positive impacts on your company through sales, awareness of the added value offered to customers and possibly partners and resellers, and perhaps even with recruiting.

Finding the right influencers can be done by working with your company's public relations department, reading trade magazines, and talking with industry associates. Getting their attention might be trickier. The public relations department might have contacts or be able to make the contact. You may need to send creative notes, phone calls, and so on to get their attention. Or you might be able to use your networking contacts to make initial introductions.

Once the introduction has been made it's important that you have a good story to tell in an interesting and enthusiastic way. Providing influencers with facts, measurement techniques, industry comparisons, and so on will often catch their attention. Many influencers make it their business to know what's going on in an industry segment. To keep their standing as influencers they need to be on the cutting edge of what's happening in that segment. The best way to initially endear yourself with influencers is to provide them with information that helps them better understand the business issue and business state. Offering a tool to measure an important industry factor that helps to differentiate companies in the sector may be seen as a valuable device for doing their job better. The tool might simply be the metrics you use to determine the health of your support business and the success of your service offerings.

Delivering interesting, well-received presentations at service and support industry conferences, writing and placing articles in service industry publications, joining and becoming actively involved in local and national service conferences and chapters, and networking with industry peers are all ways to gain the attention of industry influencers.

During the introduction of a new service offering, think of influencers as your marketing organization would if it were announcing a new product. Write and send a press release. Offer to talk with influencers about the reason for the offering; the implications of the offering on customers, resellers, and the industry; and the desired result. Send the influencer a gift such as an old fashioned wind-up alarm clock in your company's colors with the company logo (for announcing a new service offering with response time guarantees), that will make the influencer think of your company and your offering.

And always stay in touch with notes, small gifts, holiday greetings, a birthday card, or any other inexpensive way to keep influencers in touch with what you're doing. After meeting with influencers, speaking at a conference they've invited to you to, or talking with them over the phone for a publication in which your service offerings will be featured, send a thank-you note stating your appreciation for their interest in what you are doing, and the impact you hope it will have on your customers and the industry as a whole.

Regardless of to whom you're marketing and promoting, do so on a regular basis; make sure the communication is clear and concise; show appreciation for longtime supporters and customers whenever feasible; and communicate all service, marketing, and sales-related messages internally, providing anticipated objections and responses before communicating them externally.

ESTABLISHING CUSTOMER RELATIONSHIPS

Building strong, trusting customer relationships requires commitment to consistently doing the right thing, and doing what you say you will. As companies grow they evolve from entrepreneurial entities in which nearly everyone knows nearly everything, to maturing companies in which guidelines, or sometimes even policies, are implemented in response to the inability to keep nearly everyone informed of nearly everything.

Some guidelines can be good for developing customer relationships. For example, requiring that basic customer-profile information and the reason for a support contact be captured in a customer-information management system can help establish customer relationships, since it allows support organizations to be more proactive. If, upon calling for technical support, a customer keys in a customer identification number resulting in a screen pop of the customer's known information at the support representative's desk, the customer can have a better support experience. The customer does not need to repeat the same information previously provided, and if the customer is calling on a previously captured support request the customer does not have to recount, in detail, with whom they spoke, what was said, and what was done. Instead both the customer and the support representative save time, while the customer actually feels like a somebody rather than a nobody to this company.

The degree to which customer relationships are forged depends on customers' perceptions of how well you know them as separate entities from other customers, how well they believe they are being listened to, and how well they are responded to. A well-populated customer information database can make knowing a customer for the independent entity she is a relatively straightforward task. This allows the customer base to be segmented in many ways for marketing and positioning purposes. For example, a problem notification could be sent only to customers with the exact product combination and configuration known to have the problem. This allows customers to be informed before the problem is encountered, allows the message to be tailored to the customer type, and saves the company money (and reputation) by not having to notify the entire customer base of something only a percent might encounter. Customer relationships are also built with good follow-up. If customers makes suggestions, it's a valuable practice to follow up with them, thanking them for their suggestions and telling them what is being done with them. Then later when suggestions are implemented, follow-up notes telling customers their suggestions are now available, and possibly offering them something in appreciation for sharing their thoughts with you, continues to build the relationship. Building strong customer relationships can also work to increase sales. For example, if the products you sell are for children and you've captured the birthdates and ages of the customers' children, a promotional mailing can go out to those customers four to six weeks before a child's birthday, telling the parents of any new products now available for that child's age range. It also makes it cost effective to begin a customer club, giving points for purchases, which can be used for future purchases or gifts (similar to the frequent-flyer clubs the airlines offer travelers).

Inviting customers to participate in user groups and focus groups, or to be on a review team for communications of major service offering communications, and then following up to let them know what you've learned from the session and what steps will be taken as a result are all good relationship-building techniques.

Keys to Developing Strong Customer Relationships

- Do the right thing for the customer without giving away the store
- Do what you say you will
- Give as much forewarning as possible
- Segment customers to ensure the right message is communicated as clearly as possible
- Make it easy and ask customers often for feedback, then let them know what you're doing with it
- Explain why as well as tell what
- Show appreciation of longtime customers

Partners
and Affiliates

9

It's no surprise to anyone in the technical support business that the world of technical support is getting more and more complex. Most organizations are servicing larger groups of customers, with varied technology experience levels. At the same time, very few products work completely independently of other products. This leads to significant challenges in the areas of handling the volume of customer support needs, as well as the multivendor component of the system and application configurations commonly used by customers today. These challenges fundamentally have to do with providing a consistent high quality level of support in a timely manner.

One solution to these challenges is to invest in developing relationships with partners and affiliates—people or companies who take part in a common activity with another person or company. Partners and affiliates often have business components very similar or complementary to each other, and may even share the profits and the risks of the venture or market opportunity. In some cases, a partner or affiliate is viewed as an extension or branch of another partner. In others, partnerships are more purely affiliate relationships, with individuals or companies simply associating themselves with each other. Each of these possible partnership or affiliate relationships can be done in various degrees, from a very informal arrangement to a more formal arrangement, utilizing legally binding contracts.

Developing relationships with partners and/or affiliates benefits a Technical Support Organization through the leverage they provide. That leverage can take many forms, including knowledge, capacity, and scope.

Leveraging knowledge significantly helps Technical Support Organizations achieve higher levels of customer satisfaction by being able to provide solutions on issues that involve not only the company's products, but other interfacing products as well. A quick way to dissatisfy customers is by telling them you cannot help them with a problem, even though it involves your company's product, because it could be caused by an interfacing product. For example, customers using a project management application with Windows 95 on a Compaq computer while attempting to print from an HP printer does not know which of their tools is causing the problem. It could be the application itself, the operating system, a printer driver, the printer, or a number of other possibilities. Amassing and providing that information to support representatives and then to customers is nearly impossible to do well in a vacuum. However, it becomes a real possibility by working with partners and affiliates.

Partners and affiliates are also playing bigger roles in helping service and support organizations handle ever growing call volumes. These outsource, or third-party, support organizations are also beginning to offer services for providing and maintaining alternative support mechanisms, such as the Web, fax-back, computer-based training, and more.

Moreover, more and more Technical Support Organizations are being asked to not only handle the technical support issues from customers, but also do additional tasks such as selling add-on products, gather marketing data, or assisting in beta-customer relationship and feedback capture. Many partners and affiliates have also seen this trend and are positioning themselves to be an alternative provider in addition to, or in replacement of, a company's own Technical Support Organization.

OUTSOURCING YOUR SUPPORT OPERATIONS

The trend toward identifying and developing relationships with partners and affiliates is growing and taking on multiple forms. Some of those forms include outsourcing arrangements, industry consortiums, and leveraging companies' partners (such as ISVs or Integration Software Vendors, VARs or Value Added Resellers, Advisors, and a variety of others). The first, outsourcing, has become a very popular partnership arrangement for many companies, however it is not a new concept. It has been used for years by companies to allow them to focus on their core competencies while contracting with another person or company to provide skills that are not considered core competencies of the business. Each company makes the decision to outsource differently based on its view of the skills owned within the company, as well as customer type, market requirements, and cost of delivery. Nearly everything is an outsource option for one company or another. For example, some companies outsource their fulfillment efforts, others their telemarketing, others their public relations, and yet others their facility and move management components. Most Technical Support Managers make the decision to outsource based on a company decision to do so, as a way to test alternative technical support delivery mechanisms, as a way to better control costs, or as a way to staff for anticipated peaks in support request call volumes without having to invest the time and money in staffing and building an infrastructure for a short-term event. In addition, typically, the outsourcing arrangement must be a more cost effective alternative to building additional staff and systems internally.

Factors to be considered when making an outsource decision should include the company's core competencies, owned skill sets, customer type, market requirements, and delivery costs. In addition, a company's maturity and where a product is in its life cycle are also important factors.

Even when the decision has been made to outsource support, the degree to which the function is outsourced varies widely from company to company. Some companies choose to outsource overflow support requests only. And of what overflow support requests consist also varies greatly from company to company. Some companies elect to outsource their front line support requests, and handle all others. Yet others decide to outsource all support requests.

A natural progression to this outsource phenomenon has been to outsource part or all of a technical support function. As mentioned earlier, the decision to outsource is based on different factors for each company. As a result, there is no clear way to decide whether to outsource.

The advantages to outsourcing support tasks are numerous. The potential for cost savings is often a leading factor in the outsource decision. In many cases, companies can save money by outsourcing all or part of the support organization to a third party. This is partly because the delivery of technical support is the core competency of an outsource company. It is why it was founded, what its energies are focused on, and how it will stay in business and hopefully grow. Outsourcers have made the necessary investments in both the infrastructure and the people side of the equation to ensure their ability to achieve customer satisfaction ratings that are acceptable to you, otherwise they won't be in business long. Outsourcers have given serious thought and resources to all the components that make for an efficient service center, which also achieves high customer satisfaction ratings. Included in those components are the two basic components of a successful service organization: people and systems.

Outsourcers become specialists in the people and system business by necessity. They must keep the right balance between cost efficiencies and investments in people and the tools they use. Outsourcers make significant investments in staffing, training, motivating, and rewarding their personnel. They invest and bring to life a strong customer- and employee-oriented company culture, and consciously and actively create clear career paths for their Technical Support Representatives. They also invest heavily in the systems which will help their Technical Support Representatives work more efficiently and productively. In addition, outsourcers often have larger support staffs, and as a result are able to offer a more cost-efficient solution by being able to better optimize the utilization of systems and the people on their staffs.

A second advantage to outsourcing is that it gives a company flexibility in efficiently handling variable customer demand. Per a previous example, outsourcing can be used by a service provider as a mechanism for handling peaks in call volumes, without requiring the service provider to staff for peak levels. This arrangement would allow a support organization to handle the bulk of the calls, staffing efficiently for a predictably steady call load, while the outsourcing vendor handles the extra demand from customers. This partnership results in customers receiving uninterrupted service at a standard to which they've become accustomed, without the Technical Support Organization incurring the fully loaded costs (compensation, space and workstation needs, employee benefits, etc.) of staffing for these peak periods.

Conversely, a company may outsource its technical support workload when demand is expected to be low. This case may occur when a company is offering support 24 hours per day, seven days per week (24 × 7 support) to meet a customer requirement or to compete with a competitor's offering. At that point the call volume doesn't support the cost for the support organization to provide minimum staff. However, many outsource vendors are already providing 24 × 7 support, and therefore have the infrastructure already in place. This becomes an opportunity for outsource vendors to simply leverage what they already have, at a more cost-efficient rate. It also becomes a very attractive alternative to the support organization, in place of inefficiently staffing and building infrastructure specifically for a few possible calls.

Another advantage to outsourcing is that it can be used to provide a key component to the whole customer relationship for young companies that have limited resources and bandwidth but want to provide good customer service. This may be the case of a startup that has decided to allocate and focus its limited resources to development, marketing, and sales; while outsourcing the bulk of the customer support effort. It is also a very feasible scenario for organizations expanding into other parts of the world, where the focus is on establishing the company's presence through sales and marketing efforts, while again outsourcing the technical support efforts. Later as the business grows and becomes more established, the company may bring the support organization back into the company completely, or continue the outsourcing relationship in some fashion.

A fourth often used strategy for utilization of outsource vendors is for servicing sunset or legacy products. In this case, companies are still obligated to provide support for products that have been on the market for some time and have become obsolete and are no longer being invested in, but are still being used by customers. Outsourcing these typically mature and stable products allows the support organization to focus on servicing customers with newer products that are still being invested in.

A fifth benefit of outsourcing is that it allows a company to offer a broader range of services. Just as an outsource vendor can provide those services that are not considered core competencies of the company, but which are still required by customers, an outsource vendor can provide advanced technical skills in a specialty area when the company cannot justify staffing for those skill sets internally. This is especially effective when a segment of the customer base is expected to migrate or adopt a new product, such as a specific platform, where the demand is expected to be too low to warrant the investment in service staff, infrastructure, and training necessary to provide the required level of service directly.

Now that we've discussed some of the benefits of outsourcing, let's look at some of the potential drawbacks. Three of the biggest that will be discussed here include potential for loss of control over the quality of the service and support received by customers; the loss of in-house expertise—especially in understanding how customers actually use products; and the loss of valuable customer information and ongoing contact with the company.

Many technical support managers feel that someone outside the company could never understand the business and the customers' needs as well as they. Some managers are concerned that service professionals employed by an outsource vendor will not provide the same level of caring service to customers as would representatives from within the company. Yet others are concerned that valuable relationship building and information gathering will be lost if the support function is not performed in-house.

All of these potential drawbacks and concerns are real. They are also all manageable. These and other concerns can be addressed through a comprehensive review and selection process, and by taking steps to ensure that a strong, proactive, ongoing, relationship is developed with the selected vendor.

Once a decision to outsource (and what to outsource) has been made, the outsource-vendor selection process can begin. To ensure that you get what you need, the call processes, required metrics and standards to be met, data capture, report requirements, and communication processes should all be laid out and documented. This information should then be built into a Request for Proposal, or RFP. The RFP should cover the basic components of what is expected from the selected outsourcer, including scope of work, approach, pricing and contractual terms, billing mechanisms, technology issues, and other miscellaneous topics.[1] The degree of detail included in the RFP varies from company to company, but should be of a level that assures that you and the vendors who are being asked to respond to the RFP both clearly understand what is being asked for.

Typically an RFP begins with instructions to the outsource vendors (or providers as they are also called) receiving the proposal on basic information. Some of this basic information includes a discussion regarding who is liable for costs incurred in the preparation of the response to the RFP. It often states that the company has the right to reject any or all responses, has no obligation to contract for any services as a result of submitting the RFP, and may keep all RFPs and associated documents received from the provider companies. The basic instructions also outline the format the RFP response should take, the number of copies to be submitted by the provider, the location and acceptable methods of delivering the completed RFP, vendor contacts and contact information, and of course the date it is due. Finally, a nondisclosure agreement from your company should be sent along with the RFP. The executed nondisclosure agreement should be part of what is returned with the completed RFP by the outsource vendor. The reason for the nondisclosure agreement is that through the outsource selection process the company may need to disclose confidential information to assure that a complete and accurate contract can be secured. By requiring the nondisclosure at the first contact point with the provider organization, the company can be free to discuss and disclose pertinent issues to ensure that a comprehensive contract and relationship results from the process.

Generally the format of the submitted RFP, and the outsourcer's response, include the following elements: executive summary, scope of and approach to work, provider service and sales team guidelines, pricing and terms, billing methods and mechanisms, technology, success factors, due diligence on the provider's experience and references, basic understanding of the provider organization, and any other issues that may be pertinent to the selection of a provider.

The purpose of the executive summary is to provide your company's management with a concise outline of the proposed business arrangement and fees. This section is brief, three pages or less, and should cover the capabilities and background of the responding provider, benefits of the services proposed, geographic coverage, a brief discussion with supporting facts on the provider's ability to meet schedule, and a statement reflecting the commitment of the outsourcer to be a long-term, full-service provider.

The next section of the RFP would begin to discuss in detail the scope or breadth of the project, and the approach the outsourcer proposes to take to deliver against the project requirements. It may include a discussion on anticipated timelines, and resources required and intended for commitment to the project. This is where you should gain an understanding of the culture of the company and the premise upon which it does business. Although this is more clearly understood after a visit to an outsourcer vendor's operation, it does begin to tell you how this organization thinks about customers, service delivery, and overall business philosophy. This component becomes equally important in selecting an outsource partner as are the outsourcer's fee structure, investments in people, and system infrastructure.

Topics to Cover in an RFP

- Type of phone lines (toll, toll-free, 900#)
- Anticipated call volume
- Hours of operation

- Escalation levels, methods, and metrics
- Call ownership (definition of who owns escalated calls)
- Capture of customer contact information (defines if all calls or only certain calls are to be captured)
- Response requirements for answering calls
- Contact points (single or multiple, mediums)
- Languages to be covered
- Support organization (single or multilayered)
- Methodology for building, accessing, maintaining, and sharing call cause and resolution information
- Reporting requirements (standard and *ad hoc*)
- Auditable quality processes
- Training processes
- Service level requirements
- Processes for incremental improvement
- Relationship and account management
- Relationship termination

This could lead directly into a segment in the RFP intended to define the team that will be created to manage and provide the services required to fulfill the project. This team covers the project from the early proposal stages, to specific needs requirements gathering, to the infrastructure design and deployment, to staff and project organization, to service deployment, ongoing reporting, and continued maintenance and process improvements. The company submitting the RFP may also outline certain requirements about the outsourcer's project team at this point. One of the more common requirements asked for by a company is a commitment by the outsourcer that changes to the project team are made only with the consent of the company. Similarly, the company can request changes in personnel assigned to the project team, and refuse changes proposed by the outsourcer. Other specific requirements identified at this time include defining specific roles and responsibilities of key personnel on the project team, outlining the role the project team will play in a global deployment during and after implementation, when each of these key people will be available, and the length of time they will be responsible for their identified role.

Once the scope of the project, the approach to the project's deployment and ongoing management, and project team members and their roles have been identified, the fee schedule and terms of the project should be discussed. Components of the topic often include discussion of contract length and options for renewals. This is also where the terms of contract dissolution are discussed, specifically outlining what each party needs to do to terminate the relationship. In some cases this also outlines the actions necessary to continue the relationship, and any penalties which may be associated with termination of the agreement outside of the agreed upon actions. Samples of required contractual agreements and documents outlining cash flow for recurring and nonrecurring costs would also be addressed here.

Then, of course, comes the discussion on the fee structure and billing. This section should clearly outline how the outsourcer's proposed fee schedule would work, the billing cycle and methods, and the desired terms and conditions of the payment method. In order for a company to easily compare the fee structures of the various RFP responses, it is helpful to first ask for the outsourcer's preferred billing method and what it includes. Most commonly this is by call or by minute. Then also require them to provide the information by minute and by call. Some will try to convince you that they cannot comply with this request for various reasons, but ask them to provide their best response anyway. Also ask them to state what is and is not covered in each specific piece of the billing rate. This information provides you with the opportunity to compare like information from multiple respondents. It also helps to identify what is being included in a $.95-per-minute proposed fee versus a $1.20-per-minute proposed fee, allowing you to clearly understand what you're getting from each outsource vendor at their proposed rates. This provides you with a better understanding of each outsourcer's business model, where they make their money, and information to spot any hidden costs. It also provides you with the information necessary to negotiate a fair and equitable contract with the vendor you prefer.

Four Basic Factors that Drive an Outsource Vendor's Fee Structure

1. How technically challenging the product is to support
2. Service hours to be offered
3. Hour-to-hour call volume and variation
4. Response and average speed of answer requirements

Gaining assurances that the outsourcer is investing appropriately in the newest technologies designed to provide more customer-oriented yet cost-effective customer service is another aspect of the RFP process. In a section on technology, the outsourcer should be asked to identify and describe the technologies currently in use in the organization, and how they are being used and their benefit to the customer, the outsourcer's employees, and your company. A quality outsourcer will state, display, and show records of recent actions that reflect a commitment to invest in technical and procedural systems and components to meet the needs of all three entities previously listed.

In addition, check the outsourcer's ability to quickly ramp up to support new technologies on the market, which may interface with the product you are asking them to support. Ask them to define their approach and philosophy regarding how they will be handled from a service perspective, both for new implementations of technologies and for transitions, or upgrades, from current technologies. The outsource vendors should be able to speak fluently about new technologies, and be able to define a process or procedure on how the service staff handles customer queries about how or whether to upgrade or change to a new technology—subject, of course, to your approval.

Defining and communicating your company's expectations and metrics by which success will be measured is another key component to an RFP. The clearer and more comprehensive this section is, the more clearly the vendors who are responding to your RFP will understand exactly the objectives you have in mind, and more importantly, how your company will measure the success of the relationship. Key success factors should cover such areas as response time, time to resolution, provider staff accessibility to customers, quality of personnel, quality and friendliness of service delivery (as measured by customers), and what measurement tools and techniques are to be used. The success factors should also reflect the provider's ability to respond to product or program changes from your company, and the provider's ability to proactively keep you informed of developments, opportunities, and challenges before they become issues requiring resolution. The more detailed and specific this section is, the better, since detail leaves little room for misinterpretation. And that makes for a stronger partnership, which is what the outsource vendor must be in this relationship—a partner, not just a vendor.

At this point there are several main topics still needing discussion within the RFP. One is geared toward understanding the outsourcer's experience, and the second is to obtain an understanding of the size and structure of the outsourcer's organization. Gaining an understanding of an outsource vendor's experience and capability can be obtained by asking for a summary of accounts of similar size and scope, for which the outsourcer provides services. A second way to gain this understanding is by asking for and obtaining a list of references who can be contacted. Companies from both of these responses should be called for outsource vendors who have made your short list of the two or three finalists. These calls will likely be very helpful in understanding what current customers value about the provider. A third is to ask the provider for a list, again of a similar project scope, of past customers who have opted to discontinue using the provider's services. Most outsourcers are happy to provide the first two; they may not be as excited to provide the latter. How the outsourcers respond to this request will tell you something about the way they do business. For example, almost no company is successful at keeping all of its customers for a wide variety of reasons, so admitting a loss of customers should not be difficult—but may be for some vendors. If a list is not provided, it may indicate that it may be difficult to hear the whole story from the provider in the future if it is reluctant to provide all sides, successes and failures, of the topic. If the outsourcer does provide the names of companies who are no longer customers, it may be worth following up to gain a better understanding of what that company's experience was and why it left. Regardless of the reason for terminating the relationship, this provides you with another view of the outsourcer; and you can decide how applicable the issues. Again, this step becomes more important for the short-list provider candidates than for all responding to the RFP, but asking the question in the RFP is another way to see how a provider responds to an unusual request.

The last topic to be investigated in the RFP is the outsourcer's organization, and more specifically, how your project fits into the outsourcer's organizational structure. Ask for an overview of the company and the specific divisions that will be involved in the service delivery for your products. Ask for a copy of the outsourcer's recent financial reports, descriptions and examples of quality programs, employee incentive and career development programs; and any other companies, alliances, or partnerships that will be utilized to meet the contract's requirements.

Twelve Steps to a Successful Outsourcing Experience

1. Identify products and service levels to be outsourced
2. Identify success factors
3. Identify selection criteria
4. Develop and document desired call flow and process flow
5. Prepare RFP
6. Send RFP to five to ten selected outsourcers
7. Compare responses and narrow to a short list of two or three providers
8. Complete site visits, reference checks, and informal *due diligence* on remaining outsource vendors
9. Select outsource vendor based on selection criteria
10. Negotiate contract
11. Manage and monitor outsourcer relationship against success factors (utilize technology and a person responsible for the relationship)
12. Actively work with outsourcer to correct problems and identify opportunities for improvement

At this time there is no standard format for an RFP; however, there are many sources for locating RFPs already developed. The outsourcers themselves may make a sample RFP format available. Professional organizations within the service industry may have samples available. And one of the best sources are other technical support professionals who have already been through the outsource selection process. For the best RFP for your company, obtain as many different samples as possible, then build your own to meet your specifications from the ideas those samples provide, and from the requirements you've already determined.

There are many companies that offer outsourcing solutions to Technical Support Organizations. A good place to find them is in industry publications, such as *Call Center Magazine*[2] or *Service News*.[3] Periodically these publications will do a fairly comprehensive review of outsourcers, their specialties, and how to reach them. Another way to locate them is to attend industry events that host exhibits (see section later in this chapter), ask other technical support industry professionals, or do a quick search on the Internet.

Once the RFPs have been submitted to the outsource vendors for consideration, follow up with them to ensure receipt, answer any questions, and restate the due date for the completed response. In some cases, it might even make sense to call all the outsourcing vendors together to explain the project, distribute the RFP, and answer questions. The benefit of this is that all the providers get to hear the same directions and the same questions and answers at the same time.

Upon receipt of the completed RFPs combine the information into a single matrix so that each provider's responses can easily be compared to the stated success criteria and to each other. This process should be very helpful in narrowing the candidate providers down to a short list of two or three. At this point, common courtesy suggests that all respondents be contacted to let them know if they've made the short list, and if so what the next steps are, or are not.

Site visits should then be scheduled and made to the short-list candidates. Any additional details should be provided and references contacted. This is the point at which references and companies that are no longer customers of the vendors on the short list should be contacted to find out what their experience has been with the vendor, what these references see as the vendor's strengths and weaknesses, and what, if anything, surprised them about the vendor once the vendor was selected and the relationship begun in earnest. A specific question for those companies no longer utilizing the services of the vendor in question would be, Why did you terminate the relationship? A specific question for those customers still utilizing the vendors services might be asked: If you had a new project to outsource, who would you outsource to?

This is also a good point at which to do a little of your own due diligence by talking with contacts in the industry who have already outsourced, but who may not be on any of your provider candidates' reference lists. These contacts may be even more helpful in sharing their decision-making process, experience, and lessons learned for factoring into the final selection process. The selection criteria and process for each company are different since the needs and importance weighting of various factors are different for various companies, and sometimes even for product lines within a company. So factor in as much information as possible, then make the best decision possible with the information available.

An outsourcing relationship is an important business relationship that cannot easily be terminated once it is established. This is one of the reasons the details of the contract must clearly identify the scope, quality and duration of the services to be performed by both parties, the circumstances under which work will be done, the flow of information between parties, and the service level agreements and performance standards to which both parties will be held. It is also the reason why support organizations, after the hard work of defining processes, selecting a provider or providers, and negotiating the contract, must still play an active, participatory, ongoing role to ensure that what is expected out of the arrangement is what is achieved. This *trust but verify* philosophy can be established by meeting with the outsourcing vendor's management team on a regular basis, and providing timely response to issues and concerns. It can also be achieved by actively and regularly monitoring how well the success metrics are being met by both organizations, then leading review meetings to discuss possible improvements. Investing in tools to automate and enhance communication with the outsource vendor is also an important element to building a successful arrangement. This can be as simple as including each other on key e-mail distribution lists (now easily done with the Internet access available today), and deploying a client of the provider's customer information system into your Technical Support Organization so that day-to-day monitoring of call volumes, call types, root causes of calls, and so on can be viewed, obtained, and reported, as desired. It can also be done by securing access into the provider's ACD to allow for call monitoring and to provide real-time access to call volume, abandon, and hold-time statistics. A few years ago this remote monitoring was relatively unheard of or too expensive for serious consideration. Today, it is a very cost-effective option for staying involved and in touch with the selected provider organization.

Too many support organizations, after making the well-thought-through decision to outsource, and after detailed negotiations, forget this last piece: that the relationship, like any successful business relationship, needs to be managed in an active way. Too often significant time, resources, and effort go into the support organization's decision to outsource, the process of selecting an outsourcer, and the grueling task of negotiating the contract; with an additional decision to not invest in the management of the relationship. All the clichés hold true in this scenario, including What gets measured gets done; Out of sight, out of mind; and When the cat's away the mice will play. Don't make the mistake of having a great partnership turn sour because the support organization didn't invest in a resource to help manage the ongoing outsource vendor relationship. Instead, view the relationship for what it is: utilization of a partnership arrangement to better leverage the resources of the company to achieve the company's objectives. Deciding to outsource an activity that is not deemed one of the company's core competencies does not automatically mean it is also not an important business element. Remember that service and support continue to be key elements to the company's success in the eyes of the customer, and that outsourcing is simply an alternative delivery mechanism that still needs active attention if it is to do well.

The decision to outsource is a strategic decision, and as a result must be made with the specific needs and objectives of each company in mind. Similarly, just like any other opportunity, there are potential benefits and potential issues to the outsourcing strategy. All must be considered and weighed in the context of your company objectives to ensure a good decision is made.

PROVIDING MULTIVENDOR SUPPORT

Arming your Technical Support Representatives with all the information they could possibly need to provide the kind of one-stop shopping that many of today's customers prefer could be a substantial task if attempted on your own. Instead, alternatives to going it alone can include developing one to one relationships with other companies or getting involved in some of the many organizations, consortiums, and products on the market today, which are there to help do just that: share information and improve customer satisfaction.

In marked contrast with a few years ago, when Technical Support Organizations rarely shared technical support information primarily due to competitive fears, leaders of Technical Support Organizations today view sharing technical support information on their company's products a key objective. This sharing is occurring in volumes with other Technical Support Organizations and with customers directly. A variety of tools are being used to provide this information, as described in Chapter 7. And it is clear that this sharing strategy is a big win for everyone involved. Customers welcome it because they can in some cases become more self-sufficient. For others the experience of obtaining technical support on multivendor products is becoming less painful. Technical support departments and their companies embrace it, since it allows them to better service their customers who are increasingly using multivendor tools and configurations in even the most basic systems.

Providing multivendor support today is still a complex process, however a quick way to get started is by subscribing to the other technical support vendor's knowledge base CDs and deploying them within your organization so that they can easily be used. These CDs can be obtained from the company directly, and are offered by such companies as Microsoft, Lotus, Borland International, and more. A number of third-party knowledge bases are also on the market today, which are very helpful in the delivery of technical support. Explained in more detail in Chapter 7, an example of one of the more comprehensive third-party knowledge-base CDs is Support On Site from Logical Operations.[4] Additional sources for these CDs can be found in the same publications listed earlier in the section on outsourcing. They can also be found being exhibited at industry conferences throughout the year (see section later in this chapter).

There are also consortiums that have been created specifically to address the issues of multivendor support. One of these, the Customer Support Consortium, with more than 60 large technology members (including Microsoft, IBM, Dell Computer, Bay Networks, Lotus Development, and NetScape Communications) is working on a single, Internet-based universal knowledge base that contains vendor-supplied technical information. This effort has been underway for four years at the time of this writing, and the members plan to open the knowledge base to certain customer groups by late 1997. In addition the group is working on a set of standards to help all Technical Support Organizations create exchangeable online knowledge base information. A couple of other consortiums working on similar endeavors include the TSA (Technical Support Alliance), the Novell Technical Support Alliance (NTSA) and the Support Standards Working Group, which is part of a vendor-neutral, not-for-profit organization called the Desktop Management Task Force (DMTF). Which consortium, if any, will actually set the standards that the industry will adopt is yet to be determined, but the need and the opportunity to participate and help solve this issue are there.

Borland International found another way to enhance its multivendor support delivery while simultaneously building stronger customer relationships and leveraging a larger group of Borland product knowledgeable resources. The technical support team that created and managed the content of the company's bulletin board enhanced its technical support efforts by inviting select active, knowledgeable bulletin-board contributors to join a formalized bulletin-board team, called TeamBorland. The TeamBorland members continued and increased their activity on the bulletin board by helping to answer questions of other board users. These members were not employees of Borland, but simply customers who were knowledgeable about Borland products, sometimes in ways even surpassing the entire technical support team.

Advances in technology continue to offer new and improved ways for Technical Support Organizations to provide quality, comprehensive, multivendor support in a cost-effective manner. Add in the efforts of the cross-company support consortiums, and the zeal to provide customers with the ability to service themselves; and the challenges of providing multivendor support may diminish thanks to partners and affiliates with the same objectives. And who knows, one day your company's support organization may become so well tuned that it will be an outsourcer for others.

SUPPORTING THE COMPANY'S PARTNERS

Most technology companies today focus even further on their core competencies while staying as focused as possible by developing relationships with other parties. These other parties may be referred to as ISVs (Integration Software Vendors), VARs (Value Add Resellers), Advisors, or a variety of other titles. Regardless of the title, the purpose is the same: to leverage the skills of another group in getting your company's product successfully sold, installed, and used within a customer's site.

This leveraging strategy plays heavily on the concept of partnering and affiliating. As discussed earlier, partnering is the joining of people or companies to take part in a common activity with another person or company. Affiliating is to connect or associate with a person or company. These leveraging activities are gaining more and more momentum as the technology industry matures and new mini-industries spring up to take advantage of the opportunity this growth provides. The economy typically thrives on this spawning of new business opportunities that new industry offers. And typically customers, workers, companies, and stockholders all can do well in such a growth stage. However, as in any relationship, the mechanisms that are put in place to ensure good quality communication and understanding of the objectives to be achieved, as well as striving for the win-win arrangement, are what ultimately determine the success of the partnership.

In a technology-oriented company, the success of the relationship depends on many elements, including a solid contractual arrangement; clear expectations of roles, responsibilities, and rewards; analogous methods of conducting business; and clearly defined processes for timely sharing of pertinent, accurate information. The first of these elements is often taken care of within the business development, marketing, or sales organizations within the company. However, once the fundamental business arrangements have been agreed upon, it is often the Technical Support Organization that bears primary responsibility for ensuring that both parties are easily able to share information and knowledge in a timely and quality manner, which is necessary for success.

Too often these partners, after careful selection, detailed contractual negotiations, and sometimes investments of time and/or money, are treated as outsiders instead of partners. When thinking of these arrangements as true partnerships, whereby two or more entities are engaged in basically the same business enterprise, sharing its profits and risks, and acting as agents for the other, it is easier to understand the need to treat these businesses as partners.

The most effective way to accomplish this task is to create one or more support offerings, specifically designed for partners, which include establishing processes that emulate those used to keep your own service staff informed and consistently able to provide accurate, high-quality customer service. They may not be able to be exactly the same processes due to the confidential nature of some of the information; however, by keeping the objective of sharing information generally the same, and by leveraging tools, technology, and processes already in place, the chances for a highly rewarding relationship increase.

Some of these processes may include a procedure that ensures any new corporate communications, offerings, collateral, marketing programs, and so on intended for customers or channel distributors are shared first with employees, second with partners, and finally with the appropriate external audience. It may include a process whereby calls and inquiries from partners are handled by a separate group from that which handles inquiries from customers. This is often the most effective way to ensure that partners are considered and assisted in a way that best helps them do their jobs, without asking a Technical Support Representative to repeatedly have to choose between assisting a partner, which is a leveraging activity, or assisting a customer, which is a strategically important activity. If creating a group to primarily handle partner calls with a separate group primarily handling customer calls is not an option, then a strategy should be devised to service partner calls in an appropriate priority over customer calls. This is not to say that partner calls all get answered first necessarily, but it is important that the order in which calls are handled is done with serious consideration given to all options. Whichever option is selected, it is important to communicate the process to both employees and partners so that partners know what to expect. And whenever possible, utilize technology to prioritize the calls according to the strategy so that employees are not routinely put in the position of having to determine which is higher priority.

Another way to leverage current investments in knowledge and technology is to allow partners to access the same (as much as possible) information as the technical support staff. This could include information captured in a knowledge base or customer information management system. It could also take the format of inviting, or requiring, partners to become certified sources of technical support for the company's products by taking the same, or similar, product training as technical support personnel, as a part of the partnership agreement.

Creating and investing in processes to share knowledge and information are solid steps in developing a successful ongoing relationship, but they alone are not enough to ensure success. In addition, invest in creating opportunities for the technical support staff to meet partners face to face, and show appreciation and recognition of accomplishments similar to the way the sales organization might recognize a partner for outstanding sales achievements. If the opportunity exists for the technical support personnel to meet partners face to face, take it—or make it. Most companies have annual or semiannual events designed to inform partners of the company's product plans, renew their commitment to the relationship, and to say thanks to outstanding performers (all typically focused on the sales and marketing aspect of the business). Next time, secure an evening or afternoon with the partners for doing the same from a service perspective. Involve as many technical support team members as possible; give awards to recognize outstanding customer-service achievements by partners; introduce support staff members; share stories in which a partner-tech support representative effort resulted in a big win for the customer, partner, and company; and more.

An even simpler idea is to obtain pictures of the key support contacts from each partner's company, and post them in the technical support area so that people can put faces to voices and electronic messages. Whenever possible, give technical support team members the opportunity to visit partner locations, or participate in an on-site customer call with a partner.

These are just a few ideas to help initiate thinking on how to treat partners as real partners, rather than just other entities. The results of a few minor investments to leverage processes, knowledge, and technology already in place, and to personalize the relationship between the tech support organization and partners, will pay big dividends in the end.

SOURCES

The technical support industry has spawned entire new conference, publication, and membership opportunities for industry professionals. These publications, events, and associations have evolved over time to be prominent sources of information on the technical support industry. They provide exposure to new ideas and methods of delivering technical support. They provide insight into new technologies and uses of technologies that assist in the pursuit of high levels of customer satisfaction. They have played a role in increasing awareness, respect, and credibility of the critical role service and support play in a company's long-term success. They provide a way to meet others who understand the challenges faced by the technical support professional, and afford opportunities to share experiences and learning about how they turned challenges into opportunities for their company, customers, employees, and themselves.

Currently, two of the most widely read and referred-to publications are *Service News*,[5] a newspaper for computer service and support, published by United Publications, Inc., and *Call-Center Magazine*,[6] a technologies and techniques magazine for customer service, help desk, and sales and support. Other helpful publications are *CustomerCare*,[7] *Business Communications Review*,[8] *The Service Edge Newsletter*,[9] *Service Industry Newsletter*,[10] *Software Publisher*,[11] and *PC WEEK*.[12]

Many of these publications also publish buyer's guides that provide current information on various technologies and how they are being used, and how to obtain product and purchasing information. Some, like *PC WEEK*, periodically publish a buyer's guide as a section within the magazine itself. Others, like *LAN Times*[13] and *Service News,* offer a separate buyer's guide publication to their subscribers. And the publishers of *CustomerCare* also publish a survey on service and support practices in the technical support industry.

Other publications, like *Automating Your Support Center*,[14] provide information that identifies and provides basic assessments and comparisons of service automation tools. *We're Off to Seize the Wizard*,[15] a book that discusses how knowledge-based computer systems are transforming the service industry, is also very helpful in explaining the revolution occurring in America's service businesses. *Inc. Magazine's Complete Guide to Superior Customer Service*[16] is a compilation of case studies accompanied by consultant analyses covering six businesses, including Dell Computer and Intuit, Inc., that have built customer service into their corporate business strategies. Yet another, *The Call Center Dictionary*,[17] is a comprehensive guide to explaining what call-center technology and operations are and how they work.

There are also numerous organizations and exhibits in which a service and support professional could benefit from participating. Help Desk Institute[18] has an international membership group, counting in the thousands, which participates in regular local chapter, national, and international activities. Among the national events is a well-attended and still growing International Support Services Conference and Expo that has been providing for nearly a decade a place for service and support professionals to meet, learn, and share. In addition to the local chapters and the national and international conferences, HDI also offers a bounty of resource materials covering a plethora of topics helpful to the technical support professional. Some of those include a buyer's guide; a technical support industry salary survey; and white papers on staffing, scheduling, and workforce planning and benchmarking in the technical support industry. Other topics published and provided to members include how to establish and maintain service level agreements, handle difficult customers, design effective customer satisfaction surveys, and more.

The Association of Support Professionals[19] is a relatively new organization specifically created to offer regionally organized meeting opportunities for technical support professionals. The ASP was an outgrowth of OpCon, an 11-year-old conference created as a way for support professionals to meet and share ideas. Another association specifically created for the technical support community is the Software Support Professionals Association.[20] The SSPA also has annual conferences with technology exhibits, as well as organized regional events held around the country at different member locations. These regional meetings can be attended by any member and typically include a tour of the host company's facility.

A fourth association is the International Customer Service Association,[21] designed to assist service and support professionals in their roles as service providers, also offers a Customer Service Benchmark Study. And a fifth association, the Call Center Network Group,[22] was formed to provide networking opportunities for call-center professionals. It is a member-driven organization, with regional chapters throughout North America, and offers the Call Center Tech conference twice a year.

In addition to the conferences hosted by membership organizations such as HDI, ASP, SSPA, and ICSA, nonmembership conferences are alternative events to be considered. One of these, which has been growing in popularity, is Servcon—a multiday conference sponsored by the publishers of *Service News*.

Additional significant sources of information to any service and support professional are the organizations that gather and publish research and trends in the service industry. Two of the most prominent, broad-based research efforts are done by Dataquest[23] and the Gartner Group.[24] Both are extensively quoted in the press on the topic of technical support and service, both offer conference opportunities, and both often present at other conferences. In addition, both provide benchmarking studies based on their research. Among others, Dataquest offers *Outsourcing Software Support—Players, Options and Benchmarks*, which includes extensive information on detailed interviews with senior technical support executives and staffs of 25 leading third-party technical support (outsourcing) companies. It includes information on industry benchmarking and trends, outsourcer support pricing statistics, outsource provider analysis worksheets, and individual company statistics. The Gartner Group also offers a variety of similar reports.

Other organizations that gather and publish benchmarking information pertinent to service and support professionals include Prognostics,[25] Business Information Systems,[26] International Data Corporation (IDC),[27] J.D. Power and Associates,[28] and the American Electronics Association (AEA).[29] Prognostics completes benchmarking studies that include data from more than 80 companies. Business Information Systems, or BIS, does benchmark comparisons of consumer electronics service companies, and encompasses companies in 19 countries. IDC, J.D. Power and Associates, and the AEA each focus on researching and publishing benchmark studies on various segments of the technical support industry. Before investing in any of these studies, be sure they cover the type of market and information desired. They are relatively expensive but can be wise and useful investments when making vital technical service strategy decisions.

Some of the more well-known (at the time of this writing) publications, conferences and exhibits, and membership organizations are briefly discussed here. However, these sources are numerous and the number is expanding every year. By getting involved in one or two publishing subscriptions and conferences, a support professional will quickly become knowledgeable about the varied and frequent opportunities available. Then it's up to the individual to take advantage of the most interesting opportunities, and to get involved.

The technical support industry is a very close-knit community in many ways. Although each support professional has individual company, product, staff, and customer issues, the members of this consequential group have one high-level objective in common: to raise customer satisfaction to the highest level possible in the most cost-effective manner to create long-term customer loyalty and repeat purchasing of a company's products. Collectively, this group can and is playing a key role in the success of our customers, our employees, our companies, and our industry.

NOTES

1. Example from Sykes Enterprises, Inc.
2. At the time of this writing *Call Center Magazine* is located in Southhampton, PA; phone: 215-355-2886; Web site: www.callcentermagazine.com.
3. At the time of this writing *Service News* is located in Yarmouth, ME; phone: 215-788-7112.
4. At the time of this writing *Support On Site* can be obtained from Logical Operations, a Ziff-Davis Publishing Company, New York, NY; phone: 800-667-2581, ext. 112.
5. At the time of this writing *Service News* is located in Yarmouth, ME; phone: 215-788-7112.
6. At the time of this writing *Call Center Magazine* is located in Southhampton, PA; phone: 215-355-2886; Web site: www.callcentermagazine.com.
7. At the time of this writing *CustomerCare* is published by Software Strategies, Inc., located in Bridgeport, CT; phone: 203-335-6090.
8. At the time of this writing *Business Communications Review* is published by BCR Enterprises, Inc., located in Hinsdale, IL; phone: 800-227-1234.
9. At the time of this writing *The Service Edge Newsletter* is published by Lakewood Publications located in Minneapolis, MN; phone: 800-328-4329.
10. At the time of this writing *Service Industry Newsletter* is published by Dataquest located in Framingham, MA; phone: 508-370-5555.
11. At the time of this writing *Software Publisher* is published by WebCom Communications Corp. located in Aurora, CO; phone: 303-745-5711.

12. At the time of this writing *PC WEEK* is published by Ziff-Davis Publishing located in New York, NY; phone: 212-503-3500.

13. At the time of this writing *LAN Times* headquarters are located in San Mateo, CA; phone: 415-503-6800.

14. At the time of this writing *Automating Your Support Center* can be obtained by calling Knowledge Networks in San Jose, CA; phone: 408-978-5580.

15. At the time of this writing *We're Off to Seize the Wizard* can be obtained from ServiceWare, Inc., in Oakmont, PA; phone: 412-826-1158.

16. At the time of this writing *Inc. Magazine's Complete Guide to Superior Customer Service* can be obtained from Inc. Business Resources located in Wilkes-Barre, PA; phone: 717-822-8899.

17. At the time of this writing *The Call Center Dictionary* can be obtained from Flatiron Publishing located in New York, NY; phone: 212-691-8215.

18. At the time of this writing Help Desk Institute is located in Colorado Springs, CO; phone: 800-248-5667.

19. At this writing information on The Association of Support Professionals and OpCon can be obtained from Soft*letter in Watertown, MA; phone: 617-924-3944.

20. At the time of this writing the Software Support Professionals Association is located in San Diego, CA; phone: 619-674-4868.

21. At the time of this writing the International Customer Service Association is located in Chicago, IL; phone: 312-321-6800.

22. At the time of this writing the Call Center Network Group is located in Arlington, TX; phone: 800-840-2264; Web site: http://www.ccng.com.

23. At the time of this writing Dataquest is located in Framingham, MA; phone: 508-370-5555.

24. At the time of this writing the Gartner Group is located in Stamford, CT; phone: 203-964-0096.

25. At the time of this writing Prognostics is located in Menlo Park, CA; phone: 415-688-1900.

26. At the time of this writing Business Information Systems (BIS) can be reached by telephone at 617-982-9500.

27. At the time of this writing International Data Corporation (IDC) can be reached by telephone at 512-469-6333.

28. At the time of this writing J.D. Power and Associates can be reached by telephone at 818-889-6330.

29. At the time of this writing the American Electronics Association can be reached by telephone at 408-970-8565.

Index